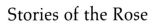

Stories of the Rose

Anne Winston-Allen

Stories
of the
Rose

The Making
of the
Rosary in the Middle Ages

The Pennsylvania State University Press
University Park, Pennsylvania

Library of Congress Cataloging-in-Publication Data

Winston-Allen, Anne, 1942–
    Stories of the rose : the making of the rosary in the Middle Ages
/ Anne Winston-Allen.
      p.   cm.
    Includes bibliographical references and index.
    ISBN 0-271-01631-0 (alk. paper)
    1. Rosary—History.   2. Confraternities—Germany—Cologne.
3. Spirituality—History—Middle Ages, 600–1500.   4. Cologne
(Germany)—Religious life and customs.   I. Title.
BX2163.W55   1997
242'.74—dc20   96-36239
                                                      CIP

Second printing, 1998

It is the policy of The Pennsylvania State University Press to use acid-free paper for
the first printing of all clothbound books. Publications on uncoated stock satisfy the
minimum requirements of American National Standard for Information Sciences—
Permanence of Paper for Printed Library Materials, ANSI Z39.48-1992.

FRONTISPIECE. *The Virgin in a Garden*, Alsatian Master, Strasbourg, Musée de l'Oeuvre
Notre Dame.

Contents

List of Illustrations   vii

Preface and Acknowledgments   xi

Introduction   1

1   Early Rosaries   13

2   The Picture Text and Its "Readers"   31

3   One for Sorrow, Two for Joy: Confraternity Writings, the Fifteen Mysteries, and the Observant Reform   65

4   Secular Love Gardens, Marian Iconography, and the Names of the Rose   81

5   Popular Promotion and Reception   111

6   Rosaries and the Language of Spirituality   133

Appendix   153

Notes   161

Selected Bibliography   187

Index   206

For Jim

List of Illustrations

Frontispiece: *The Virgin in a Garden*, Alsatian Master. Strasbourg, Musée de l'Oeuvre Notre Dame

1. *Vnser lieben frauen Psalter*, Ulm: Dinckmut, 1483 (from the plates reprinted in the 1492 edition). Reproduced here by permission of the Universitätsbibliothek Freiburg

2. The life of Christ in twenty-seven pictures, c. 1380–90. Cologne, Wallraf-Richartz Museum (Photo: Rheinisches Bildarchiv)

3. Mary's Seven Joys, woodcut, fifteenth century. Mainz, Gutenberg Museum

4. Jean Pucelle, the Hours of Jeanne d'Evreux. Metropolitan Museum of Art, The Cloisters, New York

5. Hans Schaur, Rosary Madonna, woodcut, c. 1481. Nuremberg, Germanisches Nationalmuseum

6. Madonna with the Rosary, woodcut, 1485. Washington, D.C., National Gallery of Art, Rosenwald Collection

7. The fourth joy: Adoration of the Magi, in *Die Sieben Freuden Mariae und die Leidensgeschichte Jesu*, 1460–64. Munich, Bayerische Staatsbibliothek

8. Illustrations of the Ascension and Pentecost as depicted in the *Speculum humanae salvationis* and *Von dem psalter vnd rosencrancz vnser lieben frauen*

9. Rosary fresco, c. 1500, Weilheim unter der Teck, Baden-Württemberg, Church of Saint Peter. In this set of fifteen medallions, the Adoration of the Magi has been inserted before the Presentation in the Temple (the fourth and fifth figures in the outer ring, moving

clockwise from upper left), while the Finding of the Lost Child Jesus in the Temple (usually no. 5) has been left out.

10. Wolf Traut, Rosary Meditations, woodcut, 1510. Karlsruhe, Badische Landesbibliothek

11. Franciscus Domenech, Fifteen Mysteries of the Rosary, Barcelona, 1488. Brussels, Bibliothèque Royale Albert Ier

12. Rosary antependium, c. 1484, formerly of the Dominican church of Frankfurt. The fifteenth medallion contains simply the initials IHS (Ihesus) instead of the Last Judgment. Heidelberg, Kurpfälzisches Museum, Graimberg Collection

13. Alberto da Castello, *Rosario della gloriosa vergine Maria* (Venice, 1524 ed.). The glorious mysteries. Reproduced by permission of the British Library.

14. Andrea Gianetti da Salò, *Rosario della sacratissima Vergine Maria, raccolto dall' opere del R.P.F. Luigi di Granata*, Venice, 1587. The glorious mysteries, fol. 73v. Reproduced by permission of The Newberry Library, Chicago.

15. Adam Walasser, *Von der Gnadenreichen, hochberümpten . . . Bruderschaft des Psalters oder Rosenkrantz Marie* (Dillingen, 1572). Illustration no. 15. Reproduced by permission of the British Library, London.

16. Albrecht Dürer, *The Celebration of the Rosary*, c. 1506. Prague, National Gallery

17. The Planet Venus from the fifteenth-century Italian *Codex Sphaera*, Berlin, Archiv für Kunst und Geschichte

18. Fifteenth-century love-garden tapestry. Basel, Historisches Museum (photo: Historisches Museum)

19. Illustration for "Der große Rosengarten zu Worms" from the *Heldenbuch* (Strasbourg, Prüss, 1479). Darmstadt, Hessische Landes- und Hochschulbibliothek

20. Cathedral of Strasbourg Prince of the World, "The Tempter" (detail), c. 1280. Strasbourg, Musée de l'Oeuvre Notre-Dame

21. Virgin and Child with Rosetree, c. 1300, Straubing, polychrome stone. Munich, Bayerisches Nationalmuseum

22. Martin Schongauer, The Madonna of the Rose Bower, 1473, Colmar, Saint Martin's Church. At bottom left is also a "Pfingstrose," the "Whitsuntide rose" (peony). Reproduced by the kind permission of the Conseil de Fabrique de la Paroisse Saint-Martin de Colmar.

23. Illustration of the enclosed garden (hortus conclusus) and sealed

fountain (fons signatus) signifying Mary, from the *Speculum humanae salvationis* (England, c. 1390), Morgan MS M766, fol. 25. New York, Pierpont Morgan Library

24. Woodcut illustration from the *Canticum canticorum* (Song of Songs), c. 1460–65, with banderole, "A garden enclosed is my sister, my bride, a garden enclosed, a fountain sealed" (Song of Songs 4:12). Reproduced by permission of the Pierpont Morgan Library, New York

25. Meister des Marienlebens, "Virgin and Child with Saints in a Rose Arbor," c. 1470. Berlin, Staatliches Museum Preussischer Kulturbesitz

26. Gérard David (d. 1523), "Virgin and Child in an Enclosed Garden with Saints and Donor." London, National Gallery

27. "Hortus conclusus" Annunciation scene, tapestry, upper Rhine, c. 1500. Munich, Bayerisches Nationalmuseum

28. Illustration of the legend of the monk and the robbers ("Aves Seen as Roses"), in *Der Spiegel hochloblicher Bruderschafft des Rosenkrantz Marie* (Leipzig, 1515), fol. 36v. Reproduced by permission of the Bayerische Staatsbibliothek, Munich

29. *Hoofkijn van devotien* (Garden of devotion) Antwerp, Gerhard Leeu, 1487. Reproduced by permission of the Koninklijke Bibliotheek, The Hague (No. 150 B 48)

30. Paternoster maker, *Hausbuch* (Amb. 317. 2°, fol. 13r). Stadtbibliothek, Nuremberg

31. Sixteenth-century rosary of boxwood disks and jasper, Munich, Bayerisches Nationalmuseum, and fifteenth- or sixteenth-century rosary of bone. Cologne, Erzbischöfliches Diözesanmuseum

32. Wolf Traut, woodcut, 1510. Karlsruhe, Badische Landesbibliothek

33. *Der Spiegel hochloblicher Bruderschafft des Rosenkrantz Marie* (Leipzig, 1515), fol. 107v. Reproduced by permission of the Bayerische Staatsbibliothek

34. From the Legend of the Rosary of Saint Dominic, a copy after a lost painting by Geertgen tot Sint Jans (d. 1495). Leipzig, Museum der bildenden Künste

Chapter Opening Emblems

Chapter 1: "The Virgin and Saint Dominic," woodcut, Cologne, Wallraf-Richartz Museum; Chapter 2: "Mary's Seven Joys," woodcut, Mainz,

Gutenberg Museum (see Figure 3); Chapter 3: "Celebration of the Rosary," woodcut, Munich, Staatliche Graphische Sammlung; Chapter 4: "Virgin with Child and Rose," MS 271, Colmar, Bibliothèque de la Ville de Colmar; Chapter 5: "Paternoster Maker," *Hausbuch* (Amb. 317. 2°, fol. 13r), Nuremberg, Stadtbibliothek (see Figure 30); Chapter 6: An indulgence broadside, c. 1480, London, The British Library.

Preface and Acknowledgments

This book started out as a study of gardens in medieval German literature that was going to be called "Gardens of Earthly and Heavenly Delight." But after a year of spadework on actual, physical gardens of the Middle Ages, I strayed into imaginary and allegorical ones where I have been wandering ever since.

The first such "garden" that I encountered, and the one that begins this study, was *Our Lady Mary's Rose Garden* (c. 1430), a medieval German allegory about the rosary. I was soon to learn that rosaries of various kinds were prominent features of these herb and flower plots of the imagination. But how did there come to be so many different rosary texts and how were they related to the "official" one? When, after all, did the rosary originate, and why were there so many forms all bearing the same name? Unfortunately, it was not at all clear what medieval writers meant when they referred to the practice of saying the rosary.

In the earliest reliable account of the Hail Mary, Saint Peter Damian (1007–72) tells the story of an ineffectual cleric who retained his post because he had a single virtue: every day at the altar he recited the greeting of the Angel Gabriel, "Hail Mary, full of grace, the Lord is with thee; blessed art thou among women." By the twelfth century the prayer had been lengthened to include the words "and blessed is the fruit of thy womb" (Luke 1:42). Soon worshipers who could not read were reciting 150 repetitions of it as a devotional exercise intended to simulate the 150 psalms of the Divine Office. The prayer was called the Psalter of Our Lady.

A popular legend of the thirteenth century describes how the words of the salutation are transformed into roses that form a garland or chaplet for the Virgin. Thus the practice of weaving symbolic chaplets or wreaths of verbal roses as gifts to Mary became a favorite gesture of devotion and the term *rosary*, from rose garland (*Rosenkranz*), came into use. What this practice meant to medieval worshipers and how the custom grew and changed over the three hundred years up to the eve of the Reformation is the focus of this interdisciplinary study.

The issue is complicated, as the rosary is more than a prayer in the conventional sense. It is also a literary text, a ritual and social practice, as well as an object of religious art. Getting at its meanings for medieval users goes beyond the boundaries of any one field of knowledge. Accordingly, this study is not a history but an attempt to look at the practice as broadly as possible. The devotion cannot be seen, as it traditionally has been, only as a religious practice that had a unified character and development throughout its history. Rather, it was shaped collaboratively by communities of users who revised and adapted it to changing spiritual and practical agendas.

Understanding the prayer and the world it grew out of means identifying some of these agendas in medieval writings about the practice. But while medieval rosaries are abundant, not many works have survived that explain and interpret them. What remain are a few popular songs, testimonials, exempla (sermon illustrations), pictorial works, plus some statutes and handbooks of the rosary brotherhood. These vernacular works describe or advertise the prayer and often relate stories about its medieval practitioners. By putting these pieces together—and without claiming to be exhaustive—I have explored some of the religious, social, artistic, and political implications of the rosary that illuminate what medieval users were saying and why they said it that way.

The frontispiece, a painting formerly attributed to Matthias Grünewald (c. 1480–1528), illustrates two of the motifs that are intertwined in the medieval story of the rose. Here a beautiful virgin with nimbus, perhaps the expectant mother Mary herself, sits gazing pensively and gesturing toward a rose branch—symbol of Christ and the Cross—as though sensing joys and sorrows yet to come. In this image and many others like it, the stories of Christ's Incarnation and Passion are linked to the iconographic symbols of the Virgin herself as rose and rose garden.

What the making of symbolic chaplets of verbal roses as gifts for the Virgin meant to some medieval practitioners is best described in the words of one who wrote, "We live as if in Mary's rose garden, those of us who occupy ourselves with the roses." I hope the guide to medieval rosaries provided here will serve as a useful map to those likewise interested in exploring Mary's rose garden.

For "seeding" and nurturing this project I would like to thank the Oklahoma Council for the Humanities, the National Endowment for the Humanities, and Southern Illinois University's Summer Research Fellowship program. For special help in accessing materials, I am grateful to Angela Rubin and Marta Davis of Southern Illinois University's Morris Library, Charles Ermatinger of the Vatican Film Library at Saint Louis University, Karin Schneider of the Bayerische Staatsbibliothek, and Ruth Landrock of the Universitätsbibliothek Freiburg. For helping me find my way through their special holdings, I also thank the staffs at the Library of Congress, the British Library, the Bibliothèque Nationale, and the Bibliothèque de la ville de Colmar. The Newberry Library and the Staatsbibliothek Bamberg provided friendly suggestions long-distance to augment what I had written to request. For these kindnesses and many others, I am in their debt.

Konrad Kunze talked the project over with me at an early stage, offered many helpful observations, and lent me the unpublished master's thesis of Olaf Winter (Universität Freiburg), which was extremely valuable in focusing my further research. For sharing my enthusiasm in discussions of the project, and for their special expertise on rosaries and confraternities, I thank Jan Rhodes and Virginia Nixon, who read early drafts of the manuscript. To Richard Kieckhefer and Carlos Eire I am most grateful for insightful comments and suggestions that much improved the book. For excellent practical advice I am indebted to my editor Peter Potter.

Special thanks go to Ingrid and Werner Höfel who not only tolerated my obsession with this study during five summers, but even became enthusiastic enough about it to take me on a tour of some sites of the Observant Reform movement in Alsace. For reasons that are clearer to me now, the easiest chapter of this book to write was the one drafted during two idyllic weeks as housesitter and keeper of their garden in Retzbachweg.

The best gardens, of course, are those tended by an expert husbandman, and I have been fortunate to share my life with one. For propping, nurturing, pinching, and always encouraging growth, I dedicate this book to Jim Allen.

A shorter version of Chapter 1 was previously published as "Tracing the Origins of the Rosary: German Vernacular Texts," in *Speculum: A Journal of Medieval Studies* 68 (1993): 619–36. Paragraphs from the introduction and from Chapter 4 appeared in " 'Minne' in Spiritual Gardens of the Fifteenth Century," in *Canon and Canon Transgression in Medieval German Literature*, ed. Albrecht Classen (Göppingen: Kümmerle, 1993), 153–62. In addition, some material in the introduction and parts of Chapter 5 also appeared in "German Rosary Exempla: Spirituality and 'Self-Help' in Late Medieval Popular Piety," *Proceedings of the Nineteenth International Conference on Patristic, Mediaeval, and Renaissance Studies*, ed. Thomas Losconcy, Joseph Schnaubelt, and Karl Gersbach (Villanova: Augustinian Historical Institute, 1996). Permission to draw upon these previously published pieces is gratefully acknowledged.

Introduction

> [H]e followed the noble fragrance until he came to the
> beautiful rose. . . . For the Son of the Most High saw
> this lovely, tender, fragrant rose blooming among the
> thorns of the sinful world and the sweet fragrance of
> her earnest desire wafted up to him unceasingly. He
> was caught by her eager love and so enraptured that
> he leapt from his father's lap down to this rose among
> thorns and was so sorely pierced that his hands and
> feet bled.
> —*Our Lady Mary's Rose Garden*, c. 1430

This story of the Lover and the Rose[1] seems at first glance to resemble the
Lover's quest in the popular medieval story, *The Romance of the Rose*.
Thus, it may come as something of a surprise to the modern reader to
learn that it is actually a story about the rosary prayer and that its
characters are the Virgin Mary and Christ. The work, which is attributed
to two Carthusian monks named Adolf of Essen (d. 1439) and Dominic of
Prussia (d. 1460), explains the symbolism of the rose and the uses of the
devotional exercise called a *Rosenkranz*—a garland of roses.

Like most works of the devotional garden allegory genre, this one calls
up the language and images of the Old Testament Song of Songs and
fuses them with the conventions and terminology of courtly love. The
account tells, for example, how the Son of the Most High comes to fetch
the Rose and take her to his father's kingdom "as a king's son does a
beloved bride" (lines 262–64).[2] How does this chivalrous-sounding love
story of the Rose fit with our modern notion of spirituality? Clearly,

the religious sensibilities expressed here seem alien to the twentieth-century mind.

The two fifteenth-century monks who created this work were devout members of the Carthusian religious order. At a time when discipline in most other orders had become lax and spirituality was badly in need of renewal, Carthusians were considered models of piety and frequently called on to aid in reform efforts.[3] Within Adolf and Dominic's own order an innovative prayer exercise was at this time generating considerable enthusiasm: a new kind of rosary, one to which a set of meditations reviewing Christ's acts of redemption had recently been added. Adolf and Dominic's prior, the reform-minded Johannes Rode (d. 1439), advocated this new exercise as an aid to achieving deeper spirituality, and their fellow Carthusian brothers at Trier are said to have made more than one thousand copies of the prayer, which they circulated among their own houses as well as to many Benedictine convents that Johannes Rode was tasked with reforming.[4]

Adolf and Dominic could not have foreseen that their rosary and other new forms of it would rapidly spread beyond the cloister to be taken up by the laity. Soon the rosary would spawn a brotherhood that claimed a million members (both living and deceased) on the eve of the Reformation.[5] The new brotherhood's success was not imagined even by its Dominican promoters Alanus de Rupe, Jakob Sprenger, and the scores of Dominican Observants who subsequently went out founding brotherhoods and preaching the rosary to the laity.

What message did these Observant reformers carry as they went about distributing rosaries? And what kind of spirituality was it that they preached? How is their version of the prayer related to Adolf and Dominic's and to other forms? When did these many options coalesce into the rosary that is in use today—still the most commonly said private devotion of the Catholic Church?

To the basic form of the prayer—"Hail Mary, full of grace, the Lord is with thee; blessed art thou among women, and blessed is the fruit of thy womb"—that had emerged in the twelfth century, more elements continued to be assimilated.[6] In the course of the thirteenth and fourteenth centuries the name "Jesus" was appended to the prayer, and in the sixteenth century the phrase: "Holy Mary, Mother of God, pray for us sinners now and at the hour of our death," plus also the Creed, and finally the Gloria.[7] The most distinctive feature of the devotion today is its combination of oral repetition with serial mental meditations.

The 150 Aves—divided into three sets of fifty—are recited orally in groups of ten punctuated by an Our Father. During each set of ten Aves the worshiper meditates on one of a series of fifteen mysteries, events in the lives of Christ and Mary that comprise five joyful, five sorrowful, and five glorious episodes. The joyful mysteries recount: (1) the Annunciation, (2) the Visitation, (3) the Nativity, (4) the Presentation, and (5) the Lost Child Jesus Found in the Temple.[8] The sorrowful events comprise: (1) the Agony in the Garden, (2) the Scourging, (3) the Crowning with Thorns, (4) the Carrying of the Cross, and (5) the Crucifixion. The glorious mysteries celebrate: (1) the Resurrection, (2) the Ascension, (3) the Descent of the Holy Spirit on the Apostles, (4) the Assumption of the Virgin Mary, and (5) the Coronation of the Blessed Virgin Mary as Queen of Heaven (earlier the Last Judgment or the Joys of Paradise).

Just when the first serial meditations on the life of Christ came into use remains unclear. Until recently, it was thought that these narrative meditations, which profoundly changed the character of the devotion, were first added to the Ave prayer in the fifteenth century. But in 1977 a manuscript was discovered containing a rosary with *vita Christi* meditations that dates back one hundred years earlier.[9] This discovery has raised new questions about when and how this new form of the devotion developed. Recently, Peter Ochsenbein, in a study of communal prayer among the laity in fifteenth- and sixteenth-century Switzerland, issued a call for new research into the early history of the rosary.[10]

Thus far, studies of the origins of the prayer have concentrated primarily on Latin texts because the devotion was assumed to have been composed in that language. The intriguing fact that the first Latin *vita Christi* rosaries all appeared in German-speaking areas strongly suggests, however, that vernacular works also need to be examined for what they can reveal about the prayer and its development. German rosaries dating from the thirteenth and fourteenth centuries parallel Latin ones. By looking at some of the many experiments with versions of the prayer that can be found in vernacular devotional writings, this study examines how the narrative came to be incorporated into the rosary text and why the transition to this kind of format contributed to the remarkable success of this religious exercise.

Why this particular prayer—of all the medieval experiments in devotional exercises—succeeded so dramatically has to do not only with its form but also with developments in popular religious piety, in an age when, as Steven Ozment states, the forms of piety were "never before so numerous or varied."[11] As a devotional exercise, the rosary combined elements from three older kinds of meditations to create a new, more engrossing prayer that was particularly suited to the spiritual needs of the lay faithful. As a religious practice, it influenced as well as responded to the demands of the laity for new, more individual and private forms of religious observance.

Its effect on extraliturgical piety was far-reaching. It generated (and, in turn, was affected by) a secondary literature of its own, as rosary books, testimonial anecdotes, exempla, legends, songs, and poems about it were composed. In the visual arts, it provided the theme for large numbers of devotional paintings, altars, sculptures, and block prints. To laypersons it provided a new source of spiritual guarantees, mediated by lay associations and dispensed outside of the corporate liturgical offices of the church.

As the "layperson's breviary" or "common man's hours," this private devotion served as an imitation of the monastic hours.[12] It answered both the need for a meditative exercise to supplement the mass that could be practiced in private and also for a prayer to be said during the mass by those who were not able to follow the Latin text of the celebrations. Confraternity members could recite the devotion at home privately and at the same time participate in a large spiritual brotherhood. They could share not only in the collective spiritual credits amassed by other members, but also in the benefits offered by the religious order of the Dominicans, which sponsored the confraternity and said special masses for its adherents.

The religious confraternity that was spawned by the devotion also participated in the shaping of the practice. Officially established at Cologne in 1475, it enrolled 100,000 members within the first seven years. From there it grew exponentially to become within a short time the largest such organization. Unlike most confraternities, the rosary brotherhood cost nothing to join, had no required meetings, and accepted everyone. Even deceased persons could be enrolled and prayers said on their behalf. Just as compelling as the opportunity to give aid to friends languishing in purgatory was the assurance that through this kind of self-help alliance members could guarantee prayers to be said for their own souls after death.

More than anything else, the reason so many people wanted to join the brotherhood was the acute need to provide greater security for their souls in the face of the threat of purgatory. Ironically, however, it was because of the granting of ever-greater special indulgences that the devotion fell victim to its own success. Spurious claims of indulgences for saying the prayer ballooned to outrageous proportions of up to 120,000 years.[13] Increasingly, the exercise came to be exploited as a way to stockpile insurance against prolonged suffering in purgatory. The devotional narrative meditations that had earlier been the focus of the prayer when it was promoted by the Carthusians became submerged in a host of other sets of complicated, numerical, and non-narrative meditations. Increasingly, the practice became the vehicle for a kind of legalistic "arithmetical" piety.[14] This mechanical and quantitative aspect of the exercise left it open to attacks by Protestant reformers who vigorously rejected the entire practice as fraudulent along with the indulgences and the doctrine of purgatory itself.

To be sure, there were excesses to criticize. Yet, despite the general mood of anticlericalism and dissatisfaction with religious institutions, most people still continued to accept the faith taught by the church as true.[15] The late medieval period was, in fact, a time of intense popular religious fervor.[16] Bernd Moeller has argued that in Germany, at least, the fifteenth century was "one of the most churchly-minded and devout periods of the Middle Ages." Moeller identifies this intense pious fervor and the "deep respect for the authority of the church" as prerequisites for Luther's success and as an explanation for why the Reformation took place in Germany, "a sluggish, medieval country where authority was still respected, rather than, for example, in France."[17]

Other scholars, like Stephen Ozment, agree that fifteenth-century religiosity was fervent, yet characterize it as "flawed" and "unsatisfying" because of the church's failure to provide a distinctive model of spirituality suited to the needs of the laity, a failure that—if one accepts Ozment's view—also played a role in the rosary's extraordinary success.[18] In a similar vein, Francis Oakley has suggested that while the intensity and vitality of late-medieval piety may not be in doubt, there remain many questions yet to be answered about its "quality."[19] This study will address some of these "quality" questions by looking at notions of spirituality as conveyed in vernacular writings about the rosary: the songs, statutes, exempla, and handbooks of the newly founded rosary brotherhood.

From the late-twentieth-century perspective there seems to be an unbridgeable incompatibility between late-fifteenth-century "religious fervor" and the calculations by which parishioners amassed indulgence "credits." Here particularly, an examination of devotion to the rosary serves as a useful case study of the ongoing tension between those contradictory aspects of medieval piety identified by Anton Mayer as "the sincere emotion of spiritualized faith" versus its "mechanization and resultant profaning" ("Profanierung").[20] In the linking together of meditation with quantitative prayer quotas, Ernst Schubert characterizes the rosary as "an expression of the breadth of late-medieval piety, which was able to unite the seemingly incompatible, that is, inward spirituality with calculation ['Berechnung']." Calling it "a piety that defies unequivocal labels and catchword definitions," Schubert doubts the ability of a social history of ideas to make general statements about the "externality" versus "depth" of late-medieval religion.[21]

While accepting the cautionary word about "catchword definitions," the present study sees the development of the rosary in the fifteenth century as an opportunity to examine the interaction of these two aspects of late-medieval faith. By looking at what other fifteenth-century documents said about the rosary, one can form a picture of how this religious exercise was viewed by users at the time; that is, as Anne Middleton urges, from the point of view of "practice" rather than "doctrine."[22] Accordingly, the documents consulted here include the popular media of the fifteenth century—broadsheets, pamphlets, handbooks, woodcuts, and altarpieces—vernacular "texts" that provide a much-needed late-medieval perspective on the issue of "spirituality versus calculation." It will be shown that, as Eamon Duffy has recently indicated, lay piety was perhaps not so lacking in spirituality as has generally been assumed. There is, as Duffy says, "much yet to discover about the processes and the pace of reform."[23]

As noted earlier, the bulk of the scholarship on the rosary so far has relied on Latin sources and focused on the question of authorship. Besides Jean Mabillon's (d. 1707) early investigations into the antiquity of the Ave Maria, the most significant research undertaken remains that of the Bollandist scholar, Thomas Esser, who in the 1880s established that the 400-year-old tradition attributing the devotion and its meditations to Saint Dominic (d. 1221) was a case of mistaken identity.[24] This claim unleashed a storm of protest and initiated vigorous efforts to defend the tradition and the imperiled honor of Saint Dominic. At the turn of the century, the English canon Herbert Thurston entered the debate by publishing a series of articles in *The Month* in which he argued decisively that Saint Dominic could not have been the progenitor of the rosary and refuted evidence to the contrary piece by piece.[25]

Although it was another forty years before the church accepted the weight of this evidence, a number of studies were published in the interim to reiterate Esser's and Thurston's findings, including those of Stephan Beissel, Wilhelm Schmitz, and Jakob Hubert Schütz.[26] In 1948 Franz Michel Willam published an influential study that put forward a theory of how the rosary could have developed out of Marian and Jesus psalters, while Willibald Kirfel examined the prayer's origins in relationship to similar devotions practiced by other world religions.[27] In 1969 Stefano Orlandi published several early texts of significance to the history of the rosary, including the statutes of the second Italian confraternity together with woodcuts, engravings, illustrations, and other devotions similar to the rosary. Along with these Orlandi reprinted a 1505 Italian version of the second edition of one of the earliest documents of the Cologne rosary brotherhood, the *Quodlibet de veritate fraternitatis Rosarii* (Academic disputation on the true character of the brotherhood of the rosary) that was issued together with the *Compendium psalterii beatissimae Trinitatis* (Compendium of the Psalter of the Blessed Trinity), a work attributed to Alanus de Rupe, founder of an even-earlier brotherhood at Douai.[28] An innovative study by Jean-Claude Schmitt in 1971 examined membership rolls of the confraternity chapter founded in Colmar in 1485 and signaled a new approach by exploring the interaction between the rosary text and its larger sociological context.[29]

The most controversial study to date has been Karl Josef Klinkhammer's *Adolf von Essen und seine Werke* (Adolf of Essen and his works, 1972), which ascribes the rosary meditations to the Carthusian monk Adolf of Essen (d. 1439), a prior of the Trier charterhouse. This claim has been strongly criticized by Rainer Scherschel who found no compelling evidence that Adolf of Essen wrote any of the works attributed to him by Klinkhammer.[30] Scherschel's own study investigates the commonalities between the rosary and the "Jesus prayer" and discusses the background and religious uses of repetitive prayer.

In 1975, on the five-hundredth anniversary of the founding of the rosary confraternity, the Diözesan-Museum of Cologne assembled a retrospective exhibition, "500 Jahre Rosenkranz," and published an exhibition catalogue featuring articles on the history of the prayer and on the brotherhood.[31] At the time it was still felt that the life-of-Christ rosary had originated in the fifteenth century.

The discovery in 1977 by Andreas Heinz of a rosary text with *vita Christi* meditations one hundred years older than any previous ones eliminated all certainty about who "wrote" the narrative rosary and has

left open the still unresolved question of how the devotion might actually
have evolved.[32] As recently as 1988, André Duval summarized what is
currently known about the practice and the confraternity in an article for
the *Dictionnaire de spiritualité*.[33] Duval concludes by reviewing the
various popular and charismatic movements in France that have rejuve-
nated the rosary in recent years. The practice is still very much alive and
evolving, even though the conditions of its origins remain obscure.

The approach of the present study is to demonstrate that the rosary has
always been evolving in a lively way. It is not one text but many: actually
multiple versions embedded in a constellation of texts that described,
interpreted, and marketed forms of the devotion to users who collectively
shaped and selected the ultimate version of choice. Critical to this process
was the viability of the narrative. Thus Chapter 1 traces the earliest
experiments in both Latin and German vernacular texts with adding life-
of-Christ meditations to the prayer and shows how the nature of the
text—its narrative form—exercised a decisive influence on the development of the devotion and carried the new type of rosary to popular acceptance.

Probably the most influential version of the rosary was a picture
text—the first of many picture rosaries—that appeared in 1483 as a set of
woodcuts (without an accompanying written text) inserted into a rosary
handbook printed for the brotherhood in Ulm.[34] This set of illustrations
soon appeared in other prints as well as in altarpieces and devotional
paintings throughout the German-speaking region. Although the sources
of these popular illustrations are unknown, they bear a strong resemblance
to other cycles of devotional pictures recounting the joys of the Virgin
and the Passion of Christ that are found in altarpieces, illuminated
manuscripts, and early printed books. Chapter 2 thus examines the
relationship of the rosary figures to their pictorial antecedents and consid-
ers the important role played by these pictures in the evolution of the
practice. Of particular interest is the way in which the illustrations
affected the development of the written text.

A further source of information about the devotion is found in the
statutes of rosary confraternities. These documents record how the devotion was actually practiced and how it was explained to users. Chapter 3
examines the process by which the large array of texts and formats were
supplanted by the set of fifteen mysteries that ultimately became the most
popular version. This format, which coalesced out of common sources
with the earliest picture rosaries, underscores the importance of the

interaction between pictorial and written forms in the prayer's development.

Chapter 4 examines the symbolism of the rose narrative and the popular fifteenth-century image of the Virgin in a rose garden, a genre that combines elements of secular love garden illustrations with the Marian iconographic emblems of the rose and the enclosed garden (the "hortus conclusus" of the Song of Songs—frequently the scene of the Annunciation in iconographic works). Corresponding to the pictorial images are literary texts, devotional garden allegories, of which no fewer than thirty-four were produced in German- and Dutch-speaking areas during the fifteenth century.[35] These devotional texts rely on the language and images of the nuptial dialogue between bride and bridegroom in the Song of Songs to portray the relationship between the loving soul and Christ, the beloved. As a theme and vehicle for allegory the garden embraces both spiritual and sensual images. With links to the mystical Christian iconography of the rose, the enclosed paradise garden of the Song of Songs came to be interpreted in many works as Mary herself—that virginal garden in which the rose, Christ, was planted. Ann Astell has shown how the Gospel narrative, together with the story of Mary, was used to "historicize" the Song of Songs, that is, to provide a narrative storyline for the love dialogue.[36]

The multivalence of mystical and sensual expressions adopted from the Song of Songs make many devotional works almost indistinguishable from their profane counterparts.[37] Some religious songs of the "Meistersinger" (fifteenth-century guild singers) depict, for example, scenes with Mary reposing in a beautiful garden while the Divine Lover weaves a rose garland for his beloved.[38] Because of their use of the Song of Songs nuptial garden setting it is not surprising that devotional garden allegories relied even more than many other religious writings on the language and images of connubial love. The very premise that Christ, as bridegroom, had been wounded in his heart (Song of Songs 4:9) made Christ's Passion a kind of "Liebesleidenschaft," because it occurred not out of necessity but as freely willed suffering for love.[39] Because Mary was seen as the *first* bride of Christ, she served as the model for each individual believer. Accordingly, the enclosed garden also represented the heart, locus of the soul's communion with Christ, a garden of mystical spiritual delights available to the devout soul.[40]

The bringing together of the rose emblem with the love garden, as symbol of the soul, gave rise to the activity of making for the Virgin

chaplets of symbolic roses grown in "the garden of the heart."[41] Thanks
to the competing sacred and profane connotations of both motifs, the term
"rosarium" was for a time controversial. Yet, despite this uncertainty,
the rose emblem served as an attractive signifier for the practice and
itself contributed considerably to the enormous popular appeal of the
devotional exercise.

Chapter 5 looks at popular songs, confraternity handbooks, and exempla
to discover how the rosary was promoted and the text received by users.
Jacques Le Goff has described exempla, along with the sermons in which
they were embedded, as the "mass media" of the Middle Ages.[42] Certainly
we know more about literate society than we do about the ordinary
people, for whom these sermon illustrations (exempla) were written—
those whom Aron Gurevich calls "people without archives or faces."[43]
Increasingly medieval research has been concerned with constructing a
sociology of late-medieval religion, a picture to encompass both scholarly
and popular culture. Gurevich describes sermons as a bridge between
these spheres. While sermons and sermon illustrations translated theolog-
ical and philosophical writings for a popular audience, they were themselves at the same time shaped by the language, interests, assumptions,
and demands of listeners.[44] In the same way that catechisms were defined
by the religious and moral questions of concern to lay society, so the
audience for sermon illustrations determined their content. The community exercised a form of censorship by accepting only what appealed to its
own tastes. Preachers, who themselves stemmed from the local populace—
and were often only marginally literate—shared these tastes.[45]

Many accounts of miracles that appeared in collections of exempla, like
those compiled by Caesarius of Heisterbach, were culled from area pastors.
Caesarius cites them as sources of several of his stories.[46] Many of these
are clearly tales that first circulated among the laity. Reports of miracles
performed by local saints or by the Virgin Mary migrated from oral into
written accounts as they were copied down, passed on, and reworked in
the retelling. Eileen Power calls the Virgin Mary of the exempla "a figure
of popular folklore" more than a figure of "doctrinal devotion."[47] The
miracles associated with the Virgin and her rosary grew out of common
needs. Thus they drew on the popular imagination of people for whom
the Hail Mary served as a kind of lay liturgy.

Illustrations, anecdotes, and short stories were, for obvious reasons, the
most popular parts of sermons. Some pastors of the later Middle Ages

were criticized for preaching sermons that seemed to consist of nothing but stories. For the average listener, these illustrations were needed to "prove" the point and lend validity to the message being preached. This need to have points proved by exempla is expressed, for example, clearly in the words of the novice to whom Caesarius relates his moral tales, when the novice declares, "Now I believe what has been said, but, nevertheless, I desire to have four points proved to me by illustration rather than by explanation."[48] Indeed, as Caesarius states in the prologue to his collection, exempla are for those who are "poor, not in grace, but in learning."[49] The exempla that appeared in confraternity handbooks are stories that prove the efficacy of the devotion and the authority of the rosary and its brotherhood. They advertise the indulgences to be gained, give testimony to the benefits people have already received—testimonials of the living as well as reports from purgatory—and proclaim the power of the prayer to deflect the forces of evil.

Early versions of exempla composed and circulated by the Carthusians of Trier strongly emphasized the salutary effects on morality and the spiritual life that were worked by reviewing the life of Christ and his acts of redemption in the meditations newly attached to the Ave prayer. In contrast, later versions of these same tales in confraternity handbooks scarcely mention *vita Christi* meditations and focus instead on the importance of membership in the brotherhood and on reciting the requisite number of repetitions. The comparison of early and later exempla underscores the close connection of the life-of-Christ rosary to the Observant Reform movement at the early stages of the devotion's development.

The wave of monastic reform known as the Observant movement that swept Germany in the late fourteenth and early fifteenth centuries, in which the Carthusians of Trier had participated, fostered personal prayer and what Francis Oakley terms the "more methodical meditative practices," similar to those developed by practitioners of the *Devotio Moderna*.[50] Among these exercises, the new *vita Christi* rosary—with its marriage of life-of-Christ piety and devotion to the Virgin—turned out to be such a congenial union, that the new prayer quickly was taken up enthusiastically by the lay populace. The growth and spread of this new prayer—ancestor to the modern rosary—and the changes made in it is the story of how a reformist development was taken over by larger, less reform-minded forces that adapted and promoted it to appeal to a mass market. Ultimately, these forces were in turn themselves overtaken by the more radical developments of the Protestant movement that, however ironically, served to promote the recovery of the original character of the devotion and abetted its continued rise to prominence.

Accordingly, the rosary cannot be regarded, in the way it traditionally has been, as having had an independent integrity throughout its history, but rather as a text that was packaged and repackaged to appeal to the needs of users by groups with differing spiritual agendas. Instead of looking at the rosary as a fixed practice that was handed down in definitive form, the present study examines it as a communal text that reflected—but at the same time also influenced—the religious experience of its public.

Stephen Greenblatt suggests in his description of a proposed "poetics of culture" that attention should be focused less on "the presumed center of the literary domain than at its borders." He advocates looking, for example, at how collective beliefs were "shaped, moved from one medium to another, concentrated in manageable aesthetic form, [and] offered for consumption."[51] This suggested approach is uncannily accurate in describing the nature and development of the rosary. Its simultaneous evolution as a written and pictorial prayer, as well as one that inheres in a social ritual, places it at the edge of literary studies but located at the juncture of several disciplines. As text and social ritual it participates in discourses that are both verbal and nonverbal, such as those that communicate through visual images and communal activities. An artifact belonging to two media, it illustrates well how written works can be influenced by pictorial ones. As a literary text, it demonstrates how a practice was shaped into "manageable aesthetic form" by the narrative that undergirds the ritual exercise and signifies the ongoing spiritual reality that is enacted. Looked at in terms of discourse and discourse change, the rosary serves as a vehicle for the study of the contested nature of late-medieval piety. The method employed here is a mix of cultural history and conventional philology that attempts to bring together the seemingly disparate techniques of the two disciplines to look at the "text" and late-medieval practice of the rosary in new ways.

1

Early Rosaries

In the fifty-five volumes of medieval Latin religious lyrics collected in the *Analecta hymnica*, rosaries and Marian Psalters alone take up the better part of three volumes.[1] The large number of prayers designated by these names is evidence of two things: that they were popular forms and that there was not just one rosary in the Middle Ages. But how are Marian psalters and rosaries related to each other? And how are they connected to the one(s) that the brotherhood was founded to promote? Out of so many options, how did the prayer that is said today become the "official" or standard form?

As indicated, the earliest form of Hail Mary is composed of two salutations: the Angel Gabriel's greeting to Mary in Luke 1:28 and her cousin Elisabeth's greeting in Luke 1:42. In the West, the earliest linking together of these two passages occurs in a seventh-century antiphon of the offertory of the mass for the fourth Sunday of Advent that was traditionally attributed to Gregory the Great.[2] By the eleventh century, the greeting had become well known because of its inclusion in the extremely popular Little Office of the Blessed Virgin, where the words "Ave Maria" were invoked repeatedly. Marian legends and anecdotes of the twelfth and thirteenth centuries tell of pious individuals reciting chains of 50, 60, 100, or 150 repetitions of the prayer as a religious exercise or gesture of devotion to the Virgin.[3] It was believed that hearing these words brought Mary delight by recalling to her the joy of the Incarnation.

Often these repetitions were counted on knotted cords or strands of beads. Prayer counters of beads and other materials are, of course, not unique to Western Christianity but common to many world religious. Reporting on his travels in the East Marco Polo (c. 1254–1324) noted, for example, that the king of Malabar wore a chain of 104 (probably actually 108) gems that he used for reciting morning and evening prayers.[4] Still older than these Buddhist prayer counters are the chains of ninety-nine beads used by Muslims as early as the ninth century for reciting the ninety-nine names of Allah. These counters derive from even older Hindu prayer beads associated with ancient worship of the god Shiva.[5]

While it has been assumed that the Christians first brought back prayer counters from the Holy Land at the time of the Crusades, devotional beads were actually in use in Europe before the time of the Crusades. The most prominent example is that of the famous Lady Godiva of Coventry (d. 1041) who bequeathed to the Benedictine priory she founded a set of gems threaded on a cord that she used to recite her prayers.[6] At Nevilles in Belgium another chain has been preserved that reputedly belonged to Abbess Gertrude (d. 659), daughter of Pippin I. Still older accounts tell of how Christian hermits Paul of Thebes (c. 234–347) and Saint Anthony (251–356) in the deserts of Egypt and Syria employed pebbles and knotted strings to keep track of the prayers they chanted unceasingly.[7]

Thus, while it is not known exactly how old the first prayer counters are, it is clear that the beads predate the Hail Mary and that other devotions were said on them first. Among the earlier prayers were repetitions of the Our Father from which they derived the popular name Paternoster beads, or simply paternosters. Repetitions of Our Fathers were used, for example, by lay brothers of the Carthusian and Cistercian

orders as a replacement for the prayers of the Divine Office.[8] Other
laypeople said Paternosters or Hail Marys as acts of devotion or penance.
Thus Caesarius of Heisterbach (1180–1240) reports the case of a matron
who regularly recited fifty Hail Marys and experienced a taste of wonder-
ful sweetness in her mouth.[9] Two Marian miracle stories of the twelfth
century tell of a knight who prayed one hundred Hail Marys a day in
order to rid himself of an unhappy passion for his master's wife and of "a
wife" who succeeded in ridding her husband of his mistress (although it
was the mistress who prayed the devotion!).[10] Other legends tell of people
reciting the Hail Mary 150 times over.[11]

In a Middle Low German code of Laws from 1220/35 the beads used for
keeping track of these prayers are called a "zapel" (chaplet or corona).[12]
At Ghent in 1242 beguines were required by their regulations to pray
three "chaplets" ("hoedekins") of 50 Aves daily.[13] Other religious devoted
themselves to marathon repetitions of the prayer. Thomas Esser reports
that certain Dominican nuns at the cloister of Unterlinden in Colmar
prayed a thousand Hail Marys each day, and on special days two
thousand.[14]

But the chains of Hail Marys by themselves do not yet constitute a
rosary in the modern sense; that is, a combination of verbal prayer and
an accompanying set of mental meditations. This development arose out
of the recitation of the 150 Psalms of the Old Testament in private
devotions imitating the canonical hours. In "Marian psalters," which
originated around 1130, the antiphons that preceded each Psalm in the
liturgy of the Hours and announced its theme were replaced by short
verses that interpreted each of the 150 Psalms as a reference to Christ or
Mary.[15] Gradually the devotion was shortened to recitation of the antiphons alone and either Paternosters or Ave Marias. Without the Psalms,
the connection that the antiphons had to a specific theme was lost. As a
result the antiphons themselves came to be replaced by rhymed free
paraphrases or simply by a litany of 150 verses in praise of the Virgin.
Partly for ease of recitation, the Marian psalters were subdivided into
three sets of fifty stanzas, each set of which was also designated as a
chaplet (later a "rosary").

F. M. Willam has hypothesized that the modern rosary developed out
of a combination of these two abbreviated forms of the Psalter; that is,
"psalters" composed only of 150 Ave Marias or Paternosters and the
rhymed Marian or Jesus psalters (150 stanzas representing the Psalms as
"veiled images" of Mary or Jesus).[16] The problem with this explanation is

that it leaves unanswered the question how the life-of-Christ meditations that have characterized the rosary since the fourteenth century became part of the text. A look at the Mary and Jesus psalters dating from before 1300 shows that they do not themselves contain connected life-of-Christ narratives.[17] Instead, they consist of lists of attributes of Christ or Mary keyed to the Psalms. Thus these texts alone cannot constitute the source for the narrative meditations linked to the Ave prayer that appeared in later rosaries.

That meditating sequentially on the life of Christ would eventually be joined together with the Hail Mary seems in retrospect almost inevitable given the emphasis in the late Middle Ages on reenacting the life of Jesus—particularly the Passion—in spiritual exercises and in religious pageants. Since the average layperson was regarded as incapable of higher-order imageless contemplation, reviewing the stations in the life of Jesus storywise was the form of devotional exercise recommended for the laity. And keeping the Passion ever before the mind was the primary way of training the heart in Christian virtues and of conforming the individual to Christ's example.[18] Pausing at intervals during the day to pray and reflect on the stations of the Passion was for some a part of the rhythm of the working day. The midday bell was rung (at first on Fridays and eventually every day) as a reminder of the hour of the Crucifixion.[19] Other bells called to mind the specific scenes commemorated in the liturgical Hours, depicted in pictorial works and taught in sermons and mystery plays. By serially picturing and reflecting on the stations of Christ's life and death, the laity could both sanctify daily life and participate in the collective prayer of the church at the liturgical hours and during mass.[20] Thus the mental habit of moving progressively point by point through the life of Jesus seems a natural complement to the devotional act of reciting a series of Hail Marys.

As has been indicated, it was thought until recently that the combination was first put together in the fifteenth century. This assertion was made in the 1880s by the Bollandist scholar, Thomas Esser, who established that the 400-year-old tradition ascribing the prayer to Saint Dominic (c. 1170–1221), founder of the Dominican order, was a case of mistaken identity. Noting that the Ave prayer predated Saint Dominic and that there was no evidence that he had anything to do with adding meditations to it, Esser argued that the practice was invented by another Dominic: a Carthusian named Dominic of Prussia (1384–1460) of the Charterhouse at Trier (one of the two authors to whom *Our Lady Mary's Rose Garden* is attributed).[21] In his "Liber experientiarum" (1458) Dominic of Prussia explicitly claimed to be the first to have composed a series of fifty points on the life of Christ that were to be meditated on while reciting the Ave Maria.[22] It was the addition of these meditations (later called mysteries) to the much-older Ave prayer that marked the beginning of a new form of the religious exercise.

Esser's assertion that Dominic the Carthusian was the true progenitor of the modern rosary remained undisputed until 1977, when Andreas Heinz discovered a manuscript containing a *vita Christi* rosary much older than Dominic's.[23] Dated around 1300, Heinz's text is contained in a manuscript collection of prayers that were recited by the Cistercian nuns at the cloister of Saint Thomas on the Kyll, located forty kilometers from Trier. Despite the relative proximity of Saint Thomas to Trier, there appears to be no connection between this obscure early rosary and Dominic's later, widely disseminated one, which he composed sometime between 1409 and 1415.[24] Dominic himself makes no mention of the Cistercian prayer; instead he attributes his inspiration to a passage in Mechthild of Hackeborn's (1241–99) *Liber spiritualis gratiae* (Book of spiritual grace) where Mechthild records a vision of a beautiful tree upon whose leaves were written in golden letters the entire life of Christ.[25] If Dominic actually did not know of the version already in use at Saint Thomas on the Kyll, then these two narrative rosaries must have been invented independently. A third possibility is that both were based on Mechthild's vision or another work.

Yet despite its early date[26] and obscurity, the life-of-Christ rosary used by the Cistercian nuns at Saint Thomas on the Kyll is less isolated than it might seem to be; there is also a Middle High German Mary-psalter of approximately the same time that shows a parallel development going on in the Marian psalter form. Taken together, these three experiments give a picture of the process by which life-of-Christ narratives became part of the rosary.[27]

In fact, there are good reasons for considering the possibility that the new form of the devotion might have begun as a vernacular prayer. Contrary to the long-held assumption that German rosaries are transla-tions of Latin ones, recent examination by Peter Appelhans of a large number of vernacular Marian devotional writings shows that these prayers were seldom directly related to a specific Latin source.[28] Karl Klinkham-mer, in his extensive study of Dominic the Carthusian's writings, asserts that Dominic himself actually composed his first rosary in German and

then translated it into Latin.[29] The earliest examples of both German and
Latin rosaries that contain life-of-Christ meditations are found in Middle
Dutch- or German-speaking areas where religious reform movements
were fostering increased use of the vernacular. Devotional writings of all
kinds were becoming more and more independent of Latin models.
Whether the new rosary appeared first in German or in Latin is less
important, however, than what the vernacular versions can contribute to
a picture of its development.

The Transition from Psalter to Life-of-Christ Meditation

Examples of the Ave prayer in the vernacular are almost as numerous as
they are in Latin.[30] Likewise Marian psalters in German can be found that
date from the thirteenth and fourteenth centuries and that parallel early
Latin versions. Of these vernacular Mary-psalters and rosaries, four
predate or are roughly contemporary with the Latin one of the Cistercian
nuns of Saint Thomas on the Kyll. Examining these and some slightly
later works one can form a picture of how the prayer changed to assimilate
the life-of-Christ narrative. In the three earliest examples one sees the
Marian psalter as it existed in its traditional format before biographical
scenes were added to it. But the fourth example contains a striking
innovation. Here a *vita Christi* narrative of thirty-eight verses has been
inserted into a standard litany of praises to the Virgin.

The first of these vernacular prayers is preserved only as a fragment in
a manuscript of the thirteenth century. But a complete version of the
same work can be found in a fifteenth-century copy.[31] As is characteristic
of the early Latin Marian psalters, the prayer is made up of rhymed four-
line stanzas, each beginning with the salutation "Ave Maria" in place
of—or indicating—the entire salutation. The fifty verbal "roses" consist
of Marian iconographic symbols and titles of honor each followed by a
supplication, as in the example:

> Ave Maria, rose without thorns,
> you were born to comfort me.
> A queen of high birth,
> help me that I shall not be lost.
>   (stanza 2)[32]

The titles—"rose without thorns," "bright sun," "fountain of grace," "heart's joy," and so forth—include no mention of Mary's sufferings or of events of Christ's life.

The second work dates from the late thirteenth or early fourteenth century and, likewise, is a fragment from a longer one that originally consisted of either 50 or 150 stanzas.[33] As in the earlier prayer, each of the four-line stanzas begins with the salutation "Ave Maria" followed by a meditation in praise of the Virgin, along the pattern:

> Hail Mary, branch of Jesse,
> from you came the noble one,
> Jesus, your child, whose sweet name
> took away from us all our sins.
> (stanza 11)[34]

Together the verses make up a typical list of unconnected accolades, probably derived from the psalms, Marian hymns, sermons, or litanies such as the Litany of Loreto or the Akathist hymn. At this point still no traces of a narrative are in evidence.

The third work, also from the early fourteenth century, refers to itself specifically as a "rosary" ("rôsenkranze," lines 77 and 198).[35] Instead of beginning with the Latin words "Ave Maria," each of the 50 four-line stanzas here commences with its German equivalents: "ich grûze dich" (I greet you) or "gegrûzet sîstu" (hail to you), in alternating order. It should be noted that Marian psalters center on greetings and sometimes vary the salutation, using a different word of greeting in each section or alternating between them as in this example. The prayer ends with a request that the Virgin accept the gift of this "rose wreath" ("rôsen-krenzelîn") that is being offered to her, saying:

> I greet you, Mary, my Lady.
> Accept this little rose chaplet
> that I have recited for you today.
> (lines 197–99)[36]

Like the earlier two prayers, this one contains no scenes from the life of Christ or of Mary. Instead, it is made up of epithets praising the Virgin's purity, piety, and beauty, and saluting her with titles like "heaven's rose garden," saying:

> I greet you, rose garden of heaven,
> the chosen, the pure, the tender one.
> You noble, sweet rose blossom,
> entreat God for me through your goodness.
> (lines 13–16)[37]

While Marian psalters of this traditional type continued to be written at least into the seventeenth century, their main disadvantage was the lack of connection of the individual stanzas from one to another. The 150 verses were so difficult to remember that they virtually required the use of a written text. Worse, they could become almost as monotonous as the simple Aves recited alone. What was needed was a way to focus the attention more efficiently and a way to sequence the meditations so that they could be learned and remembered better than the random lists of attributes that had lost their original connection to the Psalms. For this the life of Christ was the perfect vehicle.

In the fourth vernacular Mary-psalter, which dates from the beginning of the fourteenth century, we see for the first time just such an innovation. Here a series of scenes in the life of Christ has been inserted within a traditional litany of praise to the Virgin.[38] As in many Marian psalters, the salutation in this prayer changes with each round of fifty verses from "Wis gegrüezet" (hail) to "Vrewe dich" (rejoice) and, finally, "Hilf uns" (help us) in the last set.[39] The first two groups of fifty meditations are very much like all previous ones, listing attributes of the Virgin:

> Hail, Jesse's kin;
> angel's praise, joy, delight;
> royal child of kingly descent,
> God's daughter, Christ's wet nurse.
> (lines 69–72)[40]

The third set of stanzas, however, contains a chronological sequence of thirty-eight events from the life of the Savior. These events recount Christ's conception, birth, childhood, ministry, Passion, death, Resurrection, and end with the Last Judgment. The story is integrated within the rhymed four-line verse form that was characteristic of Marian psalters.

> Help us, because of the glances
> that he often cast at you,
> as a child toward its mother.
> Whatever you wish, he does for your sake.
> Help us, Lady, on account of the fear
> that evil Herod caused you
> through the children
> that he struck, thus frightening you.
> Help us, because of the undefiled
> flight to Egypt; the suckling,
> God's nursing at your breasts,
> which surely pleased you.
>   (lines 635–46)[41]

It progresses from scenes focused on Mary to scenes focused on Christ's ministry and Passion, such as:

> Help us, on account of the noble reception
> with palms, as Christ neared
> Jerusalem, the place he yearned for,
> as he foretold that he would.
>   (lines 675–78)

and:

> Help up, Lady on account of the agony
> that Christ suffered on death's journey,
> when Pilate washed his hands,
> that we may find a just end.
>   (lines 735–38)[42]

Here we see making its way into the Marian psalter form the same kind of connected, point-by-point narrative of the life of Jesus that is found at the same time in the Latin rosary of the Cistercian nuns of Saint Thomas on the Kyll.

That this development did not take place in isolation and likely occurred by accretion rather than all at once can be demonstrated by turning to other Latin Marian psalters, which continued to be produced on the traditional models. The best examples of this in works roughly contemporary with the two texts just mentioned are found in two psalters by Engelbert, abbot of Admont (1297–1331).[43] Engelbert's rhymed "Psalterium Beatae Mariae Virginis" includes episodes from Christ's life, distributed within a traditional Marian litany. Its companion-piece, the "Psalterium de Domino Nostro Jesu Christi"—a similar litany devoted to Jesus—also contains scenes from Jesus' life and Passion. But in neither case do the episodes make up the kind of connected sequence of events found in the Cistercian Saint Thomas text, the German Marian psalter, and the rosary of Dominic the Carthusian. Interspersed between the scenes in Engelbert's psalters are rhetorical questions, typological elaborations, laudatory passages, and reflections that break up the sequence of the narrative.

Likewise, the Latin rosaries of Ulrich Stöcklin of Rottach (d. 1443), abbot of Wessobrunn, contain a mixture of events from Christ's life alternating with meditations in the form of a litany.[44] But again these are not the concise, connected sequences seen in the German Marian psalter or in the two Latin rosaries. Although Ulrich Stöcklin's rosaries are too late to have influenced the Cistercian one, they (like several others collected in volumes 36 and 38 of the *Analecta hymnica* dating from the fifteenth and sixteenth centuries) show that the accretion of life-of-Christ anecdotes into the older Marian litany form continued for some centuries even after the first full narrative sequences appeared around 1300 in both Latin and German. As late as the sixteenth century, life-of-Christ narrative elements constitute only about 50 percent of some Marian rosaries, even after the new form popularized by the rosary confraternities had already become official.

Dominic of Prussia's Life-of-Christ Rosary

Although Dominic the Carthusian's claim to have been the first to join biographical meditations to the Ave prayer does not hold up when the Cistercian and German vernacular texts are brought into the equation, it is true that Dominic's text was the first to be widely disseminated. As noted, Klinkhammer claims that Dominic and fellow members of his order made and distributed more than a thousand copies of his prayer exercise.[45] Moreover, Dominic's is the first to consist of exactly fifty meditations (although he apparently also composed a psalter version with 150).[46] The Cistercian text, on the other hand, contains ninety-eight *vita Christi* meditations (probably originally one hundred), and the German vernacular version only thirty-eight. The next question to be asked is whether the three sets of meditations stem from a common source. The answer is that they do not. While many episodes are the same in all three accounts, the emphasis is different in each one, as is the selection of scenes that are recounted. In fact, none of the prayers seems to have drawn directly from any of the most popular contemporary works on the life of Christ. Nor can the dissimilarities be accounted for by the unequal lengths of the texts. All three are long enough to contain fairly detailed accounts of the events in the life of Jesus.

Looking, for example, at the way the narratives begin, one sees that the Cistercian rosary opens with seven scenes in Mary's life before the Annunciation, while Dominic's begins with the Annunciation itself, and the German text, rather surprisingly, opens with the story already under way, with Mary first as expectant mother (lines 627–30), then gazing lovingly at her infant (631–34). To a greater degree than in the other two works, the emphasis here is on the motherhood of Mary. A major portion is devoted to the events of the Passion, but these scenes, likewise, are portrayed from the perspective of Mary's suffering at the martyrdom of her son and of her maternal longing for him after his Ascension into heaven (771–74). Mary's own Assumption and her Coronation are not included.

In contrast, the Cistercian prayer focuses its greatest attention on the ministry and Passion of Christ (about two-thirds of the lines). Structurally, it surrounds these sober events with a joyous frame, opening with a description of God's preelection and sanctification of the Virgin Mary (lines 1–7) and closing with Christ's celestial glory and with praise of man's liberation through the merits and intercession of Christ and his mother (83–98). The tone is one of rejoicing in the redemptive plan of these events. The work links together, in telescopic fashion, temporal and eternal scenes to tell the story from an eschatological perspective.

Like the Cistercian rosary, Dominic's prayer also emphasizes the ministry and Passion of Christ (approximately one-half of the clauses). While it does describe Mary's Assumption and Coronation, it otherwise mentions her in only nine of the fifty clauses.[47] Dominic uses the Christ

theme as a counterweight to the Marian theme. This is expressed in the
different structure of his work; that is, in its fifty tags or relative clauses
("clausulae"), as a series of variations in counterpoise to an unchanging
refrain. Patrick Diehl has pointed out that medieval religious verse should
be regarded as having a structure like that of jazz, a form in which the
interest lies in the variations that are performed on a given theme.[48]
Similarly, in Dominic's rosary, the Jesus narrative provides the texture, a
kind of counterpoint to the repeated rhythm of the Ave prayer. The two
themes are bound together by the relative-clause structure, which links
the refrain and variations by means of the connecting phrase "and blessed
is the fruit of thy womb, Jesus, who . . ." (Dominic states that in his
childhood in Cracow the name Jesus was not yet part of the prayer.)[49] It
should be noted here that in German-speaking countries today the words
of each meditation are recited with every repetition of the Hail Mary.
Dominic's text is not a cradle song or an eschatological interpretation of
the life of the Son of God, but an almost matter-of-fact narrative list. A
compendium like this one, which reveals no particular bias, could have
been taken from any number of chronological accounts of the earthly life
of the Savior.

Judging from the differing conceptions underlying each of the three
narratives, it seems quite possible that each of these works drew from a
different source. The dissimilarities, in fact, argue for a theory of multiple
genesis; that is, three independent redactors acting on the common
impulse to combine a *vita Christi* narrative with an Ave devotion.

With the redaction and circulation of Dominic's version, the history of
the rosary becomes even more complicated, as variations on the idea
proliferated. "Authors" and "users" rapidly created new versions of the
devotion on both old (psalter and repetitive) and new (narrative) models.
Central to this process was the founding of the rosary confraternity,
established by Jakob Sprenger in Cologne on 8 September 1475. One of
the greatest virtues of this brotherhood was its open attitude about which
version of the rosary devotion was to be recited. The success of the
brotherhood was at least partly due to this flexibility and to the absence
of punitive regulations. Members were allowed to say the devotion when
and as they wished. The guiding spirit behind these open regulations and
behind the movement as a whole had been Alanus de Rupe (1428–75),
who died on the day before the Cologne brotherhood was inaugurated.

Alanus had founded a similar brotherhood at Douai about 1470, but it
was not until the support of Emperor Frederick III (whose name appears

on the Cologne register of earliest members) was enlisted that the organization became recognized in Rome. Although Alanus did not antici- pate the phenomenal success of the brotherhood, he had wished the organization to be easy to join and without vows or constraints. Thus, there were no penalties for failing to say the prayer, no prescribed time for saying it, and no prescribed manner. One could pray it "standing or walking."[50] Of the two earliest documents of the confraternity, Sprenger's instructions for members (1476) and Michael Francisci's *Quodlibet* (a defense of the practice against its detractors, 1476/80), neither says anything about specific meditations.[51] Members could choose any one of several recommended ways of reciting the prayer. Dominic himself had encouraged flexibility in the exercise of this devotion. One manuscript of his text, preserved at Trier, specifically grants the right to vary the meditations.[52] Though he sanctioned Aves without meditations, he sug- gested that the devotion would be much "better and more beautiful" with them.[53] Therefore, the worshiper should try to say the prayer with the meditations once a week.

As early as 1475, printed rosary books began to appear. The earliest, titled *[Dis ist] Unser lyeben frowen Rosenkrantz und wie er von ersten offkummen* (This is Our Lady's rosary and how it first came to be), contains Dominic's fifty "clauses."[54] More popular, however, was a rosary book titled *Von dem psalter vnnd Rosenkrancz vnser lieben frauen* (About the Psalter and Rosary of Our Lady, reprinted in seven editions between 1483 and 1502).[55] This book, which does not include Dominic's version, recommends at least six different ways of reciting the prayer. Designed to advertise and promote the rosary, the book encourages readers to pray the "psalter" (three rosaries) in whatever manner they please, saying, "However, if none of the six above-mentioned ways pleases you, or if you should have greater devotion by another method, take it for your own, only let this praiseworthy prayer be spoken with diligence and devotion according as it is possible and proper for each person."[56]

A look at the contents of prayer books between about 1475 and 1550 reveals a bewildering array of rosaries, forms with 200, 165, 150, 93, 63, 33, 12, and as few as 5 meditations. Many of these prayer books contain two or three "rosaries" of various kinds, rosaries to patron saints on the model of the old psalter type, Ave prayer acrostics, Marian litanies, general meditations, and narrative types. The version that won out and was made official by papal proclamation in 1569 was a scaled-down set of fifteen meditations on events in the life of Jesus. The selection of this particular one among the many versions, essentially by popular demand, was a choice for narrative coherence and simplicity. Already at the beginning of the century, however, the most popular versions of the devotion—whether with 15, 50, or 150 meditations—were *vita Christi* texts. Together they affirm the inherent advantages and appeal of the narrative format as it was tried in repeated experiments from 1300 onward.

The Significance of the Life-of-Christ Rosary

The idea of "decorating" the Ave prayer with what a fifteenth-century version calls a compendium of the life of Jesus ("jesu per compendium vita decoratum")[57] was certainly an attractive one. In fact, the addition of mental meditations to the oral chant—on the pattern of Dominic's version—was what gave the rosary its essential character. The rhythm that was set up between the repetition of the Hail Mary chant and the changes rung on an accompanying mental theme made the new devotion more challenging and more engrossing.[58] Klinkhammer maintains that the first person actually to practice this was Dominic's prior, Adolf of Essen, whose habit it was to review mentally the life of the Savior while reciting the Aves. Adolf allegedly recommended this to Dominic, who, because he found the practice too difficult, made himself a written list of fifty points as a memory aid.[59]

However Dominic may have come upon the idea for this list of fifty points, with it he serendipitously solved the major problem that had plagued older forms of the devotion all along; namely, the difficulty of maintaining one's concentration throughout the many repetitions. Worshipers had been repeatedly admonished (as, for instance, in the legend of Eulalia, a nun who mumbled her Hail Marys) to avoid distractions and not to rush through the devotion in a mechanical fashion.[60] The virtue of the narrative form was its ability to focus the attention through a logical sequence of events. As Saint Louis Marie de Montfort (1673–1716) later wrote of the rosary mysteries, the variety of virtues and conditions of Jesus had the power of rallying and sustaining the mind and of preventing distractions.[61] Mentally reviewing the events of the life of Jesus provided a logical format that led the mind forward from one station to the next. The story of the Incarnation and Resurrection provided a joyful frame for the heart-rending and dramatic events of the Passion. In narrative form, the rosary devotion became a rehearsal of an epic story, the momentous events of the Incarnation and God's redemption of mankind, essentially a compendium in condensed form of the doctrines of faith. It became possible to recite the devotion without a text while traveling or working. In short, it was the inherent appeal of this dramatic sequence that caused these narratives to make their way into the Marian psalters and then to replace them in popularity.

Besides giving a renewed logic and fervor to a religious form that had lost the connection to its roots, the addition of life-of-Christ meditations changed the nature of the devotion. Emphasis on the person of Jesus and the events of his life, in effect, transformed the Ave Maria prayer into a Jesus prayer, a shift that reflects the popular impulse toward *imitatio Christi* piety. The new meditation technique corresponded to religious exercises made popular by the Devotio Moderna movement. Instead of simple Aves, repeated ritualistically because the Virgin liked to hear them, or psalms recited round the clock in order literally to pray without ceasing, *imitatio* exercises had as their goal the conforming of the individual worshiper to the model of Christ. This shift from an outward to an inward focus was directed toward transforming the person.

With the addition of the Creed and the Gloria, the rosary became a means of summarizing the doctrines of the faith. By rehearsing the mysteries of redemption, the worshiper also practiced virtues. Eventually, each mystery became associated with a particular virtue: thus the Incarnation taught humility; the nativity instructed in the love of poverty; carrying the Cross symbolized patience, and so on.[62] In the seventeenth century the personal exercise of the rosary was seen as an individual way of achieving grace. Throughout the late Middle Ages, as private devotions increasingly supplemented public observance of the corporate offices of the church, growth of devotion to the rosary reflected this trend.

The rosary's enormous success also has something to do with the way it was popularized. Early promotional writings gave testimonials to the miraculous effects of saying the prayer. To members of the confraternities, the rosary represented protection against condemnation to eternal death. As one broadsheet (c. 1510) put it:

> Whoever wants to be of the family of Mother Mary,
> let him enroll himself in the [brotherhood of the]
> rosary.

> For I tell you, she will protect him from the
>   pain of hell.
> Indeed, she can free him from it eternally.[63]
>
>   (stanza 1.6–10)

Several popes granted indulgences for saying the rosary, and printers eagerly advertised exaggerated claims of such indulgences in order to sell copies of rosary books. One testimonial relates the story of a woman whose penance in purgatory was reduced from six hundred years to fifteen days.[64] As an additional insurance policy—if, indeed, more were needed—members could also benefit from the accumulated "credit" of other members of the brotherhood. This, for example, is promised by Saint Dominic to Benedicta, a repentant sinner, in one of the testimonial anecdotes (exempla) that were included in rosary confraternity handbooks and that themselves made entertaining reading.[65]

In practical terms, the rosary, by rehearsing the tenets of the faith, served to reinforce orthodoxy and to combat heresy. Legend asserted that Saint Dominic himself had used it to combat the Albigensians. The church approved the rosary as a further way of catechizing the unlettered in the central mysteries of the faith and thereby discouraging intrusions of heresies that continually sprouted from folk beliefs.

As a social phenomenon, the brotherhood was attractive because of its lack of class discrimination. Sprenger declared membership open to everyone, saying: "In this our brotherhood no one will be kept out, no matter how poor he may be; but rather the poorer he is, the more disdained, and despised, the more acceptable, beloved, and precious will he be in this brotherhood." In this way, Sprenger asserted, the poor, the needy, and the languishing "of this knavish world" could become "the equals of the rich."[66] Although its premier member, Emperor Frederick III, lent prestige and credibility to the organization, the membership included a broader spectrum of classes than other brotherhoods. The Colmar confraternity, for example, for which Jean-Claude Schmitt has analyzed the membership rolls, included monks, nuns, artisans (representing twenty-four trades), domestics, couples, families, children, and six lepers. While many other confraternities excluded women, the rosary brotherhood welcomed them. Membership in Colmar consisted of 57 percent females and 43 percent males.[67] The same open, nonprescriptive regulations that promoted the prayer also made membership easy. Lapsed members suffered no penalties, did not have to make up unsaid prayers, and could participate whenever they wished. The convenience of being able to say the prayer anywhere and the private character of observance also contributed to its popularity. Nor was literacy or knowledge of Latin a requirement.

The movement to supplement public observance of the corporate offices of the church with more private religious practices developed with the rosary confraternity a new kind of corporate aspect, one focused on lay association and private exercise. Members of the rosary confraternity could participate both as a group in annual festive processions (for which extra indulgences were granted) or individually, by saying the rosary in private. They might worship at rosary altars and in chapels financed by the brotherhood and enjoy participation in a spiritual brotherhood, yet do so individually, privately, and in their mother tongue.

Diehl argues that religious practice outside the official liturgy increased in the late Middle Ages in response to the progressive sequestration of church ritual from the worshipers. Unable to understand the Latin text, the populace felt excluded from participation in the divine service, "first as audience to a spectacle, then as petitioners relegated to the antechamber of a secret negotiation between the qualified and God."[68] Eamon Duffy, on the other hand, argues that the laity were able to appropriate the ritual to their own uses.[69] One way was by reciting rosaries in the vernacular language during mass. It is, thus, not surprising that from the late thirteenth century onward the vernacular increasingly became the medium for religious texts. These works met the growing demand for a more personal and subjective religious experience. As an extraliturgical, private devotion, requiring no intermediary and performable in the vernacular, the rosary was a seed that fell on fertile ground. The popular demand for such devotions and the different contexts in which they were performed shaped the kinds of works that were produced.

Paul Zumthor cautions that, in the Middle Ages, every text was designed for communication aloud.[70] In dealing with the rosary it is even more necessary to stress that the "meaning" is not "in the text" but in the context, that is, in the performance of the ritual.[71] Meditation on the narrative—on the story of man's redemption through Christ's life, death, and Resurrection—is a ritual reenactment of an ongoing reality. Changing the linguistic, symbolic performance from Latin to a vernacular dialect changes the quality of the spiritual reality that is enacted. Just as performance in a private, nonliturgical setting eliminates one intermediary agency, so does use of the native tongue eliminate another layer of mediation. In the same way that linguistic codes both mirror and create social realities, the ritual text reflects and informs the religious awareness of a discursive community.

As text and social ritual, the rosary shows particularly well the interrelatedness of text and context. While rosary confraternities participated in the changing of religious practices, the prayer that constituted the ritual was itself molded and changed by users. Hence, it was not simply the move toward more private and individual religious practices or use of the vernacular that carried the new type of rosary to popular acceptance, although these factors played their part. Rather, it was the nature of the text itself—its narrative form. Orality has certain requirements, especially where performers are nonliterate. Beyond influencing grammatical form, sounds, rhythms, shape, and length of a text, it favors mnemonic devices that aid in its performance. Besides adding focus and drama to the meditation, the sequenced life-of-Christ narrative provided a vividly logical memory aid that allowed this broader spectrum of the unlettered population to learn and to take part in the performance of the ritual. It was the selection of a coherent narrative format for the rosary meditations—in experiments that began around 1300 and continued for the next 250 years—that shaped the text and, simultaneously, the spiritual experience of the community that collectively "wrote" it.

2

The Picture Text and Its "Readers"

Wer mm fiben frewd alle tag eret
Der wirt alle zit von mir geweret
Was er göttichs hie be geret ✳ ✳
Das wirt im dort auch mit verkeret

In the still predominantly oral culture of fifteenth-century Germany, the visual media of the day—block prints, painted or carved altarpieces, and devotional panels—played an essential role in the dissemination of religious teachings to the estimated 95 percent of the population that was illiterate.[1] In his studies of popular culture in sixteenth-century Germany, Robert Scribner has pointed not only to visual media but also to participational forms such as popular festivals and to oral media—word-of-mouth, popular songs, hymns, sermons—as principal means of spreading the Word. Moreover, Scribner cautions that "overconcentration" on the role of printed texts may "seriously distort our understanding" of how ideas were communicated among the population at large.[2]

In the case of the rosary, Scribner's point is well taken, for here the visual media can be seen to have exercised a decisive influence on the development of the practice. Besides favoring the narrative as the form most congenial to users, orality also privileged visual texts—picture narratives that could be "read" by the nonliterate and used as prompts in the ritual "telling" of the beads. As late as the end of the sixteenth century, the most widely used set of rosary meditations in Germany was not a written one at all, but a picture text. This version—a series of fifteen woodcuts without any accompanying written gloss—appeared for the first time in a handbook printed in 1483.[3] Although it was only one among eight different methods of reciting the devotion, the picture rosary soon became the version of choice. Its enormous popular appeal, especially to illiterate users, played an important role in the spread of the practice and in the coalescing of competing written versions into a standard form. Even with the printing of written texts of the picture "mysteries," rosary books continued to be supplied with illustrations into the seventeenth century and well beyond.

In contrast to written rosaries, which varied widely, the picture texts changed little. Essentially the same sets of images reappeared in rosary woodcuts, engravings, altarpieces, and devotional panels over and over again with only minor variations. Thus, even after more than 150 years of experiments with different written forms of the devotion, the picture mysteries emerged almost unchanged to become synonymous with the standard version of the prayer.

Despite the persistence and apparent uniformity of these images, however, a closer look at how viewers "read" them reveals some surprising differences in interpretations of the text. Just as readers of the picture stories in early blockbooks knew the content of the narratives already from pageants, songs, hymns, or sermons, so they also "knew" the pictures—or thought they did. Certainly, they were familiar with similar images in altarpieces, devotional paintings and prints. A look at earlier cycles of devotional images helps to explain how this particular visual narrative came to be selected out of the larger body of written and pictorial *vita Christi* accounts.

The First Picture Text

The uniting of devotion to the Virgin with narrative meditation on the life of Christ, which had taken place in Dominic of Prussia's rosary and in the earlier experiments around 1300, had turned out to be such a congenial combination that the new prayer spawned dozens of imitations and variations. But at the same time that copies of Dominic's version with its fifty *vita Christi* clausulae were proliferating rapidly, other types were also being created. A rosary book from the year 1610, for example, contains no fewer than sixty-three different rosaries to vary the daily or weekly fare of the exercise.[4] Early manuals of rosary confraternities offered a variety of methods for members to choose from. While the earliest printed rosary book, called *[Dis ist] Unser lyeben frowen Rosenkrantz und wie er von ersten offkummen* (This is Our Lady's rosary and how it first came to be) and first published in 1475, contains only Dominic's method, a more popular handbook soon appeared offering several different ways of saying the prayer.[5] This was *Vnser lieben frauen Psalter* (Our Lady's Psalter), the manual published in Ulm by Conrad Dinckmut and reprinted in at least seven editions before 1503.[6] Included in this book—alongside more than seven written versions—was the first picture rosary, fifteen woodcuts depicting a sequence of events in the lives of Christ and Mary. This illustrated version of the prayer contained no written gloss but was intended to be meditated on directly by simply contemplating each of the scenes depicted while reciting Hail Marys.

Just who might have made these woodcuts and how they came to be included in the Ulm rosary manual is a question that has not been answered. The three pages of figures with brief instructions seem to have been inserted as something of an afterthought. They were not mentioned in the text proper, not counted among the seven other methods enumerated by the author, and do not correspond specifically to any of the ways of saying the prayer that the written text of the handbook describes. Moreover, they are inserted between sections, two chapters after the one in which the other methods are explained. The only thing that is clear about the illustrations is that they soon came to be preferred to the other versions.

The idea of using pictures in religious devotions was certainly not new. Even though, as Sixten Ringbom writes, Saint Bernard had regarded the use of images as a lower-order form of spirituality compared to true imageless contemplation, the majority of people found devotional pictures ("Andachtsbilder") desirable as aids to religious exercises.[7] Indeed, Alanus de Rupe, entrepreneurial promoter of his own form of the rosary, urged worshipers to recite it in front of an image of Christ or of the Virgin. Thus, the *Compendium psalterii beatissimae Trinitatis* (Compendium of the Psalter of the Blessed Trinity) recommends: "[I]n meditating Christ's

bitter Passion, thou shalt have before thee in place of a book the representation of Christ suffering or crucified."[8] Similarly, a Netherlandish rosary
manual from 1484, the *Exempelboek II* (Book of exempla), carries instructions for nonliterate users with the advice, "those who cannot read should
look at the illustrations while repeating the Ave Maria and think about
the life and Passion of Our Lord."[9]

Of the earliest printed rosaries—those before 1490—at least three were
picture texts that appeared in such widely dispersed locations as Ulm,
Barcelona, and Florence. Picture rosaries had the unique advantage that
they could be "read" in any language, and by users who were not literate
in Latin or even in the vernacular.

The Narrative Images

But where did the rosary images come from and what was the story they
told? The oldest picture rosary, the one printed by Dinckmut in Ulm,
consisted of three sets of five medallions, each medallion framed by ten
roses representing ten Ave Marias. Some surviving copies have been
tinted by hand so that the ten roses framing each roundel are colored
either white, red, or gold. The first set of five medallions (the "white
rosary") narrates the chief events in the birth and childhood of Jesus, the
second set (the "red rosary") recounts the events of the Passion, and the
third set (the "golden rosary") depicts the Resurrection and the glorious
events that followed it (see Fig. 1). Except for the final illustration, which
shows the Last Judgment, these meditations correspond to those that
emerged as standard in the course of the sixteenth and seventeenth
centuries. By the eighteenth century, variations were no longer approved.[10]

Although this set of fifteen woodcuts appeared together for the first
time in Dinckmut's Ulm handbook, the series has obvious antecedents.
Many of the same illustrations can be found in illuminated Books of
Hours, typological blockbooks—such as the *Biblia pauperum* (Bible of
the poor) and the *Speculum humanae salvationis* (Mirror of man's
salvation)—and most frequently in altarpieces, devotional paintings, and
woodcuts, all works that contain cycles of narrative illustrations recounting events in the lives of Christ and Mary.

In Books of Hours similar sets of illuminations that accompany the

F<small>IG</small>. 1a.   The birth and childhood of Jesus. From the "white rosary," *Vnser lieben frauen Psalter*. Ulm: Dinckmut, 1483 (from the plates reprinted in the 1492 edition). Reproduced here by permission of the Universitätsbibliothek Freiburg

Fɪɢ. 1b.   The Passion. From the "red rosary," *Vnser lieben frauen Psalter.*

FIG. 1c.   The Resurrection and glorious events. From the "golden rosary," *Vnser lieben frauen Psalter.*

Hours of the Virgin typically include, for example: (1) the Annunciation, (2) the Visitation, (3) the Nativity, (4) the Annunciation to the Shepherds, (5) the Adoration of the Magi, (6) the Presentation at the Temple, (7) the Massacre of the Innocents or the Flight to Egypt, and conclude with (8) Mary's Coronation. Those illustrating the Hours of the Passion normally show (1) the Betrayal by Judas, (2) Jesus before Pilate, (3) the Flagellation, (4) the Carrying of the Cross, (5) the Crucifixion, (6) the Deposition, (7) the Entombment, and finally (8) the Resurrection or Christ in Majesty.[11] Yet, while these two narrative cycles of illustrations might at first seem to be closely related to the rosary mysteries, they actually contain only about half of the images that appear among the fifteen rosary pictures. The same is true of the typological blockbook illustrations of the *Biblia pauperum* and the *Speculum humanae salvationis* that likewise resemble the rosary pictures. Although the total number of images devoted to the life of Christ in these blockbooks is much larger (thirty-five to forty), the *Biblia pauperum* and *Speculum humanae salvationis* still lack four of the fifteen rosary scenes.[12]

Similar sequences of illustrations narrating the life of Christ or of Mary can be found in altarpieces and serial devotional panels. These works—very popular in the fifteenth century—are made up of multiple scenes linked together to form a sequential story that was used to guide serial meditations. Several examples from the Cologne area featuring 15, 19, 27, or 31 panels can be seen in the rich collection of late-medieval altarpieces in the Wallraf-Richartz Museum of Cologne[13] (see Fig. 2). These include many of the same images, but none the same set of fifteen contained in the Ulm medallions.

Another group of illustrations that more closely approximates the rosary set can be found in devotional pictures celebrating the joys of the Virgin—usually five or seven happy events in Mary's life, but also frequently nine, twelve, fifteen, or more.[14] These picture sequences occur not only in altarpieces and panel paintings, but also in woodcut illustrations for printed books and broadsides. Depictions of the seven joys differ from illuminations in Books of Hours showing the seven Hours of the Virgin in that the latter typically focus only on the infancy of Christ and then leap ahead to Mary's Coronation, so that only four of the same scenes are found among the rosary pictures. Cycles of illustrations of the seven joys, on the other hand, contain (besides Christ's infancy) also the Resurrection, the Ascension, and Mary's death and Assumption—all scenes that *do* occur in the picture rosary.

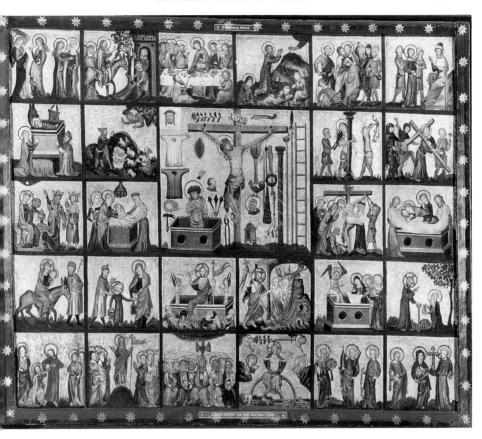

FIG. 2.   The life of Christ in twenty-seven pictures, c. 1380–90. Cologne, Wallraf-Richartz Museum (Photo: Rheinisches Bildarchiv)

A typical example is a woodcut series depicting Mary's joys, found in a fifteenth-century broadside now held by the Gutenberg Museum of Mainz. This print contains seven medallions arranged in a circle that show (1) the Annunciation, (2) the Nativity, (3) the Adoration of the Magi, (4) the Presentation at the Temple, (5) the Resurrection, (6) the Ascension of Christ, and (7) the Death and Coronation of the Virgin[15] (see Fig. 3). Except for the Visit of the Magi, all of the same illustrations are present in the fifteen medallions of the Ulm picture rosary. Stephan Beissel has pointed out that the Magi came to be displaced from cycles on the joys in Netherlandish and German manuscripts as greater attention was paid to the Assumption and coronation of Mary.[16]

Wer mir liben frewd alle tag eret

Der wirt alle zit von mir geweret

Was er götlichs hie be geret ✳ ✳

das wirt im dort aik nit verkeret

FIG. 3.   Mary's Seven Joys, woodcut, fifteenth century. Mainz, Gutenberg Museum

In addition, illustrations of these five or seven happy events were frequently also paired with a companion series on the sufferings of Christ or on Mary's own sufferings as witness to them. As it turns out, the Gutenberg Museum woodcut showing the seven joys described above is actually one-half of a set that depicted seven sorrows on its companion page.[17] Accordingly, Beissel and Gilles Meersseman have suggested that meditations on the five joys first originated as a complement to sets of devotions on Christ's five wounds. Eventually these five "gaudes" were expanded to seven with the addition of the Assumption and the Coronation. In a parallel development, Mary's sorrows also were increased to seven and were frequently represented as seven swords piercing her heart.[18]

While it is not unusual for devotions on the happy events in the Virgin's life to appear together with a companion set on her sufferings or the Passion of Christ, normally the two cycles are not merged. Yet, in some Books of Hours such as the famous Hours of Jeanne d'Evreux, illuminations of the Hours of the Virgin and the Hours of the Passion can be found arranged so that they stand juxtaposed on facing pages. Thus illustrations of the Betrayal of Christ and of the Annunciation end up opposite one another as alternate meditations for Matins (see Fig. 4). This kind of merging of two interlaced sets leads to the hypothesis that the rosary picture series could have developed by the merging of similar cycles of meditations on the joys and sorrows. Just such a series of interlaced illustrations does, in fact, exist comprising a rosary—one with ten scenes—that is found in a broadside made by Hans Schaur now held by the Germanisches Nationalmuseum in Nuremberg. Schreiber dated Schaur's woodcut (no. 1128) sometime before the end of 1481 when Schaur left Ulm for Munich.[19] In this set of matching pictures and text, two cycles depicting five happy events in the Virgin's life and five sufferings of Christ have been interjoined so that they are to be meditated on in alternating order, as follows:

    I. ("Ave" meditation): the Annunciation
       (Passion meditation): Christ in the garden of Gethsemane
   II. ("Ave"): the Visitation
      (Passion): the Flagellation
  III. ("Ave"): the Nativity
     (Passion): the crown of thorns

Fig. 4.   Jean Pucelle, the Hours of Jeanne d'Evreux. Metropolitan Museum of Art, The Cloisters, New York. *Top left:* Fol. 15v, The Betrayal; *top right:* Fol. 16r, The Annunciation; *bottom left:* Fol. 68v, The Crucifixion; *bottom right:* Fol. 69r, Adoration of the Magi

IV. ("Ave"): the child Jesus found teaching in the Temple
(Passion): Christ carrying the Cross
V. ("Ave"): The Death (and Assumption) of the Virgin
(Passion): the Crucifixion

In the center of the ring of ten roundels is a large illustration of the Virgin being crowned with a corona of red and white roses.[20] (See Fig. 5. Fig. 6, dated 1485, shows the same set of roundels more clearly.)

The hypothesis that the rosary pictures grew out of integrated sets of meditations on the joys and sorrows goes a long way toward locating the rosary illustrations in a larger pictorial context. But there remains one important difficulty: the presence in the Ulm picture rosary of a scene that is usually not found in depictions of the joys and sorrows, namely, the final rosary illustration—the Last Judgment. Just how the Last Judgment image might have become part of the series can be explained by looking at another, similar type of pictorial text, one that pairs Mary's joys with a longer passion sequence.

Just such a combination ending with the Last Judgment is found in one of the very earliest printed books, an anonymous work titled *Die sieben Freuden Mariae und die Leidensgeschichte Jesu* (The seven joys of Mary and the Passion of Christ) published between 1460 and 1464, possibly by Numeister in Mainz.[21] This book contains 26 full-page, metal-cut illustrations that recount seven scenes of Mary's joys, which are joined together with a longer set of nineteen scenes of Christ's Passion. Each picture is accompanied by a written text on the facing page[22] (see Fig. 7). The interesting thing about the linking of the two cycles here is that even though they are put together serially and not interlaced, as in the two merged cycles in Hans Schaur's broadsheet, the sequence produced is still not chronological but overlaps, so that Mary's Assumption ends up coming before Christ's entry into Jerusalem. In the Ulm picture rosary it is particularly the tighter chronology and narrative coherence that distinguish this series from its close relatives. Indeed, the much greater popularity of the Ulm rosary over that in Hans Schaur's broadsheet (the version used, for example, by the rosary confraternity at Colmar) seems to parallel the displacement of non-narrative versions by chronologically more coherent narrative ones already described for written texts.

But, while the Ulm rosary medallions are in the right sequential order, they represent only select episodes in the life of Christ. Understandably, the complete story could not be portrayed in only fifteen scenes. Yet the

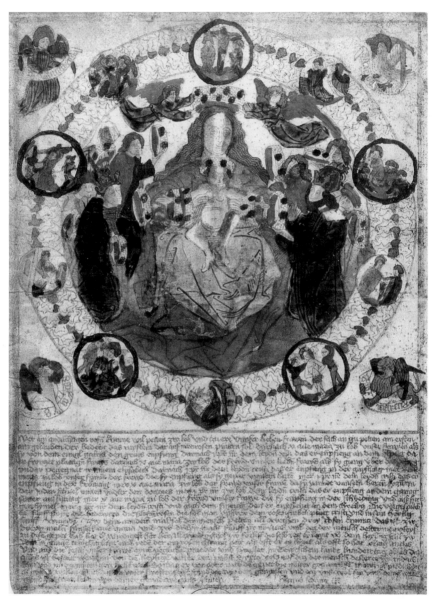

FIG. 5.   Hans Schaur, Rosary Madonna, woodcut, c. 1481. Nuremberg, Germanisches
Nationalmuseum

F<small>IG</small>. 6.   Madonna with the Rosary, woodcut, 1485. Washington, D.C., National Gallery of Art, Rosenwald Collection

Omaria cin guctigc muctcr
crifti ocin victoc frcivo haft
oiu cupbangcn oa oiu haft
gcbort uno gcfctcn fo cin
loblictc tycivgmuf ocr hcilige
orcy lunig uon ocinctu fuc:
oic fur in uyocr viclcn uno
iu an pcttcn uno in crkano
tcn ivarcn got uno nicufrhe
uno im oppbcrtcn gaftlict
gab ivcyract golo uno mir
rcn Oguctigc muctcr crifti:
ict crnian oirt ociucr vicr
tcn frcivo oao oiu ocin fun:
fur mict pitcy in civigkait:

F<small>IG</small>. 7.   The fourth joy: Adoration of the Magi, in *Die Sieben Freuden Mariae und
die Leidensgeschichte Jesu*, 1460–64. Munich, Bayerische Staatsbibliothek

reasons why only fifteen scenes—instead of 50, 33, 12, or 7—ultimately
became the standard number of tableaux and why specific events were
chosen over others highlight the agenda of the rosary narrative and some
of its appeal.

The Picture-Rosary Narrative

What is conspicuously missing from the rosary illustrations is the entire
public life of Christ—events such as the Baptism, the Temptation, the
Miracles of Jesus, the Triumphal Entry into Jerusalem, and the Last
Supper—scenes that are present in the written experiments with *vita
Christi* rosaries. While lack of emphasis on Christ's public ministry may
distinguish the picture rosary from its written antecedents, it is not
inconsistent with the devotion's pictorial relatives. Indeed, narrative altarpieces, woodcuts of the joys and sorrows, typological blockbooks, and

Books of Hours all generally contain very few depictions of the public life of Christ.[23] Instead, these works focus almost exclusively on the Incarnation and the Passion while leaving out Christ's ministry and his role as teacher—both significant facets of his mission that come to the fore in the post-Reformation period.[24] Like its iconographic and typological relatives, the rosary concentrates on the most joyful and tragic events. Josef Stadlhuber has emphasized that the Man of Sorrows image, which so preoccupied the late-medieval popular imagination, attempted to depict the magnitude of the Savior's love by showing in the most graphic way the extreme agony he endured for it.[25] Ernst Schubert, likewise, has pointed out that the more excruciating the representation of the sufferings of Christ, the more powerful his love was perceived to be and the greater was the treasury of grace that was available to be drawn upon through the church.[26] As a mechanism for drawing on this treasury, the rosary and its confraternity were particularly well suited to the lay public. Attractive and immediately accessible, the picture rosary could serve as a kind of substitute "Hours of the Virgin" and Passion meditation for nonliterate laypersons.[27]

The Late-Medieval Viewer and the Images

How, after all, did late-medieval readers use the picture sets? Fortunately, two fifteenth-century glosses on the rosary figures have survived that reveal how two users "read" and interpreted the figures (differently, it turns out). These two contrasting glosses, both in German and composed within three years of one another by Sixt Buchsbaum and Johannes Lambsheym, constitute unusual examples of a visual text influencing a verbal one. The first of these works is a song called "Vnnser lieben frawen Rosenkrancz" (Our Lady's rosary), which Buchsbaum set to a contemporary secular melody known as Duke Ernst's melody ("herczog ernsts meladey").[28] Although none of Buchsbaum's other writings has survived, this work of his enjoyed considerable popularity. It was issued as a broadside as early as 1492, reprinted several times during the next twenty-five years, and was published in at least nine collections of religious lyrics between 1574 and the end of the following century.[29] The work affords a unique opportunity to see how a written text was composed to go with the rosary pictures and how one literate late-medieval viewer interpreted them.

Buchsbaum makes it clear that his description of how to pray the rosary is based on the fifteen printed figures. He states plainly at the end of his first set of five meditations: "There you have the fifth figure" (stanza 8.1). And in introducing the second set, he says: "You must have fifty red roses and also the five figures" (stanza 9.2–3). "The figures" is the term used to designate the woodcuts in the heading on the pages inserted in the Ulm handbook. All of Buchsbaum's meditations correspond exactly to the fifteen scenes represented in the picture text. The fact that Buchsbaum undertakes to tell people how to "read" these figures and that his interpretation differs from the gloss made by Lambsheym confirms the lack of an established written version of the picture rosary in Germany in 1492. Indeed, even as late as 1514, Marcus von Weida's manual, *Der Spiegel hochloblicher Bruderschafft des Rosenkrantz Marie* (Mirror of the excellent brotherhood of Mary's rosary), still does not include the fifteen mysteries among its offerings.[30]

Buchsbaum's idea of interpreting the illustrations was to write dialogue for the characters in the woodcuts and to describe their actions. While keeping to the outline dictated by the figures, his written descriptions expanded the pictorial narrative by filling in the gaps between the scenes with details not contained in the simple woodcuts themselves. In constructing a more detailed narrative to surround each of the fifteen figures, Buchsbaum produced a devotion more like Dominic's popular text of fifty meditations. But his source cannot have been Dominic alone, for he has included episodes not found in Dominic's fifty scenes from the life of Christ. Instead, Buchsbaum cites Saint Bernard, John Chrysostom, the Gospels of Mark, Matthew, and John, and other texts. He recounts, for example, the apocryphal story of Veronica's meeting with Christ on the road to Golgotha. From another source, identified only as "the knights" ("die ritterschafft"), Buchsbaum reports that Christ carried his cross for 1,000 paces (stanza 12.1). Moreover, he informs us specifically that the distance from the square to the Jerusalem city gate is 350 paces; the number of steps from there to Calvary is 500; and that Christ received 6,666 blows and suffered 462 pains. What Buchsbaum seems to have done is to have condensed one or more detailed accounts of the Passion story into a narrative to accompany the images. What he produced by using the figures as his outline was a short, but vivid and lively story focused in fifteen "action-packed" stanzas—no doubt one of the reasons for the song's appeal.

A comparison of Buchsbaum's gloss to the pictures themselves makes the program of the Ulm woodcuts stand out more clearly. Already the earliest additions of *vita Christi* meditations to the "Ave Maria" prayer in written versions had changed the nature of the devotion from a simple celebration of the Annunciation into a more complicated explication of "the benefits of the incarnation," as the text of the Cistercian sisters of Saint Thomas on the Kyll claims.[31] In another work, the "Zwanzig Exempel," Dominic describes his own fifty rosary meditations as a review of Christ's acts of redemption.[32] Similarly, the emphasis in the picture rosary is strongly Christological. Here Mary is missing from scenes in which she ordinarily would be represented prominently, for example, at the Ascension, in the Pentecost scene, and at the Last Judgment. A comparison of the woodcut figures with very similar images in the *Speculum humanae salvationis* shows Mary to be present there where she is absent in the rosary series. In fact, of the fifteen illustrations in the Ulm picture rosary and its later editions, eight of the medallions do not include Mary at all (see Fig. 8).

As if in an attempt to restore the Marian focus, Buchsbaum's gloss on the figures gives Mary a much stronger role to play. While keeping to the fifteen picture episodes as his outline, Buchsbaum takes pains to include Christ's mother in the narrative—even where she is not shown in the figures. At the scene of the Crucifixion, for example, Buchsbaum relates how the Virgin "kissed her dear son / and bathed him in hot tears" (stanza 13.12–13). Although Mary is not depicted in the medallion showing the Pentecost scene, Buchsbaum points out that the Holy Spirit was sent "to Mary and the disciples." Moreover, despite her absence in the illustration representing the Last Judgment, Buchsbaum asserts that on the Day of Judgment "Mary will faithfully stand by [members of her brotherhood]" (stanza 19.12–13). Besides enlarging Mary's role in the narrative itself, Buchsbaum adds extra material at the beginning and at the end of the song to create a sort of frame for the work. He explains how the Virgin herself founded the confraternity, how she acts as its protectress and as advocate for its members. In this way the author has made Mary the heroine of a story that begins and ends with her.

The song's obvious agenda is to promote membership in the burgeoning organization and to advertise its benefits. Clearly, broadsides like this one

FIG. 8.   Illustrations of the Ascension and Pentecost as depicted in the *Speculum humanae salvationis* and *Von dem psalter vnd rosencrancz vnser lieben frauen*

A. The Ascension
Top left: Speculum humanae salvationis (Speyer: Drach, c. 1475). Reproduced by permission of Bayerische Staatsbibliothek, Munich.
Top right (detail): Von dem psalter und rosencrancz unser lieben frauen (Augsburg: Sorg, 1490). Reproduced by permission of the Universitätsbibliothek Freiburg.

B. Pentecost
Bottom left (detail): Von dem psalter und rosencranz unser lieben frauen.
Bottom right: Speculum humanae salvationis.

A.

B.

were made to be sold and did so by advertising results. Buchsbaum's song promises that Mary will meet the members of her brotherhood at the gate to heaven where she will say with authority, "Let my dearest guest in!" (stanza 21.13). Similarly, printers of rosary manuals advertised the indulgences—as well as rumors of indulgences—associated with their wares. And they reprinted the picture medallions in order to appeal to an audience, only a small percentage of which could read, but a larger portion of which could afford to purchase a picture book or broadside. Natalie Davis has pointed out the "almost complete illiteracy" of well-off merchants and especially urban women in sixteenth century France.[33] Many of these urban women and merchants might, however, buy a manual with pictures for use in private devotions. The less well off bought broadsides, which they pasted on the walls of their cottages.[34] But it was not simply the advantage afforded by pictures as prompts for illiterate users that made the illustrated rosary so attractive. Equally important was the power that these images had to add immediacy and drama to the devotion. This was true not just for nonreaders but even for readers as well.

Readers, Printers, and Illustrators

Stephen Nichols has cautioned that illustrations too often are regarded as mere interventions in a text that serve only to confirm a work's intentionality when, actually, a double narrative—one with two and more voices—is going on.[35] Buchsbaum's work provides not only a good example of voices at variance with one another, but also an interesting reversal of the usual situation. Here the pictures are not interventions in a written work. They *are* the text, and the narrative is written around them.

By virtue of their open-endedness, illustrations contribute to divergent verbal interpretations. Rather than merely confirming the intentionality of a work, they point up the difficulties of imputing "meaning" to it. A good example can be found in the second gloss on the popular Ulm picture rosary, the one by Johannes Lambsheym. It is contained in his rosary manual, *Libellus perutilis* (A very useful little book), published in Mainz in 1495.[36] The intriguing aspect of this particular work is the way its author has constructed an alternative version by "misinterpreting" one of the figures in the picture series and by construing differently the order in which the figures were to be "read."

The figures Lambsheym used were the woodcuts in the 1495 edition of *Unser lieben frawen psalter unnd von den dreien rosenkräntzen* ([Of] Our Lady's Psalter and of the three rosaries) that was printed by Zeissenmair in Augsburg (and reprinted in 1502), which contain the same illustrations as the Ulm picture rosary yet with some of the medallions in a different arrangement. In the first set of five pictures, the figures are arranged so that the fifth one is located in the center instead of at the bottom right as in the other two sets in the handbook. Thus, Lambsheym has assumed that the center figure is the third one instead of the fifth one and has arranged the chronology of his text accordingly. The result is that his rosary presents an "illogical" sequence of events with the following order: (1) the Annunciation, (2) the Visitation, (3) the Lost Child Jesus found in the Temple, (4) the Nativity, and (5) the Circumcision.[37] Not only are the scenes here out of line, but Lambsheym has interpreted the figure showing the Presentation of the Infant Jesus in the Temple to be the Circumcision. The result is a sequence that seems to make little sense: the finding of the lost child Jesus teaching in the Temple comes before the Nativity and the Circumcision.

Even though keyed to the same series of figures that Buchsbaum used, Lambsheym's text results in a drastically different version. Given this example of variant interpretations by two highly literate "readers" of the picture text, one wonders what kinds of divergent interpretations uneducated users may have made for themselves and what kinds of alternative "texts" resulted. The Lambsheym example shows how the open-endedness of pictorial images allows for alternative meanings and secondary associations to be read into a text. Clearly, as Nichols asserts, the illustrations that make up a "text matrix" cannot be ignored; they offer a useful perspective on the multiple "meanings" and possible interpretations of a work.[38]

Just why the rosary illustrations should have had such a decisive impact on the formation of the ultimate form of the devotion has a great deal to do with printing and with the ever-widening circle of bookowners and broadsheet buyers. As Robert Scribner points out, the influence of printing was not, after all, limited to or even primarily dependent on printed words. To those unable to read well—or unable to read at all—the picture series served as devices for imagining or telling a story with which they were already thoroughly familiar. As with illustrated blockbooks in general, a prior knowledge of the text was assumed. Still, the Lambsheym and Buchsbaum examples show to what degree users actually created their own texts.

Indeed, in the case of the rosary, illustrated versions constitute an indispensable source of information about the development of the practice. Where written texts fail, pictures show how changes occurred, how the practice was shaped in various media, and how these representations affected each other. A good example is the shift from Last Judgment to Coronation of the Virgin as the final rosary mystery that occurs first in picture sets and only later in written ones.

Later Rosary Illustrations

In Germany written forms of the fifteen mysteries appear very late. The glosses that Buchsbaum and Lambsheym made for the pictures, in 1492 and 1495 respectively, show that a standard written gloss was still not attached to the picture rosary in the 1490s. Nor were the fifteen mysteries yet the most widely accepted form. Thomas Esser looked in vain for written texts of the fifteen mysteries in German rosary books up through the first quarter of the sixteenth century.[39] What Esser did find were a myriad of other types of rosaries, variations on Dominic's fifty meditations, sets with 150 meditations, and a host of other types. Yet, even without a written gloss, the rosary images continued to be reproduced in altarpieces, wall paintings, and broadsides.[40]

Although the pictorial versions show far less variety than written ones, the picture sets too were subject to experimentation. Besides the shift in the final scene from Last Judgment to Coronation, the most common variation was substitution of the Adoration of the Magi in place of one of the other events of Christ's childhood (see Fig. 9). Some versions leave out the Visitation, as does, for example, a set of woodcuts made by Wolf Traut in 1510. Here, instead of the Visitation and the Flagellation, both usually in the second position, Traut includes the Lazarus episode and Christ before Pilate (Fig. 10). The instructions that accompany this woodcut are revealing in that they show how fluid the devotion still was as late as 1510. In Traut's woodcut there are only general directions for use of the figures, and the viewer is left to figure out for herself specifically

FIG. 9.   Rosary fresco, c. 1500, Weilheim unter der Teck, Baden-Württemberg,
Church of Saint Peter. In this set of fifteen medallions, the Adoration of the Magi has
been inserted before the Presentation in the Temple (the fourth and fifth figures in the
outer ring, moving clockwise from upper left), while the Finding of the Lost Child
Jesus in the Temple (usually no. 5) has been left out.

Fig. 10.   Wolf Traut, Rosary Meditations, woodcut, 1510. Karlsruhe, Badische Landesbibliothek

which event is represented in each of the fifteen pictures.[41] That this could lead to some startling variations has been shown by Lambsheym's gloss.

The most significant shift, however, was the replacement of the Last Judgment scene. This figure had already begun to change by the time the second and third picture rosaries were printed in Barcelona and in Florence, respectively. The Barcelona picture rosary appeared as a single-sheet engraving, dated 1488 and signed by its Dominican engraver, Franciscus Domenech.[42] Here, for the first time, one finds the Coronation of the Virgin as the closing meditation (see Fig. 11). The third picture rosary to appear was a set of fifteen full-page engravings printed in Florence sometime before 1490, probably by Francesco Roselli.[43] Like the Barcelona engraving, this set also has replaced the Last Judgment with the Coronation.

The substitution of the joyful scene for the somber and fear-inspiring one may have to do with the devotion's close kinship to picture cycles on the joys of the Virgin, which also end with Mary's Assumption or coronation. Practically speaking, the replacing of the Last Judgment image—showing Christ seated on a rainbow with a sword and a lily proceeding from his mouth—amounts to a sort of victory of "the lily" over "the sword" or, in Eileen Power's words, of "love" over "justice."[44] Most people preferred the happier ending because they hoped for clemency from Mary rather than for justice. This accords with the Virgin's more active role as merciful intercessor on behalf of members of her brotherhood that is not only advertised but even guaranteed in the songs, stories, and testimonials used to popularize the confraternity as will be seen.

The strengthening of this emphasis is reflected also in rosary altars, wall paintings, and engravings, which often group the fifteen medallions around a central image of the Virgin. An early example of the shift from Last Judgment to Coronation can be observed in a painting from approximately the same time as the Barcelona engraving. This work forms part of an altarpiece made sometime between 1484 and 1490 for the Dominican church at Frankfurt.[45] Here the fifteenth medallion, which in German rosaries still usually contains the Last Judgment, is blank. Instead of a pictorial scene, it contains simply the initials IHS (Ihesus). In the middle of this painting and forming the center of the circle of five glorious mysteries, is a larger depiction of the Coronation (see Fig. 12). This coronation scene is, in fact, strikingly similar to that in the Barcelona engraving. It is a scene celebrating the Virgin's apotheosis that focuses attention on her as the recipient of the Aves. From there it was only a

FIG. 11.   Franciscus Domenech, Fifteen Mysteries of the Rosary, Barcelona, 1488.
Brussels, Bibliothèque Royale Albert Ier

short step to its placement within the series itself as the culminating
image.

   In rosary books having both text and illustrations, the transition occurs
more gradually. Here, however, the same resonance can be observed

FIG. 12. Rosary antependium, c. 1484, formerly of the Dominican church of Frankfurt. The fifteenth medallion contains simply the initials IHS (Ihesus) instead of the Last Judgment. Heidelberg, Kurpfälzisches Museum, Graimberg Collection

between the arrangement of the glorious mysteries and a larger central image of the enthroned Virgin. Three examples from Italian rosary books printed between 1521 and 1573 illustrate the trend. In 1521, Alberto da Castello published a very popular and richly decorated manual, *Rosario della gloriosa vergine Maria* (Rosary of the Glorious Virgin Mary), that went through eighteen editions.[46] Among the more than 190 illustrations in this book are the fifteen picture rosary medallions, displayed in three groups, each representing the five petals of a large rose. In Castello's fifteen roundels the fifteenth figure still shows Christ in glory, but in the center of the rose itself sits the enthroned Virgin wearing a crown (see Fig. 13). Another rosary book, *Rosario della sacratissima Vergine Maria* (Rosary of the Most Holy Virgin Mary), published in Rome in 1573 by Andrea Gianetti da Salò, shows the medallions grouped as blossoms on three rosebushes.[47] Here the fifteenth flower shows Christ with God the Father and the Holy Spirit, but a larger oval-shaped illustration in the center of the bush—not yet itself actually one of the roses—depicts the glorified Virgin (see Fig. 14). In the third book, however, Gaspar Loarte's *Istrutione e avvertimenti per meditar i misterii del Rosario della Santissima Vergine Madre* (Instructions and notes for meditating on the mysteries of the rosary of the Most Holy Virgin Mother), published in 1573 (and subsequently translated into French, Portuguese, German, Latin, and English), the transition is completed. Here the Coronation of the Virgin has become part of the series as mystery number fifteen.[48]

In German-speaking countries the Last Judgment image persists still longer. An interesting example is a German rosary book by Adam Walasser published in 1572 and titled *Von der gnadenreichen, hochberümpten . . . Bruderschaft des psalters oder Rosenkrantz Marie* (About the beneficent, famous . . . brotherhood of the Psalter or rosary of Mary), which shows the same Last Judgment figure found in the first German picture rosary of nearly a century earlier.[49] Interestingly, however, the written text that should correspond to this Last Judgment illustration labels the meditation "the eternal glory of the heavenly paradise"[50] (see Fig. 15). The fact that the written words and the illustration do not exactly match here suggests that the pictures were likely reprinted from an earlier version. But their continued acceptance indicates that they were still in use as an alternative form in Germany and underscores the persistence of their influence. In fact, as late as 1577 Peter Canisius commented that the Coronation was usually—but not always—the fifteenth meditation.[51]

Thus, not only did images influence and compete with one another in

PATER·NOSTER

FIG. 13.   Alberto da Castello, *Rosario della gloriosa vergine Maria* (Venice, 1524 ed.). The glorious mysteries. Reproduced by permission of the British Library.

FIG. 14.   Andrea Gianetti da Salò, *Rosario della sacratissima Vergine Maria, raccolto dall' opere del R.P.F. Luigi di Granata*, Venice, 1587. The glorious mysteries, fol. 73v. Reproduced by permission of The Newberry Library, Chicago.

FIG. 15. Adam Walasser, *Von der Gnadenreichen, hochberümpten . . . Bruderschaft des Psalters oder Rosenkrantz Marie* (Dillingen, 1572). Illustration no. 15. Reproduced by permission of the British Library, London.

the formation of the picture series but, as will be shown in Chapter 3, they interacted and competed with written versions. This latter competition—sometimes even within the same printed edition as in Walasser's rosary manual—highlights the nature of the text "matrix" (to use Stephen Nichols's term) as "a place of radical contingencies: of chronology, of anachronism, of conflicting subjects, of representation."[52] Where plates in a printed edition are of an entirely different date or venue from the typesetter's text and represent an independent visual-textual tradition, the visual art, far from merely confirming the verbal form, contests it. The two kinds of "reading" that Nichols identifies at work here—that of "reading text" and of "interpreting visual signs"—mean, however, that even highly literate users like Lambsheym who were familiar with the written context were prone to give primacy to the illustration. Clearly, it is not solely for nonliterate users, but even for literate ones, that the impact and immediacy of the images contributed substantially to the making of the text's meanings and ultimately to the process of selecting the most congenial version.

3

One for Sorrow, Two for Joy: Confraternity Writings, the Fifteen Mysteries, and the Observant Reform

In a series of eight articles published between 1904 and 1906 Thomas Esser made public the results of his exhaustive but unsuccessful search for the written origins of the fifteen rosary mysteries.[1] After examining every available document, Esser concluded that the first appearance of these mysteries was in the Ulm picture rosary of 1483. What he was unable to trace was its connection to any direct antecedent in earlier works except for a general similarity to the writings of Alanus de Rupe. These he discounted, however, because the many (and confusing) methods proposed by Alanus in his writings did not indicate that he had envisioned a way of reciting the prayer like the fifteen mysteries of the Ulm picture rosary.[2] Similarly, Herbert Thurston also concluded that "no trace" of the mysteries was discoverable in Alanus's various works.[3] And André Duval, in a 1988 review article in the *Dictionnaire de spiritualité*, asserted that none of the earliest documents of the rosary confraternity alluded to the fifteen mysteries.[4] If, therefore, the association's founders did not themselves propose this form of the devotion, who did?

The earliest documents of the confraternity, it is true, do not yield the clear link between the picture rosary and the written version that Esser was seeking. A reexamination of these early writings in view of some more recently discovered ones, however, shows how the development of the fifteen meditations was affected by the establishing of a brotherhood devoted to the prayer. While the rules and rationales for its performance are not the prayer itself, they are in a sense an extension of it. The recommendations put forward for "enacting" the prayer highlight the degree to which it evolved in interaction with users, particularly the organizers and leaders of the Observant Reform movement.

Although Dominic of Prussia and his fellow Carthusians had been extremely successful in the first half of the century in propagating their new rosary with *vita Christi* meditations attached, the credit for establishing a brotherhood goes to Alanus de Rupe, the Dominican who around 1470 founded a "Confraternity of the Psalter of the Glorious Virgin Mary" at Douai—five years before Jakob Sprenger established another, more famous one at Cologne. Alanus rejected both the term "rosary" and the Carthusian short version with only fifty Aves, objecting that this "truncated" form of the prayer was a threat to the traditional Marian psalter of 150 Aves. Claiming that the prayer and its confraternity actually dated back to the days of the Virgin Mary herself, Alanus announced that the Virgin had personally commissioned him to revive her prayer and its languishing confraternity.[5] The statutes—the *Livre et ordonannce* (Book and Ordinance)—of the new confraternity that Alanus established at Douai record eight days of Alanus's preaching there and recommend a method of reciting the prayer that harks back to an older one used in the thirteenth century. A similar method can be found described in an English exemplum in British Museum manuscript Digby 86 dated about 1275. The exemplum—in English, despite its French title, "Comment le sauter noustre dame fu primes cuntroue" ("How our Levedi [Lady's] Sauter was first founde")—recommends dividing the 150 Aves into three sections of fifty by meditating in the morning on the Annunciation and Incarnation, at noon on the Nativity, and in the evening on Mary's Assumption.[6]

The method described in the Douai confraternity statutes uses the same three divisions except, instead of three joyful themes, it contains two joyful meditations and one sorrowful one; that is, (1) the prophecies of Jesus, (2) his childhood, and (3) the Passion.[7] A second version suggested later on in the same document also recommends marking off the Aves with fifteen Paternosters. In this way (the statute asserts) the number of Paternosters recited over the course of a year will equal the total number of wounds that Jesus suffered as reckoned by Saint Bernard, namely, 5,475.[8] Neither of these schemata very closely resembles the fifteen mysteries of the picture rosary.

While the statutes of Alanus's Douai brotherhood present only two versions of the prayer, his *Liber Apologeticus ad Ferricum episcopum Tornacensem* (Defense before Bishop Ferricus of Tournai), a work defending Alanus's teachings, contains a bewildering number of variations on the prayer, including meditations on Christ's wounds, on the limbs (head to toe) of Christ and of Mary, on the virtues, friends and benefactors, the duties of office, saints, the altars of the church, a review of one's own sins, and other similar topics.[9] This confusing array led Esser to conclude that Alanus did not have in mind the form of the devotion that later emerged in the fifteen picture mysteries. Rather, it remained for a better organized communicator to interpret Alanus in a way that promoted the best of his ideas.

This communicator was Michael Francisci. During the years 1465–68, Michael had been at Douai where Alanus was first preaching the Psalter of Our Lady.[10] From 1469 until 1481 Michael was active in Cologne promoting the confraternity established there by Jakob Sprenger. In December 1475 Francisci, then professor of theology at the university, presented a set of lectures defending the devotion and the brotherhood against their detractors. The lectures were published—apparently at Sprenger's urging—in two editions, the first edition under the title *Sequitur determinatio quodlibetalis facta colonie* (Here follows the scholarly disputation held at Cologne, 1476), and the second under the title *Quodlibet de veritate fraternitatis rosarii seu psalterii beatae Mariae virginis* (Academic disputation on the true character of the brotherhood of the rosary or Psalter of the Blessed Virgin Mary, 1480).[11] It was in Michael's work that Alanus's ideas were interpreted to a larger public in a form that was attractive and practical. Out of the many methods proposed by Alanus in his characteristically frenetic manner (contemporaries describe Alanus as a manic personality), Michael compiled one usable version.

The method Michael proposed was a composite of the models outlined in the Douai brotherhood's statute, *Livre et ordonnance*, combined with the first of the several forms that Alanus himself had proposed in his *Liber apologeticus*. Michael's hybrid of the Douai and Alanus's methods contain three meditations comprising a joyful-sorrowful-glorious sequence, including (1) Mary's earthly joys, (2) her Passion sorrows, (3) her heavenly joys. In addition, Michael incorporates the Douai format of marking off the tens with fifteen Paternosters to the wounds of Christ, in commemoration of the fifteen hours, persons, places, parts of Christ's body, instruments, and other aspects of his suffering.[12]

At first glance Michael's version of the prayer likewise would not seem to provide much of a link to the mysteries of the Ulm picture rosary, for neither the fifteen Paternosters to the Passion nor the three Ave-meditations identify individual scenes that are to be focused on.

Jakob Sprenger's German Statutes

Influenced by Alanus's and Michael's suggestions, Jakob Sprenger recommended in his statutes for the new brotherhood (published the year after Michael Francisci presented his *Quodlibet* at Cologne) a format similar to Michael's but without the three Ave-themes. Sprenger states that each week members are to pray "three rosaries" (that is, one psalter) each consisting of fifty Aves with five Paternosters. Calling the Aves "white roses" and the Paternosters "red roses," Sprenger explains: "[A]fter ten white roses, insert a red rose, by which is meant a Paternoster. And at the same time meditate on the rose-red blood of Christ Jesus, that God, Our Father, wished to be shed on our behalf."[13] Although Sprenger's text links the Paternosters to the Passion of Christ, it does not specify particular Ave-meditations. It is interesting to note, however, that the 1477 edition of Sprenger's German statutes contains bound together with it (but printed separately) Dominic's fifty life-of-Christ rosary meditations—an indication of the continuing popularity of the Carthusian *vita Christi* text.[14] Clearly, the idea here—even though Sprenger himself does not suggest it—was for these fifty meditations to be used as Ave-tags. In other statutes, however, such as those of the brotherhood in Colmar (founded 1485), Sprenger's instructions have been interpreted quite differently, here using, instead, the format of Hans Schaur's pictorial broadsheet. The Colmar statutes call for five joys (ten Aves each) and five sorrows (one Paternoster each).[15] While this antiphonal format of ten merged joys and sorrows also does not yet represent the full fifteen mysteries that make up the rosary today, it does enumerate roughly two-thirds of them, that is, the "joyful" and "sorrowful" ones. What is lacking is the last third, namely, the "glorious" mysteries.

Subsequent experiments with Alanus's three-part format in other handbooks combined Mary's earthly and heavenly joys together in different ways with a Passion sequence to produce variations that were less narrative in character and, probably for that reason, less appealing. A late-fifteenth-century manuscript of the University of Giessen includes—among nine methods offered in the manual—one that pairs seven earthly joys and five earthly sorrows with an unspecified number of "heavenly joys."[16] Another handbook printed in Ulm by Schäffler and titled *Ein GAR nützlich Büchlein von dem Psalter oder Rosenkranz Marie* (A very useful little book about the psalter or rosary of Mary) contains this same format with nineteen meditations.[17] The "heavenly joys," however, constitute a non-narrative list of aspects of Mary's radiance in paradise. Here the formula tried in Hans Schaur's pictorial broadsheet and the Colmar statutes has been expanded on, but with scenes that have lost the narrative thread.

The Ulm Picture Rosary and Johannes of Erfurt's Venice Statutes

At the time that Esser conducted his exhaustive search for the origins of the fifteen mysteries, it was thought that there existed no other example of the fifteen meditations other than the picture rosaries that are found in woodcuts, engravings, altarpieces, and devotional paintings. According to Esser, the earliest appearance of the fifteen meditations in written form was in Alberto da Castello's Italian rosary book of 1521. In 1965, however, Stefano Orlandi published the statutes of a rosary brotherhood founded in Florence in 1481 that contain a method of praying the rosary that is almost the same as that in the Ulm picture rosary—with the exception of the fifteenth meditation.[18] And in 1977 Meersseman, in his extensive study of Italian confraternities, published the statutes of a rosary brotherhood that was founded in Venice in 1480—a year earlier than the Florence confraternity.[19] The statutes of the Venice confraternity are likewise very similar to those of the Ulm picture rosary except for the last meditation.

The most likely connection between these Venice statutes and the German picture texts can be found in the person of the chaplain and founder of the Venice rosary brotherhood, Johannes of Erfurt (Giovanni d'Erfordia), a German Dominican who was himself an alumnus of the convent in Cologne. On his way back from a trip to Rome, where he had obtained a license to preach the rosary and a copy of the just-issued bull of indulgence, Johannes stopped over at Venice where—not able to speak Italian—he preached the rosary in his native language to the large community of German artisans and merchants living and working there. So favorable was the response in Venice, that Johannes promptly established a confraternity and remained for the next two years as its chaplain.[20] This same brotherhood later commissioned Albrecht Dürer to make for its chapel the rosary painting *Das Rosenkranzfest* (The celebration of the rosary), a work that was completed in 1506 (see Fig. 16). Frances Oudendijk-Pieterse has shown that Dürer's painting was modeled on the woodcut that first appeared in Jakob Sprenger's German statutes of 1476.[21]

In the statutes of the Venice brotherhood, there appears for the first time in written form a complete set of fifteen specific narrative meditations resembling those in the Ulm picture text. Exactly who made this text is not known. Possibly Johannes brought some form of it with him from Cologne. What is clear, however, is that the compiler of the Venice statutes was familiar with Sprenger's German handbook, which he cites, and probably also with Michael Francisci's *Quodlibet*.[22] Indeed, it would have been a simple matter to have adapted the suggestions in Sprenger's statutes to Francisci's three-part joyful-sorrowful-glorious format. In this way the experimenter could have combined meditations on Christ's Passion with any one of several popular sets on Mary's joys. Perhaps Johannes or the redactor used something similar to Hans Schaur's broadside and simply expanded the five joys and five sorrows to fifteen by adding five more joys. Another possibility is that the compilers of the Venice and Ulm texts could have adapted some of the vernacular songs ("laude") performed by Italian confraternities or similar "Meistergesang" lyrics (of German singers' guilds) that likewise tell of the Virgin's joys and sorrows and commemorate the Passion of Christ. Philipp Wackernagel's five-volume collection of German religious song includes several texts of Mary's five or seven "Freuden," one of which, from the fourteenth century, includes the words "Ave gracia plena" after each line.[23]

FIG. 16.   Albrecht Dürer, *The Celebration of the Rosary*, c. 1506. Prague, National Gallery

Where the Ulm and Venice texts differ is in the final meditation. In the Ulm picture text it is the Last Judgment, but in the Venice statutes it is "the glory of paradise" ("la gloria del paradiso"). Most likely, the phrase "the glory of paradise" for mystery 15 in the Venice statutes harks back to Michael Francisci's format in his *Quodlibet*, which ends with the joys in heaven above all the saints and the "joys of paradise."[24] In contrast, one of the five methods proposed by Alanus de Rupe in his *Liber apologeticus* ends with the Last Judgment.[25] But where might Alanus himself have come up with a format that concluded with the Last Judgment? Closer examination of Alanus's recommendations leads back to Dominic of Prussia.

Dominic of Prussia and Alanus de Rupe

It was, after all, because of the rapidly growing popularity of Dominic's rosary of fifty Aves and fifty *vita Christi* clauses that Alanus first began to promote his "more authentic" Psalter of Our Lady. Although Alanus publicly rejected Dominic's form of the prayer, in actual practice, whether consciously or unconsciously, he made use of it. The legend stating that "Saint Dominic" received the rosary from the Virgin actually originates in Alanus's own writings where accounts of "Saint Dominic's vision" first appear. Before Alanus's time no connection existed between Saint Dominic and the rosary or the Psalter of Our Lady. Perhaps Alanus thought it necessary to create an "author" for an authorless practice. Or perhaps, as Herbert Thurston suggested, Alanus may have mistaken a vision reported in Dominic of Prussia's autobiographical "Liber experientiarum" (Book of experiences, 1458)—recounting how a fellow monk saw the Virgin reciting the rosary—for a reference to "Saint" Dominic.[26] Alanus himself reported recurrent visions of his own in which the Virgin charged him with preaching the method she had taught to "Saint Dominic." The method the Virgin describes to Alanus calls for him to meditate on the "articles of the life and Passion" of her son, a description that sounds very much like Dominic of Prussia's fifty narrative life-of-Christ clausulae.[27]

That "Saint Dominic's method" was generally considered to be a *vita Christi* type can be seen in the suggestions given in the Ulm handbook of 1483. Of the several versions described in this handbook, the one labeled "Saint Dominic's method" is the only one that contains a coherent chronological account.[28] Unlike any of the other models enumerated in the manual, it is clearly based on that of Dominic of Prussia.[29]

Despite Alanus's opinion that Dominic's method of fifty Aves was unacceptably short and that it constituted a dangerous rival to the longer Psalter of Our Lady, its length was, in actuality, the chief disadvantage of Dominic's text. Even though versions of Dominic's narrative rosary persisted into the early seventeenth century, fifty meditations were simply too many for most people to remember, and ultimately Dominic's text lost out to still shorter ones. The narrative form, however, remained and was even more successful in these briefer formats.

Some unsuccessful attempts had been made to adapt Dominic's fifty-clause method to Alanus's three-part division, as, for example, one by Justus Landsberg (d. 1535).[30] But even this version was still too long for most people to learn and remember. What the compilers of the pictorial and written fifteen-part rosary text managed to create was a genial synthesis of both Dominic's and Alanus's methods, one that put together a sequential narrative on Dominic's *vita Christi* model but condensed it into only fifteen scenes by using Alanus's three-part division punctuated by fifteen Paternosters and thus preserving the symbolic psalter-format that Alanus had insisted on (see Table 1).

In the end no one person can be credited with the definitive innovation in the growth of the rosary in any of its forms. The link missing in Esser's chain turns out to be several links, represented by several contributors. The "authors" include redactors and illustrators, but most particularly "users"—the lay public and Observant reformers concerned with the care of souls—who played a role collectively and incrementally, by consensus in selecting the most viable version.

The Observant Reformers

Tracing the development of these various experiments with the rosary meditations, one is struck repeatedly by the close connection of all the early innovators to the Observant Reform movement. Indeed, from Dominic of Prussia onward, each of the devotion's initial promoters— including Johannes Rode, Alanus de Rupe, Michael Francisci, Jakob Sprenger, Johannes of Erfurt, and others—was intimately and actively involved with the Observant movement, an initiative that affected all of the major religious orders in the fifteenth century. One of the indirect results of the reform was an increase in attention to the spiritual life of the laity. Indeed, both Alanus de Rupe and Jakob Sprenger hoped by promoting their confraternities to engender pious devotion among the lay populace. Both felt that in "reviving and reestablishing" (Sprenger's words) a prayer that had fallen into disuse they were rekindling a form of spirituality from which men and women of their day sadly had fallen away.[31] Among the religious orders themselves, the reform sought a return to strict discipline and piety in religious observance.

Having begun in the 1330s among Franciscans in Italy, the Observant reform was promoted among the Augustinians in the 1380s, Dominicans in the 1390s, and had reached the German-speaking provinces by the turn of the century.[32] In 1391 Raymund of Capua, the leader of the movement

TABLE 1 Elaboration of Meditations

Texts	Meditations		(x = not elaborated)
Digby MS (1275)			
Annunciation	*Nativity*	*Assumption*	
x	x	x	
Douai Statute (1475)			
Incarnation	(Mary) *earthly joys*	(Mary) *passion sorrows*	
x	x	x	
Liber apologeticus Rupe (1475)			
	(Christ)	(Christ)	
Incarnation	*Passion*	1. *Resurrection*	
x	x	2. Ascension	
		3. Holy Spirit	
		4. Glorification	
		5. Judgment	
Quodlibet Francisci (1476)			
earthly joys	*passion sorrows*	*heavenly joys*	
x	x	x	
Sprenger (1476)			
	150 *"white roses"* (Aves)	15 *"red roses"* (passion) (Paternosters)	
	x	x	

Colmar Statutes (1485) and Hans Schaur (c. 1481)

joys (Aves)	*passion* (Paternosters)
1. Annunciation	1. Agony in Garden
2. Visitation	2. Flagellation
3. Nativity	3. Crown of Thorns
4. Finding	4. Carrying Cross
5. Assumption	5. Crucifixion

Texts	Meditations	(x = not elaborated)

Büchlein
(1501)

earthly joys	sorrows	heavenly joys
1. Annunciation	1. prophecy	1. glory
2. Visitation	2. child lost	2. with trinity
3. Nativity	3. arrest	3. honored
4. Magi	4. crucifixion	4. illuminatrix
5. Presentation	5. burial	5. wishes united
6. Resurrection		6. wishes served
7. Ascension		7. eternal joy

Venice Statutes (1480) and Ulm Picture Rosary (1483)

joys	sorrows	glory
1. Annunciation	1. Agony	1. Resurrection
2. Visitation	2. Flagellation	2. Ascension
3. Nativity	3. Thorns	3. Pentecost
4. Presentation	4. Carrying	4. Assumption
5. Finding	5. Crucifixion	5. Glory of Paradise/ Judgment

SOURCES:

Digby MS: Carl Horstmann, ed. *Altenglische Legenden: Neue Folge*, (1881; repr. Hildesheim, 1969), 220–24.

Douai Statute: Gilles Gérard Meersseman, *Ordo Fraternitatis: Confraternite e pietà dei laici nel medioevo*, 3 vols., Italia Sacra 24–26 (Rome, 1977), 3:1163–69.

Liber apologeticus: *Magister Alanus de Rupe, sponsus novellus beatissime virginis Marie . . . et immensa et ineffabili dignitate et utilitate psalterii precelse ac intemerate semper virginis Marie* (Gripsholm, 1498), fols. R6r–X3v.

Quodlibet: Stefano Orlandi, *Libro del Rosario della Gloriosa Vergine Maria* (Rome, 1965), 141–80.

Sprenger: Jakob Hubert Schütz, ed. *Die Geschichte des Rosenkranzes: Unter Berücksichtigung der Rosenkranz-Geheimnisse und der Marien-Litaneien* (Paderborn, 1909), 25–28.

Colmar Statutes: Jean-Claude Schmitt, "La Confrérie du rosaire de Colmar (1485): Textes de fondation, exempla en allemand d'Alain de la Roche, listes de Prêcheurs et des Soeurs dominicaines," *Archivum Fratrum Praedicatorum* 40 (1970), 103–24.

Hans Schaur: Stephan Beissel, *Geschichte der Verehrung Marias in Deutschland während des Mittelalters* (Freiburg, 1909), 531–32.

Büchlein: *Ein GAR nützlich Büchlein von dem Psalter oder Rosenkranz Marie* (Ulm, 1501), fols. B1r–B2v.

Venice Statutes: Gilles Gérard Meersseman, *Ordo Fraternitatis: Confraternite e pietà del laici nel Medioevo*, 3 vols., Italia Sacra 24–26 (Rome, 1977), 3:1215–18.

Ulm Picture Rosary: *Vnser lieben frauen Psalter*. [Psalterium Virginis Mariae] (Ulm, 1483), fols. C5v–C7v. See also Walter L. Strauss, *The Illustrated Bartsch*, vol. 84, *German Book Illustration before 1500*, Part 5: *Anonymous Artists, 1482–1483*, eds. Walter L. Strauss and Carol Schuler (New York, 1983), 42.

among the Dominicans and general of the order (1380–99), mandated that in each province one cloister should be set aside for those who wished to live in strict observance of the rule of the order and in accordance with its early ideals.[33]

The first Dominican house in the north to institute the observance was the convent at Colmar in Alsace where prior Conrad of Prussia and thirty like-minded brothers resolved together to implement this model of strict discipline and piety.[34] To a large degree the reform was retrospective in focusing on measures such as a return to the rule of silence, enclosure, required participation in choral prayer, the wearing of rough woolen clothing, abstinence from meat, and the relinquishment of all private property.[35] Beyond the initiative to reinstate a stricter way of life, however, the movement also undertook a renewal of spirituality. In at least a few convents this also included the practice of daily communion.[36] Raymund of Capua, Johannes Meyer, and Johann Geiler of Kaysersberg, among others, all stressed in their writings that the reform was not to be a matter of external observance—that is, of "eating and drinking"—but, as Geiler of Kaysersberg put it, of "inwardly dying to self and living for God."[37] Particularly in the mendicant orders the movement was accompanied by a wave of revivalist preaching and a recommitment to attend to the sacramental life of the laity.[38] It was this revival of attention to the care of souls that led to the energetic efforts among Dominicans to promote the rosary and to found brotherhoods devoted to it.

Although the Observants never succeeded in reforming even a plurality of monastic houses, they were in a few places briefly in the majority (for example among the Dominicans in the province of Teutonia where in 1475 thirty-two of the fifty-four houses were reformed).[39] What is most striking, when one looks at the first generation of preachers of the rosary is that every one of its earliest propagators was a member of an Observant house, and many were themselves leaders in the reform movement. Although most were Dominicans, the first group to promote the rosary in an organized fashion was not the Dominican order but, as indicated, the Carthusians at Trier, members of the only order generally regarded by its fifteenth-century contemporaries as not in need of reform. Indeed, it was the Carthusians who served as models to Observant activists and were frequently enlisted to visit houses of other orders and to aid in the effort.[40] A prime example is Johannes Rode (d. 1439), prior of the charterhouse of Saint Alban's in Trier, who was drafted by Archbishop Otto von Ziegenhain to institute the reform among the Benedictines of his district. On visits to Benedictine convents, Johannes Rode took with him a new manner of reciting the rosary, one that featured Dominic's fifty life-of-Christ meditations, which he promoted as an aid to achieving a deeper spirituality.[41] The text of this new rosary was disseminated in numerous copies made by the Carthusian brothers at Saint Alban's.

Among the Dominicans, the Observant reform spread out from Colmar to Nuremberg, Bern, Vienna and throughout the German-speaking provinces. In the far north, a number of convents wishing to institute the strict observance banded together to establish what was called the Congregation of Holland, an association that soon included houses from as far west as Lille in France to as far east as Greifswald in the province of Poland.[42] When Alanus de Rupe first received his commission from the Virgin to revive her rosary, he was living at the Holland Congregation's original house in Lille. The sites of his subsequent work and preaching—Rostock, Douai, Ghent, Zwolle—read like a list of the early memberhouses of the association.[43] It was Alanus's reading of a copy of the Carthusian rosary that motivated him to draft his own text of the prayer and to organize the brotherhood for laypersons at Douai. Subsequently, Alanus's prayer was introduced to the other houses of the strictly Observant Holland Congregation where it came into widespread use at least two years before Jakob Sprenger founded his now famous rosary brotherhood, at Cologne in 1475.[44]

The ideal of spiritual revival drawn from Alanus's writings is found in the Ulm handbook, which itself claims to be based on the work of "Maister Alanus." The text states that through her psalter, Mary wishes to "renew the world . . . and bring it back to the laws and the gospel of God."[45] Similarly, the establishing of a rosary brotherhood a year later at Frankfurt is attributed by eighteenth-century chronicler Franciscus Jacquin to the "revival of fervor" brought there by the Observant movement.[46] In an account of the reform among the Dominicans, called *Buch der Reformacio Predigerordens* (Book of the reform of the Dominican order), written in 1468, Friar Johannes Meyer (1422–85) describes how the rekindling of religious ardor spread by the Observants resulted in dramatic increases in the number of professions to enter convent life, and in the founding of new houses dedicated to the stricter piety.[47] Although clearly a partisan account, Meyer's book gives a sense of the enthusiasm of the movement's committed adherents and of the zeal that motivated them to send out preachers of the rosary and to found devotional associations for the laity.

In cities where both reformed and unreformed houses of Dominicans coexisted, it was characteristically at the reformed ones that the rosary confraternities were established (in the case of Strasbourg, for example, it was at the Observant women's convent of Saint Nicholas in Undis).[48] In Augsburg, where the Dominicans had not joined the reform, the rosary brotherhood was founded not at a Dominican convent but at the church of Saint Moritz by the charismatic pastor, Johannes Molitoris. Molitoris was commissioned to start this chapter by Jakob Sprenger who was at that time vicar-general of the Observants in Brabant.[49] Pastor Molitoris was later investigated and censured for administering daily communion to his parishioners.[50] Indeed, the zealousness of some houses in propagating the brotherhood is exemplified by the convent at Gebweiler in Alsace, which founded forty-six rosary chapters in local churches of the surrounding area.[51]

It was, after all, to preaching that the Observants were committed and in which they particularly excelled.[52] Accordingly, the earliest licenses to preach the rosary were issued to members of the strictly Observant Holland and Leipzig Congregations. Records show that in 1479 Conrad Wetzel of the convent at Leipzig received a license to preach the rosary, as did Friar Hennig Quitzkow of the Holland Congregation's house at Wismar in 1481 and a year later Johannes of Chemnitz of the Leipzig Congregation's house at Freiburg in Saxony.[53] Johannes established rosary brotherhoods in Grottkau and Wroclaw (then Breslau), Poland.[54] Perhaps the most improbable, but ultimately the most significant, of these early foundings was that of the first Italian rosary brotherhood. This chapter was the one organized at Venice in 1480 by the German friar Johannes of Erfurt, a member of the Holland Congregation's convent at Greifswald in the province of Poland, when Johannes undertook a trip to Rome in company with Albertus Pieters, known as the "Reformer of the North," who was soon to be appointed vicar-general of the Holland Congregation.[55] Further foundations followed in 1481 in Florence and Rome.[56] The activities of these many Observant preachers reveals the degree to which the early organized promotion of the rosary confraternity was associated with reformist outreach to the laity. But just what was the message that the preachers carried as they went about distributing rosaries, and what was it that inspired them to go?

For Jakob Sprenger and Alanus de Rupe it was, as has been indicated, a vision of engendering a new spirituality among the laity. By founding their respective lay brotherhoods, Sprenger and Rupe were both adapting the model of Observant monastic spirituality to a larger public with the aim of encouraging laypersons to take up a more devout lifestyle and to win grace for their souls. The rosary was particularly appropriate because it combined an "imitatio" exercise—contemplation of the life and Passion of Christ—with a quantitative expiatory ritual, one that was backed by an indulgence. In the statutes of his new brotherhood, Sprenger concedes that "self-interest motivates people best," but what he hoped for was that through the practice of prayer and meditation on the Blood of Christ, laypeople would, as he says, become eager and obedient to God's commandments, persevere in good works, and ultimately "receive the grace of justification of sins."[57] By setting up an organization with no membership dues and an open admissions policy that even the poorest could join, Sprenger hoped to encourage more people to pray. Indeed, his stated goal in founding the brotherhood was to provide prayers for the souls of the many for whom, he lamented, not enough was being done.[58] By joining the confraternity, anyone could guarantee that prayers would be said for his or her soul after death. Furthermore, members were assured that the Dominicans who sponsored the organization would hold quarterly prayer-vigils for the souls of all deceased confraternity members in perpetuity.[59]

Five years earlier Alanus de Rupe's brotherhood at Douai had offered a similar benefit to members. The Douai statutes are accompanied by a decree issued in 1470 by Johannes Excuria, vicar-general of the Holland Congregation, promising members of the brotherhood a share in all the spiritual "goods" accumulated by the Observant congregation.[60] Following this model, Sprenger's confraternity likewise offered its members a part in all the meritorious works accrued by the Dominicans.[61] In 1475 General Leonardus Mansuetis confirmed that all who would pray the rosary would be participants in the offices and merits of the order.[62] In many cases the services of Observant friars as chaplains and confessors posed an attractive alternative as well to the ministrations of unreformed local priests.

Although the rosary generally is not thought of as an instrument of reform but rather has been criticized as a mechanical attempt to achieve grace by quantitative means, when looked at from the point of view of its fifteenth-century Observant promoters—those concerned with care of the souls of the poor for whom, as they said, not enough was being done—the rosary becomes an important instrument of evangelical outreach. Meditation on the Passion and the shedding of Christ's Blood for mankind would, it was hoped, encourage spirituality among the laity, obedience to God's commandments, and allow those who persisted to receive the grace of justification of sins. How this initial impetus worked out in the further propagation of the prayer will be the focus of the chapters to follow.

André Vauchez attributes the attraction for laypersons of membership in confraternities partly to the "prestige of monasticism." By imitating monastic practices, members could live as semireligious and thus in a sense "become clerics while remaining lay."[63] Similarly, Richard Kieckhefer has pointed out that the rosary, along with books of hours and meditations on the Passion "were so many lay imitations of the monastic hours."[64] The adoption of a format for the rosary resembling a kind of ersatz Hours in a symbolic "psalter" arrangement was thus a doubly attractive design. For his part, however, Steven Ozment sees this appropriation of the monastic model as a telling reflection of the church's failure to put forward alternative forms of piety suited to the laity.[65] If numbers are an indication of demand, the exponential growth of Sprenger's confraternity shows how lively was the interest in religious associations for the laity. The 1476 edition of Sprenger's statutes cites enrollments during the confraternity's first year in Cologne of 8,000 and in Augsburg of 3,000. The second edition printed a year later reports Augsburg enrollments at 21,000.[66] This sevenfold increase, if reliable, registers the enthusiasm for the kind of affiliation Vauchez describes.

While the early confraternity documents written by Observant promoters outlining nonprescriptive regulations and suggesting various forms of the practice are not the ritual text itself, they are contiguous with it. The open-endedness of confraternity regulations and their application encouraged experimentation in attempts to create congenial forms of the exercise that would fit the spiritual needs of the membership. Ultimately, the text that won the day was the miniature mystery-play format of fifteen *vita Christi* scenes, one that easily could be enacted by illiterate practitioners. Ironically, although now shorter in length, this successful minidrama (recapitulating in brief compass Christ's "acts of redemption") fulfilled the original intention of the life-of-Christ rosary as Dominic had described it. For illiterate users (by far the majority) the picture images displayed in confraternity chapels formed the most immediate basis for their mental performance of the ritual. Thus the "text" for most people was both a visual and a verbal one. More than any other, it was the success of the picture version that made the ritual text so attractive to so many. The prayer not only served as a comforting recourse against anxiety about purgatory, but with its dramatic and two-thirds joyful content, it was an uplifting exercise that ideally suited the Observant reformers' efforts to foster spirituality among the laity.

4

Secular Love Gardens, Marian Iconography, and the Names of the Rose

The conflicting conceptions that Dominic of Prussia and Alanus de Rupe had as to the nature of the devotion that they collectively promoted extended even to its name. While Dominic called it a "rosary" ("dat Rosenkrentzge geziert mit gedechtnisse des leuens und lydens christi"), Alanus adamantly opposed this label and insisted on calling it a "psalter."[1] Why did Alanus reject the term "rosary"? And, given such strenuous opposition, why did Jakob Sprenger continue to use it? Why, in fact, were roses connected to the devotion at all?

Alanus makes it quite clear that his reservations involved more than simply the wish to preserve the psalter model and, thereby, a more traditional form of the devotion. His opposition to the term "rosary" ("rosarium") stems rather from the profane associations attached to the rose chaplet. In his *Liber apologeticus* Alanus objects that the names "rosarium," "corona," and "sertum" (for chaplet) all have "vain and worldly connotations."[2] A look at the conflicting profane and religious typologies at work here will explain why Dominic's term "rosary" was controversial, but also why it ultimately prevailed over the competing term, "psalter," in popular use.

The Rose in Pre-Christian and Germanic Traditions

The rose is an ancient emblem with a long history in both Christian and non-Christian traditions. In ancient Rome the "rosalia" was a spring festival honoring the dead that was celebrated when the roses began to bloom. The blossoms were placed on graves and strewn on the ground where relatives banqueted in the spiritual presence of the departed.[3] Spring festivals of the Middle Ages, especially those that celebrated the month of May, featured flower hoops suspended on maypoles and chaplets of roses and other flowers that were donned as headdresses. These wreaths symbolized the maidenly status of the women wearing them, even though members of both sexes—including the clergy—readily bedecked themselves with garlands of flowers during such festivals. Emile Mâle points out that chaplets were traditionally presented by vassals to a lord on festive occasions as a sign of homage.[4]

In Greek tradition the red rose was associated with the blood of a god. It was said to have originated when a thorn pierced Aphrodite's foot.[5] As the flower of Aphrodite, it became associated with the Roman cult of Venus, particularly with the bower of Venus, archetype of the paradisiacal love garden. A fifteenth-century illustration of the planet Venus in the *Codex Sphaera* (Book of the spheres) shows Venus holding a rose and wearing a chaplet of red and white roses. Below couples amuse themselves in a traditional, enclosed love garden[6] (see Fig. 17). From ancient times down to the *Roman de la rose*, an orchard or garden protected by a rosehedge constituted the ideal "locus amoenus" for romantic encounters. Love garden illustrations, a popular genre of the fifteenth century, frequently picture lovers in a rose-trellised enclosure. Frank Crisp has suggested that the term "rose garden" was applied to orchards and

FIG. 17.   The Planet Venus from the fifteenth-century Italian *Codex Sphaera*, Berlin, Archiv für Kunst und Geschichte.

pleasure gardens because they were enclosed with a hedge or fence of roses[7] (see Fig. 18).

"Rose gardens" figure prominently in two Middle High German tales of adventure called *Der große Rosengarten zu Worms* (The large rose garden at Worms, c. 1250) and *Laurin* or *Der kleine Rosengarten* (The small rose garden, c. 1250/75).[8] In Kriemhild's garden at Worms, knights do battle in a garden or grassy plot well supplied with rosebushes (stanza 47.1). Here the winner of each contest receives a kiss and a "Rosenkranz" from Kriemhild, mistress of the tournament.[9] The woodcut illustration accompanying the first printed edition (1479) shows a typical love garden scene with a couple embracing before a background of roses (see Figs. 19 and 20). Kriemhild's garden is enclosed by a silken thread as is that belonging to the dwarf Laurin in *Der kleine Rosengarten*. When the thread is broken and his flowers trampled, the enraged owner rides out to avenge the trespass.

In another forbidden-garden adventure, *Garel vom dem blühenden Tal* (Garel of the Flowering Dale, c. 1250/80), a knight, Eskilabon, tells how he has defended a flower plot against all comers who would attempt to pick a blossom, forcing the loser in each unsuccessful challenge to carry a wreath of red flowers to the lady of the garden, the queen of Portugal.[10] For the victorious challenger the prize is to be the hand of Eskilabon's sister, Flordiâne. Entering the garden and despoiling the flowers is the gesture that calls forth the knight Eskilabon, protector of the garden, into battle. In a figurative sense, what is being defended here is a lady's maidenly honor: in medieval German the phrase "rose brechen" or "picking a rose" had the similar connotations to those that the term "deflower" has in English.[11]

Grimm's *Deutsches Wörterbuch* lists five uses of the term "rose garden." These include, besides the literal meaning, (1) a designation for a burial ground, (2) the embodiment of joy and delight, (3) a title of the Virgin Mary, (4) a literary anthology, and (5) the diminutive form, "rosengärtlin," an obscene usage.[12] This last meaning is made clear in a fable by thirteenth-century writer, Johannes von Freiberg, called "das redelîn" (The little wheel). In this tale a clever farmhand comes upon an exhausted serving maid who is sound asleep. The knave gingerly raises up the sleeping girl's shift to see her "rose garden" ("Bis ûf der rôsen gertel"). Then with lamp black he carefully paints a small wheel on her belly, above her "little rose bush" ("Ob wendik dem rôsen büschelîn").[13] If any more clarity is needed, the reader is directed to Neidhart of

Fig. 18. Fifteenth-century love-garden tapestry, detail. Basel, Historisches Museum (photo: Historisches Museum)

FIG. 19.   Illustration for "Der große Rosengarten zu Worms" from the *Heldenbuch* (Strasbourg, Prüss, 1479). Darmstadt, Hessische Landes- und Hochschulbibliothek

FIG. 20. Cathedral of Strasbourg Prince of the World, "The Tempter" (detail), c. 1280. Strasbourg, Musée de l'Oeuvre Notre-Dame

Reuental's (c. 1185–1240) obscene song praising a wreath of brown roses.[14]

Perhaps the best-known example of the profane use of rose imagery is found in Guillaume de Lorris's (c. 1212–37) *Roman de la Rose* (Romance of the Rose) and Jean de Meun's (c. 1237–1305) bawdy sequel to Guillaume's work.[15] The strenuous objections that this romance elicited, especially those expressed by Christine de Pisan, had to do with the less-than-flattering view of women that the work presented and with its generally unedifying character. Reactions against it were strong enough to induce Pierre d'Ailly (1350–1420) to compose a contrafacture that deliberately recasts the profane romance as a religious one. This text, d'Ailly's *Jardin amoureux de l'âme dévote* (The pious souls' garden of love), contains all the details of the dream garden in the *Roman de la Rose*: the wall decorated with pictures, allegorical guides, the search for the "ami," the lovers dallying in the garden.[16] But in d'Ailly's work the false God of love, Cupid, is overtly contrasted with Christ, the true God of love. And the company of lovers learns of true love in Christ's garden school. Perhaps the reaction against the *Roman de la Rose* was also triggered in part by objection to its use of rose imagery that was associated in religious circles with the sacred themes.

The Rose in Christian Iconography

The symbolism of the rose also has a long history in Christian tradition extending back to patristic writings that identified the rose with the Virgin Mary. Saint Ambrose (339–397), in his *De virginibus* (Of Virgins), referred to Mary as the "rosa pudoris" (rose of modesty), while the fifth-century Christian poet, Sedulius, in his *Paschale carmen* (Paschal song), proclaimed her a rose "among thorns" ("e spinis").[17] In the earliest Greek litanies Mary bears the title "mystic rose," a name that reappears in the twelfth-century Latin litany of Loreto.[18] By far the richest sources of such floral references, however, are Latin hymns and sequences that praise the Virgin with a profusion of titles like "noble rose," "fragrant rose," "chaste rose," "rose of heaven," "rose of love," and "never-wilting rose." The fifteenth-century sequence, "De gaudiis beatae Mariae" (Of the joys of Blessed Mary) for example, repeats the salutation "rosa" in every stanza.[19]

Vernacular German "Marienlieder" sing of Mary with similar praises, calling her the "pure rose," "bright rose," "summer rose," "rose of virtue," "Rose of Jesse," and "rose in heavenly dew." The early twelfth-century "Marienlied" of Melk hails Mary as the "Rose of Jericho," a term borrowed from the matins reading from Sirach 24.14 in the Little Office of the Virgin.[20]

Besides representing the flower itself, the Virgin is also depicted as a rose garden—the garden that bore Christ. In Latin hymns she is called "God's rose garden."[21] The Minnesinger, Frauenlob (d. 1318), in his "Marienleich," calls Mary "wolgemuoter rôsengarte" ("pleasant rose garden" [stanza 12.8]).[22] In what is certainly the best known such reference to the Virgin, Dante (1265–1321) lauds her as the "Rose in which the Word of God became flesh" (*Paradiso*, canto 23.73–74).[23]

In Christian tradition the rose stands not for Mary alone but also for Christ. The familiar sixteenth-century advent hymn, "Lo, How a Rose Ere Blooming," relates how both Mary and her son are roses that sprang from the tree of Jesse.[24] A fourteenth-century German song discloses the name of the rose, saying: "The rose is named Christ, / Mary, the garden so fair."[25] Accordingly, sculptures from the thirteenth and fourteenth centuries place Mary and the infant Christ beside a rosetree; in the fifteenth century they are shown seated in an arbor covered with roses—a scene that later becomes a popular genre setting for devotional paintings, as a kind of holy love garden[26] (see Figs. 21 and 22).

The Enclosed Garden of the Song of Songs

The primary source of these images was the Old Testament Song of Songs, which was the most commented-on book of the Bible in the Middle Ages, and the fourteenth century's most frequently quoted text. The Song is a love dialogue between bride and groom. In it the bride praises her beloved as the "rose of Sharon," and the bridegroom admires his bride as "a lily among thorns" (2:1–2). (In later references to this passage, the "lily" was replaced by the more alluring flower, rose, which also echoed the groom's title.) The lover goes on to eulogize the chastity of his undefiled bride, likening her to an enclosed garden and a sealed fountain. He sings: "A garden enclosed is my sister, my spouse, a spring shut up, a fountain sealed" (4:12).

Fig. 21.   Virgin and Child with Rosetree, c. 1300. Straubing, polychrome stone. Munich, Bayerisches Nationalmuseum

Fɪɢ. 22.   Martin Schongauer, The Madonna of the Rose Bower, 1473, Colmar, Saint Martin's Church. At bottom left is also a "Pfingstrose," the "Whitsuntide rose" (peony). Reproduced by the kind permission of the Conseil de Fabrique de la Paroisse Saint-Martin de Colmar.

In the earliest commentaries, the speakers in the Song were most often identified as Christ and his church or as Christ and the individual soul.[27] By the twelfth century, however, the bride had come to be popularly identified with the Virgin Mary, who is a type of the church. While most commentators continued to depict the nuptials as those between Christ and soul, the figure of Mary continued to be firmly linked to the Song of Songs, since she was seen as the *first* bride of Christ and, hence, the model for each individual believer.[28]

In religious typologies, the enclosed garden ("hortus conclusus") thus became the symbol of Mary's untainted virginity and developed into one of the most frequently used symbols in medieval devotional writings to depict the mystery of the Incarnation. Typological picture books such as the *Speculum humanae salvationis* (Mirror of man's salvation) contain images of a locked, walled garden representing the "hortus conclusus"[29] (see Figs. 23 and 24).

At least by the institution of the feast of the Immaculate Conception (c. 1140), the enclosed garden had become the standard symbol for Mary's womb. In *Das Sankt Trudperter Hohe Lied*, a twelfth-century vernacular commentary on the Song of Songs, the Christ child recalls that his mother's womb was "the best garden."[30] It was into this garden that the Christ child sprang and then fell asleep "covered with roses," says the late fourteenth-century German poet, Der Harder, in his *Guldin Schilling* (Golden schilling).[31]

Mary is herself not only the enclosed garden, but is also frequently shown seated in a walled garden. In these images the walled garden has become fused with the garden of heavenly paradise where Mary is now enthroned. Devotional pictures of this garden of heavenly love typically show Mary and the infant Savior seated together alone or with various saints (see Figs. 25 and 26). The garden of the incarnation, the "hortus conclusus," was traditionally contrasted with the garden of earthly paradise (Genesis 2:8), which Brun von Schönebeck's interpretation of the Song of Songs (*Das Hohelied*, 1276) says was "not locked" ("unbeslozzen").[32] In the same way Mary was contrasted with Eve and the Fall juxtaposed to man's redemption. Just as the name "Eva" reversed spells the word "Ave," so was Eve's sin reversed by Mary, the new Eve.[33] Stanley Stewart has characterized the incarnation by saying that "the answer to man's Fall and Expulsion is God's entrance into the Mary-garden."[34]

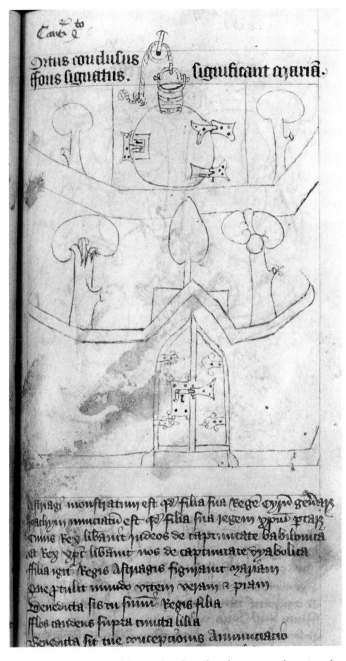

FIG. 23.   Illustration of the enclosed garden (hortus conclusus) and sealed fountain (fons signatus) signifying Mary, from the *Speculum humanae salvationis* (England, c. 1390), Morgan MS M766, fol. 25. New York, Pierpont Morgan Library

FIG. 24. Woodcut illustration from the *Canticum canticorum* (Song of Songs), c. 1460–65, with banderole, "A garden enclosed is my sister, my bride, a garden enclosed, a fountain sealed" (Song of Songs 4:12). Reproduced by permission of the Pierpont Morgan Library, New York

The "Hortus Conclusus": Scene of the "Mystical Unicorn Hunt"

The connection between the Virgin, the rose garden, and the rosary proceeds via the iconography of the "hortus conclusus" in its permutations as emblem of the Incarnation, in particular the Annunciation scene. This scene pictures Mary herself seated within an enclosed walled or fenced garden with a unicorn approaching her or in her lap. The angel Gabriel, with horn and hunting dogs, pursues the unicorn. This scene, known as the "mystical unicorn hunt"—to distinguish it from other unicorn tales—was condemned by the Council of Trent in 1563 and subsequently faded from use.

Popular songs and other accounts, however, tell its meaning. The

FIG. 25.   Meister des Marienlebens, "Virgin and Child with Saints in a Rose Arbor,"
c. 1470. Berlin, Staatliches Museum Preussischer Kulturbesitz

unicorn represents Christ (the rose planted in the enclosed garden). They
relate the story of an animal so wild and swift that no man, only a pure
virgin, could catch it. Konrad von Megenberg (c. 1309–74) explains, for
example, in his *Buch der Natur*:

Fig. 26.   Gérard David (d. 1523), "Virgin and Child in an Enclosed Garden with Saints and Donor." London, National Gallery

it is such a powerful and wild animal, that no hunter can catch it by force . . . but it can be caught by a chaste virgin. If she sits alone in the forest, it will come to her . . . place its head in her lap and fall asleep. . . . The animal signifies our Lord Jesus Christ, who was angry and filled with fury before he became man because of the angels' pride and man's disobedience on earth. He was caught by the most praiseworthy maiden, Mary, that is, by her chaste purity, in the midst of this desolate and sick world, when he sprang from heaven down to her pure womb.[35]

Konrad von Würzburg (1220–87) explains that "the heavenly hunter" sent his only begotten son down into this deep, vile "forest of many sins" where he sought refuge in Mary[36] (see Fig. 27). The unicorn, a type of Christ, is destined to be killed by hunters. A woodcut in the Bibliothèque

FIG. 27. "Hortus conclusus" Annunciation scene, tapestry, upper Rhine, c. 1500. Munich, Bayerisches Nationalmuseum

Nationale, Paris, shows a virgin seated with a unicorn in her lap and a large branch of white roses (white for chastity) arching over them.[37] In a German popular-song version from 1536 the events of the story are set in a landscape of red roses.[38]

In other works, the association of the garden with Eve and man's fall becomes a symbol of man's seduction by woman. *Our Lady Mary's Rose*

Garden explains how Christ "like the unicorn" was drawn by the noble fragrance of Mary, the rose, who "like a wise virgin," bound him so that he could not escape. But, "unlike women who trick and deceive men," Mary captured Christ by her virtue and her great and ardent love.[39] This garden, however, also contains thorns. Indeed, the author reminds us that Mary was "a rose among thorns" and that Christ was wounded by the thorns. He was pierced on the rosetree of the Holy Cross (lines 111–12, 509–12).

Roses as Wounds: The Rosetree of the Cross

In mystical devotional writings, the rosetree is identified with the Holy Cross. *Our Lady Mary's Rose Garden* describes the five-petaled red roses of the garden as the wounds of Our Lord Jesus Christ that grow "on the rosetree of the cross" ("uff dem rosebaume des cruczes" [line 731]). The *Nürnberger Garten* (early fifteenth century), another spiritual garden allegory, describes Christ as the most beautiful rosebush "decorated with beautiful red roses of his holy wounds."[40] A similar devotional work, the *Rosengarten des Leidens Christi* (Rose garden of Christ's suffering, c. 1450) makes use of the rose-garden metaphor to sequence meditations on Christ's Passion.[41]

The theme of being wounded by the darts of love, a theme that was incorporated into Christian writings by Origen (c. 185–254), was later transformed into veneration of the wounds of the Savior. The *Vitis mystica* of Saint Bonaventure (c. 1217–74), for example, likens Christ's Passion to a "bleeding rose" and the *Nürnberger Garten* describes Christ's wounds as red roses that are wide open "from the heat of love."[42] In these works the Savior's suffering was portrayed as freely willed suffering for love, a theme that became a leitmotif of mystical writings, and in particular of the "bridal" mysticism of allegorical devotional gardens. These works, based on the Song of Songs, celebrate in the language of connubial love the relationship of the devout soul to Christ the Bridegroom.

The roses symbolizing Christ and Mary are typically red and white. In the Song of Songs, the bride sings, "My beloved is white and ruddy" (5:10). White was interpreted as signifying purity, red as love or suffering. Thus, Saint Bernard (1091–1153) writes, "The rose Mary was white for virginity, red for love ("caritatem")."[43] In other writings, roses signify the mystical love-suffering of the fervent heart, as in the case of Henry Suso (1295–1366) who is seen in a vision by a fellow mystic wearing a crown of red and white roses. The friend interprets the white roses as Suso's purity and the red roses his suffering.[44]

Devotional Garden Allegories

A theme closely related to the enclosed garden of Mary's virginity is the garden of virtues. To Saint Jerome (c. 350–420) Mary is a "garden of delights into which are sown all kinds of flowers and spice plants of the virtues."[45] Conrad von Haimburg's song "Hortulus B. V. M." (c. 1360) describes each one of the plants in the garden of Mary's virtues.[46] In devotional gardens the rose is the favorite symbol for the virtues of the Virgin. A fifteenth-century German poem called "Marien krentzelin" describes ten roses as ten virtues that grow in Mary's garden.[47] The *Nürnberger Garten* describes seven virtues and the seven kinds of roses they represent.[48]

In other works, the garden represents the soul of the individual Christian and the trees and flowers are the virtues to be cultivated there. Although in early religious writings the soul is depicted as "a paradise," in later medieval texts it is more often a garden.[49] In a thirteenth-century collection of sermons attributed to the Preacher of Sankt Georgen, for example, the "garden" is the human heart.[50] Earlier Saint Bernard had compared the flowers in the garden of the Song of Songs to the believer's good works.[51]

In the fourteenth century—primarily in German- and Dutch-speaking areas—numerous allegorical works begin to appear with titles like "Little Rose Garden," "Spiritual Flower Garden," or "Rose Garden of the Heart."[52] When the garden has become the soul—or the soul a rose garden—the image of picking spiritual flowers from it to offer to the Virgin is a logical step. From there it is only a small step to the concept of the rosary.

Aves as Roses: The Rose Chaplet

The transformation of words (Aves) into roses comes through the identi-
fication of the rose with Christ and Christ with the Word. The Gospel of
John (1:14) declares that "the Word was made flesh and dwelt among us
. . . the only begotten of the Father." Thus, as *Our Lady Mary's Rose
Garden* explains, "The rose is the Word that the first gardener, who
planted paradise in the beginning, sowed and planted in Mary's earthly
womb. . . . The word from the mouth of God is our Lord Jesus Christ"
(lines 74–76, 88–90). The Ave Maria, which is spoken to commemorate
this event, is itself "a rose." It is made up of five phrases and has five
petals that represent the letters MARIA (lines 64–65, 190–91).

The earliest mention of Aves taking the form of roses and comprising a
chaplet occurs in the legend called "Aves seen as Roses," which appears
in the latter half of the thirteenth century in Latin, Catalan, and German
versions. It is included with many of the manuscript and printed copies of
Dominic of Prussia's rosary of fifty meditations to explain how the prayer
originated and how it was improved on by the addition of Dominic's fifty
meditations. The legend was also printed together with Jakob Sprenger's
German rosary statutes in 1477, and in many later rosary handbooks.
Dominic's version of the tale, titled "Wie der rosenkrantze ist funden"
(How the rosary came to be), states:

> A good, simple, secular man had the custom of making every day
> a chaplet of roses, or flowers, or rue, or of whatever he could,
> according to the season, and placing it on the head of an image of
> Our Lady. This he did with great enjoyment and pious devotion.
> The Virgin saw the good intention of his heart and, wanting to
> help him further it, gave him the desire to take up the religious
> life. And so he became a lay brother in a cloister. But in the
> cloister he was given so many tasks to perform that he no longer
> had time to make Mary her chaplet as he was accustomed to do.
> Because of that he became dissatisfied and was about to leave the
> order and go back into the world, when an older priest became
> aware of his distress. The priest wisely advised him that he should
> recite each day fifty Ave Marias in place of the chaplet and
> convinced him that Queen Mary would prefer that to all the rose
> chaplets that he had ever made. The lay brother followed the
> advice and continued in it for some time. Then one day he was

sent on an errand that required him to ride through a forest which
harbored thieves. In the forest he tied his horse to a tree, knelt
down, and was reciting his fifty Ave Marias when thieves saw him
and decided to rob him and steal his horse. But as they approached
him, they saw from a distance a wonderfully beautiful maiden
standing by him, who, every little while, took from his mouth a
beautiful rose and added it to a chaplet that she was making. When
the rose chaplet was complete, she placed it on her head and flew
off to heaven. The robbers were thoroughly amazed and ran to the
brother asking him who the beautiful maiden was that they had
seen beside him. The lay brother replied: "I did not have any
maiden with me. I have only been reciting fifty Ave Marias as a
chaplet for Queen Mary, as I was instructed. And that is all I
know." When the robbers told him what they had seen, the lay
brother, and the robbers too, realized that it was the most revered
Mother of God who, in person, had accepted the rose chaplet that
we are accustomed to send to her daily through our angel. Then
the brother rejoiced from the depths of his heart and from that day
forward made a spiritual rose chaplet of fifty Ave Marias for Queen
Mary daily and instructed other good people in the practice. In this
manner the rosary was created and made known to us. And one
may believe that the robbers bettered their lives as a result, because
God's grace had permitted them to behold the Mother of Mercy.[53]

Some variations on the legend report the roses being carried to heaven by
an angel or by white doves, rather than received by the Virgin herself.
Yet the transformation of words into symbolic flowers is common to all
of them (see Fig. 28).

As early as the fourth century, Gregory of Nazianzus writes of weaving
a chaplet for the Virgin Mary.[54] By at least the early thirteenth century
the term was used to designate a chain of fifty Aves (one-third of an Ave-
psalter). Beguines at Ghent in 1242 prayed three such "hoedekins"
(chaplets) each day.[55] That these, however, were not yet referred to as a
"rosarium" is indicated by the fact that the thirteenth-century versions
of the legend "Aves Seen as Roses" in Latin use the term "corona" or
"sertum" for the wreath of roses. The version in King Alfonso's *Cantigas
de Santa Maria* uses the term "guerlanda."[56] The earliest German versions, dating from 1280/1300, however, employ the term "Rosenkranz,"
which appears to have been translated back into Latin in later versions as

FIG. 28. Illustration of the legend of the monk and the robbers ("Aves Seen as Roses"), in *Der Spiegel hochloblicher Bruderschafft des Rosenkrantz Marie* (Leipzig, 1515), fol. 36v. Reproduced by permission of the Bayerische Staatsbibliothek, Munich

"rosarium." Before this time the term "rosarium" was used to designate an anthology of texts (like a "florilegium"), or a rose garden, but not generally in use for a chaplet of Aves.[57] Yet the transition from "psalterium" to "rosarium" is seen taking place almost automatically in a work like Engelbert, the abbot of Admont's (1297–1331) "Psalterium beatae Mariae Virginis" where each of the 150 stanzas begins with "Ave, rosa," in effect, enacting the legend.[58]

The act of constructing and giving spiritual gifts for the Virgin— especially clothing and jewelry (even a temple)—made out of words is an old and particularly attractive idea. Marian miracle stories of the thirteenth century describe praying the Ave-psalter as making dresses for the Virgin.[59] Konrad von Würzburg (c. 1225–87) forges a golden garland of verbal "gems" and "blossoms" for her in his *Goldende Schmiede* (Golden Ornament, lines 1–9, 60–85), and Albrecht of Scharfenberg (late thirteenth century) lovingly constructs a "temple of words" for the Virgin.[60]

The Aves recited for the Virgin in the legend "Aves Seen as Roses" were said without the addition of meditations. Dominic of Prussia points this out and contrasts this old method of saying the rosary with his new method. To show how pleasing the new exercise, with meditations added, is to God and to the Virgin, he reports a vision experienced by one Carthusian brother at Trier in which the monk was transported to heaven and witnessed there the saints and angels reciting the rosary and its new meditations with great devotion. He recounts that after each clause in the life of Christ the heavenly host sang an "alleluia."[61] Another of Dominic's exempla asserts that this new rosary is like "a ribbon that ties all one's good works [and spiritual exercises] together into a bundle so that they can be placed into the hands of the Virgin and presented by her to God."[62] The new rosary with meditations soon became a fixture of devotional gardens like Ulrich Pinder's *Der beschlossen Gart des Rosenkrantz Marie* (The enclosed garden of the rosary, published 1489–1505), and the theme for religious songs such as *Der geistliche Blumengarten* (The spiritual flower garden, c. 1500).[63]

The Allegorical Narrative of the Rose

The version of fifteen meditations that developed out of devotions on the joys of the Virgin and the passion of Christ is the three-part story of

God's love, sacrificial death, and triumph. The first act, the white rosary, celebrates the Incarnation of the Divine Child, who like the unicorn was attracted by Mary's purity and love. Seen through the mystical filter of the Song of Songs, the figures are also bride and bridegroom. In mystical terms the bridegroom is both old and young, the infant and bridegroom are one. Thus *Our Lady Mary's Rose Garden* can assert that Mary "drew and, in a way, forced the Son of the most high God to come from heaven to fetch her, as a king's son does a beloved bride, that he wishes to lead to his eternal father's kingdom" (lines 261–64). Tropologically, the garden also represents the devout soul, and the infant savior is also the soul's bridegroom. The *Rostocker Gardengebet* addresses Christ, "the rose," as "You blooming bridegroom, you firstborn of the Virgin."[64]

The red roses of the Passion sequence depict the Savior's tears, sweat, blood, and agony, willingly suffered for love. Christ's acceptance of humiliation at the hands of man to be mocked, beaten, crowned with thorns, and hung on a cross, is witness to his supreme love. Allegorically, the wounds are seen as the roses of love. It is through his wounds that man is healed. The golden roses sing the triumph of divine love that is stronger than death. The risen savior, having survived the ordeal and proved himself worthy to save man, returns to his father's land in triumph as a hero. The spirit of God descends to man. The Virgin ascends to the heavenly kingdom.

The earliest picture rosary did not focus so much on the apotheosis of Mary as on that of Christ at the Last Judgment. Some versions, like those in the Venice and Florence statutes, emphasize the hero's glorious return and his approbation among the saints, who themselves exemplify virtue and martyrdom. But the most popular ending—and that which ultimately comes to dominate—focuses on Mary's reunion with Christ and on her apotheosis as queen of heaven. Through her, paradise is regained, says the author of *Our Lady Mary's Rose Garden*, for "when this beautiful rose, Mary, began to bloom, the winter of our sadness passed away, the summer of eternal joy began to arrive, and the May of eternal delight to shine. And with her was given back to us the greening, delightful paradise" (lines 205–9). Earthly paradise and heavenly paradise become connected through the "hortus conclusus." Figuratively, devotional gardens like *Our Lady Mary's Rose Garden*, where religious exercises are performed, become the meeting place of the soul and Christ (see Fig. 29). The enclosed garden symbolizes both Mary's virtue and the mystical spiritual delights available to the devout soul.

In secular literature as well, the walk in the garden was a standard feature of "Minneallegorien" (love allegories). Thus erotic-spiritual writings like those of Frauenlob (d. 1318) and even some religious "Tagelieder" (dawn songs), which show Mary reposing in a beautiful garden while the Divine Lover weaves a rose garland for his beloved, seem to be almost indistinguishable from their profane counterparts.[65] The multivalence of mystical and sensual expressions adopted from the Song of Songs makes distinctions in these works problematic if not impossible.

In German vernacular paraphrases of the Song of Songs, as well as in mystical writings from Hadewijch down to Henry Suso, the enclosed garden is the loving soul, and the rose in works like the *Münchner Minnegarten* (Munich love garden, c. 1470) represents the burning love that the soul has toward God ("brynnende mynne nach got").[66] Clearly, as Peter Dronke has pointed out, it was not always easy to separate sacred from profane uses of popular images.[67]

Alanus's Objection, Michael's Accommodation, and Sprenger's Vision

In certain writings, says Kurt Schmidt, the rosetree (the cross) has become "contaminated" with the maypole.[68] Perhaps this was the feeling that Alanus had about the symbol of the rose chaplet. Given the contradictions between sacred and profane connotations attached to the rose wreath, it is easy to see why Alanus might have objected to the term "rosarium" as too worldly and therefore unsuited to the devotional practice that he envisioned. But why did Alanus's campaign to substitute the term "psalter" for "rosary" fail?

Even after the founding of the brotherhood in Cologne, with great fanfare and the emperor present, there was still no agreement as to the most appropriate title for the devotion and for its confraternity. Michael Francisci himself offers three different names in his *Quodlibet*, calling it "fraternitas de rosario," "fraternitas de serto (chaplet)," and "fraternitas de beatae Mariae virginis psalterio" and goes on to explain their origins.[69]

To define "rosario," Michael cites not only biblical and apocryphal references to Mary as the "Rose of Jericho" and the rose springing "out of the thorns"; he also calls on two legends that show the connection of spiritual roses to verbal prayers. The first legend tells the story of a

Fig. 29. Above and opposite: *Hoofkijn van devotien* (Garden of devotion), Antwerp, Gerhard Leeu, 1487. Reproduced by permission of the Koninklijke Bibliotheek, The Hague (No. 150 B 48)

simpleminded lay brother who was able to recite only one prayer, the "Ave Maria," which he prayed constantly and earnestly. Upon his death there grew from his mouth a rose bearing the words of the "Ave" salutation in golden letters. The second legend, a variation of the story "Aves Seen as Roses" story, tells how a dove carried to heaven roses from the mouth of an abbot as he recited the prayer while walking in the woods. This was witnessed by a thief who was lying in wait for him there.[70]

The actual "Aves Seen as Roses" story is the example that Michael uses to explain the second name, "serto" (chaplet). Finally, Michael traces the third term, "psalterio Mariano," to the practice of reciting 150 "Ave Marias" in place of the Psalter of David. According to Augustine, the Virgin Mary is herself a psalter (a harp) that soothes the ire of God.[71]

Michael does not voice a preference. And, at least as late as the time of his 1480 revised edition, the issue had not yet been settled. In France the brotherhood continued to be referred to as the "fraternitas de serto" and in Italy as "de capelleto," even though the proclamation of the papal legate in 1476 and the papal bull of 1478 both used the term "rosario."[72] As late as 1572, Adam Walasser still includes both of the terms in the title of his rosary manual, *Von der gnadenreichen hochberümpten . . . Bruderschaft des Psalters oder Rosenkrantz Marie* (About the benevolent, very famous . . . brotherhood of the Psalter or rosary of Mary).[73]

Jakob Sprenger seems not to have wavered, however, in his preference for the term "Rosenkranz" in his handbook of instructions. This preference registers his recognition of the attractiveness and utility of associating the rose symbol with the devotion. He underscores the relationship by designating the Paternosters as fifteen "red roses" representing the wounds of Christ.[74] At the end of Sprenger's booklet on the art of dying (his "Sterbebüchlein") attached to the 1476 edition of his German rosary manual, he exhorts the brotherhood's members to "hurry, hurry and make chaplets before the roses are gone." The text urges members to "run after the fragrant Virgin Mary with sweet-smelling garlands, up to that place where she now resides, where she leads those who are pure in heart as they follow the path of the Lamb to the cool spring of life."[75] This passage shows how effectively Sprenger made use of the rose and rose chaplet as poetic symbols of the devotional practice he was seeking to establish. Sprenger's decision to keep the term in spite of Alanus's opposition shows his realization of the appeal and importance of the rose symbol to the devotion and for its propagation.

Ultimately, however, Alanus's campaign to substitute the term "psalter" for "rosary" failed because of the attractiveness of the rose symbol itself and because of the propensity of its mystical religious connotations to assimilate profane meanings to spiritual ones. In an atmosphere in which the Song of Songs was the most frequently quoted book, use of this idiom of the day resulted in a mode of expression in which sensual love terminology became the accepted emotive idiom of the realm of the spirit. The ability of the term "Rosenkranz" to draw upon the body of popular spiritual rose-garden imagery helped to create an ethos that benefited its growth. Works like Ulrich Pinder's *Der beschlossen Gart des Rosenkrantz* (Enclosed garden of the rosary, 1489–1505) and Vincentius Hensberg's *Viridarium Marianum* (Marian garden, 1615) show the continuing influence of the image. Perhaps Dominic of Prussia, too, foresaw this; he wrote in a set of promotional exempla for his version of the devotion: "We live as though we were in Mary's rose garden, all of us who occupy ourselves with the roses."[76]

5

Popular Promotion
and Reception

From its inception onward, the rosary devotion was intimately tied to the string of beads that came to represent it. The many uses and attractiveness of rosary beads were conducive to the prayer's success. Indeed, they lent the devotion an added aesthetic dimension and a certain concreteness, even as simple as the tactile comfort of something to grasp onto in times of trouble and especially in the final hours. While the founding of the confraternity may have served to heighten demand for rosary beads, it in turn benefited from their attractiveness as a symbol of the devotion and as a way of promoting the practice. This chapter will examine the various means used to "romance" the rosary to a wider audience.

By 1482 at least 100,000 people had joined the rosary confraternity.

Probably most members used some kind of device for keeping track of their prayers, but even if only a portion of them used beads for counting, the result was an increase in demand for what was already, before the founding of the confraternity, an item of medieval "mass merchandise" and a flourishing business.[1] As early as 1277–78 makers of bead-chains called "paternosters" are recorded in London.[2] These beads were so named because of their use in saying repetitions of Our Fathers—the uneducated person's version of the 150 Psalms. Thomas Esser cites the names of London streets, Paternoster Row and Ave Maria Lane, as evidence for the early existence of the craft[3] (Fig. 30). At about the same time in Paris, Etienne Boileau's *Livre des métiers* (Book of trades, 1268) lists "paternoster" makers by groups, according to the materials they specialized in: bone and horn, coral and mussel shell, or amber and polished brown coal (gagat)[4] (see Fig. 31). In the fifteenth century, beads make up a significant portion of the items recorded, for example, in the account books of Ulm merchant Ott Ruland, for the years 1446 to 1462, who, besides wooden "Paternosters," dealt in helmets, daggers, pigs, horses, wines, and oats.[5] As a cottage industry, the manufacture of beads offered the possibility of a viable trade for women. Gerlind Ritz cites the example of a widow in Nuremberg who in 1606 made and sold 10,000 glass beads in the form of blackberries.[6]

Chains of varying lengths and types—longer for women, shorter for men—were in use. Exemplum 10 in the Ulm handbook of 1483, for example, tells how a knight was instructed to make a set out of five stones: (1) a multicolored stone to signify one's manifold sins; (2) a light one to represent unpredictable death (which is, indeed, certain in the future); (3) a red one for the Last Judgment; (4) a black one for hell; and (5) a golden one to represent the glory and joy of the saints.[7]

Certainly it was not detrimental to their popularity that prayer beads constituted religious jewelry that even the most pious could wear. Chaucer's description, for instance, of the tasteful prioress, Madame Eglantine, relates that she wore a set of small coral beads with green markers (gaudys) attached to a gold brooch.[8] Some bead sets contained a filigree pomander that could be filled with perfume paste, a recipe for which can still be found in a verse by the Meistersinger Hans Folz (c. 1450–1515).[9]

To curb ostentation in the wearing of fine religious jewelry, sumptuary laws specified what was not permitted. Fifteenth-century ordinances of the city of Nuremberg stipulated "no married or unmarried woman shall any longer wear a Pater Noster which is valued at more than twenty

FIG. 30.   Paternoster maker, *Hausbuch* (Amb. 317. 2°, fol. 13r). Stadtbibliothek, Nuremberg

FIG. 31a.   Sixteenth-century rosary of boxwood disks and jasper. Munich,
Bayerisches Nationalmuseum

FIG. 31b.   Fifteenth- or sixteenth-century rosary of bone. Cologne, Erzbischöfliches Diözesanmuseum

Rhenish guelders," lest she be fined "the amount by which the Pater Noster exceeds the value of twenty guelders."[10] The manner of wearing beads was also regulated. They were, for example, to be worn around the neck or arm, or on the belt, but not hanging down in back "uber den ars."[11]

Alanus de Rupe advocated displaying Ave-beads publicly in order to remind those who might see them of their sins "great and small" and of death and the pains of hell.[12] The *Livre et ordonnance* of the brotherhood in Douai offers an indulgence of 10,000 years for wearing or carrying them, "pour donner bon exemple."[13] Adam Walasser's rosary book of 1572 likewise advises members of the brotherhood to carry the beads in their hands or wear them on a belt or around the neck.[14]

Besides devotional and decorative uses, rosary beads were carried because they were thought to have the power of an amulet to ward off evil. In 1496, Michael Nielsen, author of the Danish rosary text, *Om Jomfru Marie Rosenkrands* (About the Virgin Mary's Rosary), advised:

> If you will keep the devil's wiles at bay
> Then you should have this chain and wear it.
> If you would not fall prey to the devil's tricks,
> Never let it leave your side.
> For if you wear it on your arm,
> It will protect you from sin and harm.[15]

By being kept for a time near a picture of the Virgin or being consecrated in a church, the beads gained greater strength to fend off evil powers or to help the wearer to achieve a particular aim.[16] Rosary manuals report cures of illness and insanity accomplished by placing rosary beads around the necks of affected sufferers.[17] It was not uncommon for people to sleep with a rosary around the neck so as not to be overtaken by death in the night without this vital link to the Virgin. Most of all, when the hour of death came, people held the beads in their hands as they died.[18]

As both comforting talisman and attractive item of apparel, the beads constituted the confraternity's best advertisement. With the official founding of the brotherhood in Cologne by Sprenger in 1475 and its approval by Papal Legate Alexander of Forli in 1476, it quickly spread to other cities, not only in Germany (Rostock, 1475; Augsburg, 1476), Brabant and Flanders (Lille, Ghent, 1475), but also to cities as far away as Lisbon (1478), Venice (1480), Florence (1481), and Barcelona (before

1488).[19] Since each chapter of the brotherhood was independent, any location could start one. It was only required that members should sign a membership roll with their name, marital status, and whether they were religious or laypersons.[20] In Germany, those who lived in isolated places could join at a distance by having their name sent in to Ulm. An early promotional flier advertises: "Whoever wants to be enrolled in the brotherhood of Mary's psalter should come to the Dominicans in Ulm. But anyone who cannot come to Ulm should humbly request his name and surname to be written out on a piece of paper and sent to Ulm to the Dominican cloister which has been authorized by the pope to accept brothers and sisters and to enroll them."[21] Marcus von Weida's rosary handbook from 1515, *Der Spiegel hochloblicher Bruderschafft des Rosenkrantz Marie* (Mirror of the praiseworthy brotherhood of Mary's rosary), equates the signing of one's name with "offering oneself as a special and willing servant to the most worthy Mother of God . . . in the same way that a knight or soldier swears fealty to his lord with his name." Moreover, signing one's name in the book is an incentive to others to join.[22] And numbers were, to be sure, important. Sprenger himself asserts in his handbook that 10,000 prayers are better than 1,000.[23]

Although earlier medieval confraternities tended to be predominantly artisan in membership, fifteenth-century confraternities broadened in social composition.[24] Women, who had been excluded for the most part from many other societies, were welcomed into the rosary brotherhood. In his study of *Italian Confraternities in the Sixteenth Century*, Christopher Black characterizes rosary confraternities as both "female-centered and popular." He states, "It can be assumed that the saying of the Rosary and the contemplation of the Mysteries was more predominantly—though certainly not exclusively—a female devotion." Black cites, for example, membership rolls from the confraternity of Parabiago for the years 1576 to 1596 that contain 2,952 women and only 1,224 men and whose officials were all female. At Legano in 1589 there were 561 women and 162 men members.[25]

While devotion to the rosary appears to have been bitterly resented by some husbands, membership was tolerated for women because this type of society did not involve "common masses, processions, or banquets—merely prayer."[26] Illustrated rosary manuals and broadsides made it possible for more women to participate in this kind of devotional activity. The investment required was about forty-five minutes a week (Marcus von Weida's manual asserts that it took only fifteen minutes to pray one-third of a psalter) and this could be carried out at home, even while working.[27] A second important consideration for women was the confraternity's no-cost admission policy. The rosary manual titled *Ein GAR nützlich Büchlein von dem Psalter oder Rosenkrantz Marie* (A very useful little book about the psalter or rosary of Mary), from 1501, states clearly that to be a member one "need pay no money at the beginning, in the middle, or at the end."[28] Likewise, Marcus von Weida's manual stresses the absence of any annual fee. Once a member, always a member, says Weida.[29]

Optional processions, for which extra indulgences could be gained, took place on the feast days of the Virgin. A painting of a rosary confraternity procession showing women participating—with putti scattering roses—can be found in the church of the Canons Regular at Krasnik. This work was painted by the Venetian artist Tommaso Dolabella (1560–1650), probably while he was in Cracow.[30] Similarly, Dürer's *Rosenkranzfest* (1506) shows women in attendance.[31]

In addition to works such as these, confraternities commissioned paintings of the rosary mysteries such as the series painted on the vault of the chapel of the Capranica family in S. Maria sopra Minerva in Rome and donated to the use of the rosary confraternity there.[32] Numerous similar altarpieces, sculptures, and frescoes made it possible for more illiterate women and those who had no books or prints to learn and practice the narrative meditations in beautiful settings that doubtless further encouraged membership and participation.[33]

Why People Joined the Confraternity

The benefits of the association, as set forth in the 1483 Ulm handbook, were broadly conceived. Not least among its stated goals and accomplishments was the fostering of virtue. The Ulm handbook declares:

> This confraternity frees from hatefulness and enlightens blind spirits. It fortifies the person in good thoughts, protects from distractions and from hindrances to devotion in prayer and meditation. This brotherhood produces fruitfulness of virtue and curbs cursing tongues. It fills the soul with good works and increases purity of spirit. Indeed, through this association quarreling and

disunity, envy, hate, and offensiveness are banished. Help comes
to the poor, prisoners are released. Worldly and carnal individuals
become godly people and children of God like unto the angels. To
be sure, this brotherhood generates good and averts evil, and
Christians are drawn to the praise and love of Christ and his dear
mother. . . . For this is not a brotherhood of earthly riches but of
the spirit and of the achievements of virtues and of all spirituality.[34]

Similarly, Michael Nielsen's Danish rosary text, *Om Jomfru Marie Rosenkrands* (About the Virgin Mary's rosary), asserts that by praying the
rosary one gains a penitential frame of mind and thereby the mercy of
God.[35] Another manual, contained in a late-fifteenth-century manuscript
of the library of Donaueschingen, relates the example of how practicing
the rosary by meditating on the five stones of different colors (described
above) caused a knight to repent his sinful life and to attain to great piety
and grace from God. By contemplating the end of life, says the handbook,
one can "avoid sin and practice virtue," for "he who ponders life's end
will not sin anymore."[36] The next enumerates fifteen virtues or "good
works" that the psalter of Mary accomplishes in those who recite it.
   In addition to fostering virtues, the handbook goes on to say that
reciting Mary's psalter brings special spiritual rewards from the Virgin. It
cites promises, first made by Alanus de Rupe, that whoever serves Mary
by reciting her psalter "will be protected by her from 150 snares of the
evil spirit, will receive 150 assists in combating sin and vice, will be
comforted 150 times in death's distress against the evil spirit, will escape
150 pains of hell, and will be granted 150 joys in heaven."[37]
   But beyond such spiritual rewards, faithful members could expect to
receive important temporal benefits. These rewards are enumerated in the
Livre et ordonnance of the Douai brotherhood, which promises Mary's
protection from "arson, lightning and thunder, brigands, thieves, murder-
ers, and from all the assaults of enemies from hell."[38] Michael Nielsen's
Danish handbook promises as well that those who pray the devotion will
be blessed by God, saying, "their fruit, their grain, whatever they
plant will grow and stand sturdily in the field, [and] God will increase
their harvest."[39]
   Not only does the psalter bring material benefits; it holds at bay
punishments that God otherwise would visit on the earth. *Ein GAR
nützlich Büchlein von dem Psalter oder Rosenkrantz Marie* recounts a
well-known vision attributed to Saint Dominic (see Fig. 10) in which three

lances are aimed at the world. The lances are "pestilence, famine, and war." The booklet counsels men to turn from their sins, to found brotherhoods, and to pray, in order that Mary will intercede with her son to avert the lances. "For where of old this brotherhood was established and preached and where members turned from their sins and prayed the psalter or rosary, all plagues were averted and stopped."[40]

Certainly, an extremely attractive incentive for joining the brotherhood was the member's privilege of drawing on the special treasury of merits accumulated by the Dominican order, the confraternity's sponsors. Indeed, the 1501 booklet promises, "Members will have a part in all the acts of service such as fasting, prayer, and singing, that are carried out in all Dominican cloisters."[41] Besides sharing in the treasury of spiritual assets accumulated by the Dominicans, members also had a share in the "fruits" that thousands of lay members of the brotherhood had "harvested" in their prayers collectively.[42]

There were advantages to being part of a large praying community. Members of a spiritual brotherhood could aid and protect each other through their collective supplications. But it was in praying for the dead that the confraternity had its most important role and performed its most valuable service. In life, people could rely on their own prayers and penances to expiate their sins, but after death they were dependent on the prayers of others to help them out of purgatory. Unfortunately, relatives and friends could not always be relied on, for they might fail to pray enough or to keep on praying. Spouses might die in the meantime. Far more certain was membership in an organization whose sole purpose was to pray for its members and that could be counted on to do so. This special kind of association provided for friends to pray one another into heaven and for those who had reached heaven already to pray, in turn, for the living, thus forming a kind of prayer chain or pact. Marcus von Weida's handbook describes this kind of solidarity, saying, "certainly there are and have been many [nobles and clergy] who in their lives have pleased God and, because of this honorable brotherhood, have after their deaths, come to rejoice in eternal blessedness and continue to do so, and do faithfully pray for the others who are still on earth."[43]

As a self-help association providing supplementary insurance (in perpetuity) against the pains of purgatory, the brotherhood met a pressing need. Other confraternities offered similar benefits, but because the rosary confraternity required no fees, it was available even to the poor. It is clear from Sprenger's statutes that he intended the organization to address this issue. For he writes, "Many people are dying in these days, for whose souls little is being done." Thus he advises, "To protect and defend oneself against this selfsame neglect, one can join this brotherhood."[44]

The rosary brotherhood offered not only the safety of numbers but also the spiritual support of its sponsoring religious order. The pamphlet *Ein GAR nützlich Büchlein* claims that, besides the number of prayers that are daily offered collectively by the brotherhood's members, "400 or 1000, 2000, or more masses are being said for all the brothers and sisters of this praiseworthy confraternity" in Dominican cloisters.[45] Sprenger's statutes promise that the members of the Cologne Dominican convent will hold four special prayer-vigils every year for all of the souls of deceased members of the brotherhood.[46]

In some brotherhoods members themselves organized around-the-clock prayer vigils. A pledge sheet titled, *Bericht, Uhrkund, Gedenckzaichen, ewiges Rosenkrantz Gebetts, von der heiligen Ertzbruderschafft Rosarii für die sterbende im 1640 Jahr allhie auffgericht, und einverleibt* (Report, document and reminder of the perpetual rosary of the holy archbrotherhood established and founded for the dying in the year 1640) printed in Salzburg, has spaces to fill in a name, plus the day and hour during which a member would promise to take part in a perpetual rosary vigil to be said for the souls of the dying.[47] Considering the extent of mass mortality from plague and other causes, such support was much needed. Christopher Black cites, for example, statistics for the city of Venice that show that 46,721 people died of the plague there in 1575–77 and another 46,490 with its return in 1630–31.[48] The assurance that prayers would continue to be said for one's soul after death—prayers by the thousands—was a powerful inducement for many people to enroll.

While most people could hope to escape the eternal death of hell through confession and absolution of the guilt of sins ("Sündenschuld"), the temporal penalty for sins ("Sündenstrafe") still had to be paid.[49] And since the sum total of one's sins was known only to God and reckoned at death, medieval Christians might justly worry about how many venial sins they would have to expiate. Certainly, all but the most pious could expect to spend a term in purgatory where such sins would be shriven. R. W. Southern has stated that last testaments from the late Middle Ages "show very clearly that the dying were no longer overpowered by a fear of hell as they had once been. Instead they trembled at the prospect of prolonged purgatorial pains."[50] Accordingly, most Christians were concerned about just how long and how much they would have to suffer, and were vitally interested in means to reduce their future pain. For this the rosary offered a special remedy: indulgences that could be earned by reciting it.

The first of many rosary indulgences was granted in 1476 by the papal legate Alexander of Forli who offered forty days (one quarantine) for reciting the prayer. This was followed by an announcement of seven years and seven quarantines, granted by Pope Sixtus IV in a bull promulgated in 1478, or five years and five quarantines in a bull issued in 1479. In addition, Cardinal Raymundus granted one hundred days and even Archbishop Albrecht of Mainz added forty days for each Ave and Pater-noster, totaling for each rosary 7,700 days.[51] Many more grants are listed in Marcus von Weida's handbook, which in 1515 enumerated indulgences that had been issued up to that time. Alanus de Rupe's reputed claim, however, of an indulgence of 60,000 years from the Virgin Mary was apparently felt to be too questionable to be endorsed outright in von Weida's handbook.[52]

Praying the rosary was certainly not the only way one could earn indulgences, but it was less expensive than pilgrimages, a journey to Rome, or simply purchasing them. One might, as Emile Mâle explained, go to confession and afterward recite the prayers of Saint Gregory before an image of the man of sorrows, in this way earning at least six thousand years of "true pardon."[53] But the rosary was more convenient. No image was required, and it could be said anywhere and at any time.

In 1476 Pope Sixtus IV extended indulgences to apply to souls already suffering in purgatory and, by this action, added a major incentive to membership in the confraternity.[54] It was now possible to enroll deceased friends and family members in the brotherhood and to say on their behalf prayers to lessen their present sufferings in purgatory. Both Francisci's *Quodlibet* and Sprenger's statutes announce this option.[55] Besides earning indulgences for friends in purgatory, one could enroll other persons—even without their knowledge—and accumulate benefits for them or pray for their "betterment."[56] The Colmar statutes suggest enrolling children, the sick, and those who are not able to pray.[57]

The Handbooks: Reading Between the Lines

The chief way of proclaiming the organization's benefits as well as its practices was through printed handbooks and broadsides. In addition to explaining how the devotion originated, its significance, and how to recite it, the manuals contained stories that illustrated how people could profit from membership in the brotherhood. These promotional materials overtly appealed to the interests and to the most pressing concerns of their audience.

Stories make up the largest part of the materials in the manuals. The Ulm handbook of 1483, for example, contains nineteen exempla and twenty-seven shorter anecdotes that together constitute two-thirds of the contents of the book. Not all manuals contain the same stories. While the Ulm manual features tales attributed to Alanus de Rupe, Marcus von Weida's manual includes selections from Caesarius of Heisterbach, Thomas of Cantimpre, the *Speculum exemplorum*, and other unidentified collections of exempla. The 1501 pamphlet *Ein GAR nützlich büchlein* has condensed versions of most of the same stories as the Ulm manual, but also tales from a source it identifies as the "Mariale blesensis."[58] While many handbooks include one or two of the Carthusian exempla that were circulated along with Dominic of Prussia's rosary of fifty life-of-Christ meditations, by far the most frequently encountered stories stem from the writings of Alanus de Rupe. Fifteenth- and sixteenth-century rosary books that contain Alanus's tales include Johannes Lampsheym's *Libellus perutilis de Fraternitate Rosarii* (1495), the anonymous *Speculum rosarium* (1497), Jodocus Beyssel's *De rosacea augustissimae Christiferae Mariae corona* (1500), Alberto da Castello's *Rosario de la gloriosa vergine Maria* (1521), and Adam Walasser's *Von der gnadenreichen, hochberümpten . . . Bruderschaft des Psalters* (1572), among others.[59]

Like Dominic of Prussia, Alanus de Rupe used exempla to promote his version of the rosary devotion. The stories in the Ulm handbook come mostly from the *Compendium psalterii beatissime Trinitatis* and the *Sponsus novellus* compiled by Alanus's followers after his death.[60] The stories are adaptations of older Marian legends dating back to the twelfth century but also new ones that Alanus composed himself.[61] Unlike Dominic's exempla, which are more didactic than fantastic, Alanus's tales cross the line from pious illustration to hard-sell and market the devotion with claims of benefits, both spiritual and material. Twenty-seven short anecdotes, told in the first person (each only about five lines long), advertise the good things that have already happened to users. The narrator recounts, for example, how farmers' crops have been protected from destruction by storms (no. 16), a poor woman became rich and then shared her wealth with the less fortunate (no. 27), evil spirits were exorcised (no. 22), and a raving madman calmed (no. 31). Prostitutes and money lenders have been transformed into honest people (nos. 12 and 36) and persons given to evil and cursing have curbed their tongues and come to lead honorable lives (no. 13); apostate members of religious orders have returned to the fold and become devout (no. 15); people who mistreat the poor have become compassionate and generous (no. 19); feuding rivals have been transformed into the most amicable of friends (no. 21). A man formerly overtaken by despair now surpasses all others in hope (no. 20). All of these things were witnessed by the narrator firsthand.[62]

In case these testimonials should not be enough to convince people to take up the prayer, there are also nineteen longer tales in the handbook that are more colorful, more flamboyant, and more exotic in their settings. A number of them are set some three hundred years in the past, in the days of Saint Dominic, who figures prominently in them. They contain more descriptive detail and are longer than the average sermon illustration. Indeed, some would take too long to recount as part of a sermon and must have been designed to be read alone. The story of Benedicta (no. 9) is nineteen printed pages long. Like the others, this story is not told solely for the purpose of illustrating a didactic point about the efficacy of the prayer, but regales its audience with the outrageous exploits and lurid details of the protagonist's life. Virtually all of the tales in Alanus's collection, in fact, deal with noble, rich, beautiful, or educated people of high social standing. They include a cardinal, a count, knights, kings and queens, wealthy merchants, scholars, and one schoolmaster. The modern reader senses a certain tabloid delight in the relating of these tragedies of the rich and famous. Certainly, the ability of the tales to shock, to amaze, and to entertain contributed greatly to the popular success of this and other confraternity handbooks.

In the story of Benedicta the details of the heroine's worldly life and upbringing are depicted with great relish. Benedicta is the daughter of a count, a stubborn, willful young woman of spectacular beauty, intelligence, musical talent, vivacity, and athletic prowess. Unusually tall, she is an Amazon who possesses the strength of several men and excels at jousting. In the same way that the tale revels in sketching its larger-than-life heroine, so too does it relish her spectacular fall. After a career as a notorious courtesan, Benedicta contracts leprosy. As the disease progresses, she becomes blind, disfigured, and is attacked by worms. Yet even though reviled, abandoned, and malodorous, she stubbornly refuses to repent. Eventually Saint Dominic hears of her case and persuades her to join the brotherhood of Mary's psalter and to pray the devotion. Before long she is healed of the six plagues that beset her. But the tale does not end here. Once restored by the Virgin Mary to health, Benedicta marries the king of Castile and converts all of her kingdom to pray the Psalter of Our Lady. At her death hundreds of birds flock to her castle and accompany her soul to paradise with songs of joy.[63]

This may seem an outrageous tale to be used to market the confraternity, yet it must have appealed to medieval audiences, since it was one of the stories chosen to be copied out in its entirety and included in other confraternity manuals, such as that of the brotherhood in Colmar which contains only a few of Alanus's exempla.[64] Its attractive message is that Mary will heal those who sincerely pray her psalter and that moral deficits can be made up by drawing on the accumulated "credit" (merits) of the other members of the brotherhood.

In exemplum no. 6, the story of a cardinal who rescues the pope with Mary's psalter, the text gives a striking account of penance, one that must have fascinated even medieval audiences used to such extremes with its voyeuristic description of profuse weeping and unrestrained flagellation.[65]

Exemplum no. 12, that of Mary, the charcoaler's daughter, is a romantic Cinderella story in which a very virtuous woman, black from head to toe with coal dust, catches the attention of the dauphin—not because of the coal dust, but because she prays her psalter incessantly. He falls in love with her, they wed, and she becomes queen of France.[66] In this story the Virgin Mary is cast in the role of good fairy and the heroine, as queen, brings peace and prosperity to her realm. Whether or not hearers may have been at all convinced by this story, they were undoubtedly entertained by its fairy-tale structure and plot.

More often than dramatic conversions and exemplary piety, however, the theme in these exempla is the supernatural power of the psalter: both that wrought by reciting it and by its mere physical presence when worn, displayed, or even painted on walls and armor. Everywhere it has the power to defeat the forces of evil, whether they be armies of heretics, heathen, or demons. In one episode (exemplum no. 6) it actually rescues the pope who has been deposed by rebellious Romans, but is saved and restored to his office after he and his fellow captives are taught how to pray the Mary psalter. Later, it holds an entire army of 100,000 soldiers at bay.[67] A newly converted Jew (exemplum no. 1) who wears a rosary on his belt is attacked by devils in the form of a black hunter with a pack of black dogs, but they cannot bite him on the side where he wears the psalter. He defends himself by swinging the beads and succeeds each time in driving them away.[68] The knight who was taught by Saint Dominic (no. 10) how to make a psalter of colored stones wields his beads against a devil who tries to choke him. He knocks the devil down and agrees to let him go only if he promises no more damage. To protect his castle from an evil spirit that haunts it, he paints psalter beads on the walls and the devils are driven out.[69]

Indeed, reciting Mary's psalter is so salutary it can save a captured heathen nobleman (no. 14) who does not understand its meaning but is tricked by Saint Dominic into reciting it—doubtless in the same way that some unlettered Christians did who recited the prayer in Latin without knowing the exact meaning of the Latin words. Because of his prayers, the Virgin Mary intercedes on the heathen Eleodorus's behalf. When God objects that "in his whole life he never did anything good," Mary replies, "He prayed six psalters." The words count, even though Eleodorus said the prayers uncomprehendingly and thought they were "not against his religion." Eventually, however, they cause him to repent and become baptized.[70]

Even a rosary recited "insincerely," that is, without true devotion but "out of fear," protects the wearer. In one such tale Mary defends a knight who only wears her beads as an amulet (no. 15).[71] Here she is cast in the role of a warrior-goddess, and shoots arrows at an opposing army of heretics. In several stories (nos. 8, 15, 16) Mary functions as a protectress who rewards devotion to herself and sincere repentance, no matter how evil the life of the penitent may have been.

Sinners can even be rewarded for a good intention that has not actually been carried out. Exemplum no. 8 tells of Alexandra of "Arrogonia," a beautiful but self-centered woman who is notorious for taking a whole hour to dress herself each morning. Knights vie for her attentions. When she hears the preaching of Saint Dominic, she is moved to join the brotherhood of the psalter, but afterwards prays the devotion only rarely and does nothing to alter her vain lifestyle. After two knights kill each other in a joust for her hand, Alexandra is beheaded by their angry retainers who throw her head into a well. One hundred fifty days later Saint Dominic retrieves the head, which begs to receive the sacrament. It seems that Alexandra's soul is beset by demons attempting to take her to hell. Because of her membership in the brotherhood, however, she has been protected from these devils by the Virgin Mary. Alexandra is permitted to receive the sacrament and is spared hell, but is sentenced to seven hundred years in purgatory for the deaths of the two knights and for her bad example to others. But thanks to the powerful prayers of the brotherhood and to the collective merits of its members, Alexandra's sentence is commuted to only fifteen days. At the end of two weeks, she appears to Saint Dominic again, this time as a shining star on her way to paradise. She thanks the members of the brotherhood for their help and urgently entreats everyone to join, adding that the saints and angels in heaven rejoice greatly over it.[72]

Here, even a good impulse that was never fully realized is rewarded by the Virgin Mary. It is not surprising that the story of Alexandra should have had great appeal to those who had been weak in keeping resolutions and who feared a long stay in purgatory. The tale was well liked enough to be circulated in abbreviated form as a popular song advertising the confraternity.[73]

The Confraternity in Popular Song

Like the ballad of Alexandra, there were several other popular tunes that promoted the confraternity. Some are found in handbooks such as one in a fifteenth-century manuscript of the library of Donaueschingen. This rosary manual contains a song that first sums up the rosary indulgences and then assures listeners: "If you will say three rosaries faithfully / for the benefit of a soul in purgatory, / that's how much sooner it will be released."[74] Five other confraternity songs can be found in Wackernagel's *Das deutsche Kirchenlied von der ältesten Zeit bis zu Anfang des 17. Jahrhunderts.*[75] Most of these texts feature generous claims of indulgences, which, however, differ radically even in versions of the same song. One example, called "Ein new lied von dem Rosenkrantz vnd bruderschafft Marie" (A new song about the rosary and brotherhood of Mary), states:

> If you will pray the holy rosary
> every day through for a week,
> indeed, the indulgence amounts to
> one hundred thousand and five thousand days
> plus fifteen, I tell you
> In Jesus's name.

But another version of the same text, dated 1513, advertises only 15,000 days.[76]

An important theme in the songs is the assurance that faithful members of the brotherhood will not be damned but will be guaranteed the opportunity to make confession and to receive the sacrament before their deaths. This is the theme of the song version of the story of the beheaded Alexandra, which states that members can be assured, "whoever enrolls himself in the [brotherhood of the] rosary . . . will not die in mortal sin. He is guaranteed that he will receive the sacrament from the hands of a priest before his final end, for the salvation of his soul."[77] Another song reports that some members who have prayed the devotion very faithfully have even been given a fifteen-day warning in advance of their deaths.[78] A similar text advertises that Mary herself, along with a host of angels, will attend members of the brotherhood at death and help them through their distress.[79] Sixt Buchsbaum's song promises that Mary awaits members at the gate of heaven to tell the gatekeeper: "Let my brother in."[80] All of the songs intimate that Mary intercedes on behalf of those who serve her. One goes so far as to claim that people in the past who have prayed the rosary "have received honor and good fortune in life." This song also quotes Saint Dominic as saying, "whoever has angered God, let him take up [Mary's] psalter, [and] God will overlook it."[81]

In all of these songs as well as in the exempla of the handbooks the most important theme by far is minimizing or avoiding time in purgatory. In these texts Mary is cast in the role of helping people to circumvent purgatory. She gives those who serve her through her psalter and in her brotherhood a second chance to repent and to escape punishment. The moral that evil does not pay is overshadowed in the exempla by another theme, namely, that it is repentance—rather than virtue—that is rewarded. Several exempla show that an entire lifetime of misdoing can be outweighed by repentance and just a few rosary-psalters. As Eileen Power suggests, Mary stands in popular miracle stories for "faith and not for good works, for love and not for justice."[82] She is loyal to those who serve her and she stands for clemency. Such a message was clearly appealing to a fifteenth-century populace extremely anxious about the fate of souls in purgatory. Indeed, in many respects it overshadowed other aspects of the devotion.

Of all the songs advertising the confraternity, only Sixt Buchsbaum's intimates that specific meditations are associated with devotion. The others either do not mention meditations at all or cite only the three general themes of Mary's purity, Christ's suffering, and Christ's (or Mary's) Ascension.[83] In the Ulm handbook, only two of the nineteen exempla propose that any meditations should accompany the Aves. These two texts mention dividing the 150 repetitions into three sections to honor the Annunciation, the Nativity, and the Assumption—with no mention of the Passion—(exemplum no. 2) or in honor of the Incarnation, Christ's suffering, and the seven sacraments (no. 6).[84] In the expository part of the manual, seven ways to meditate are proposed, but only one contains a chronological narrative of the life of the savior like Dominic of Prussia's or the picture rosary. In the handbook the narrative meditations become lost in a forest of alternative sets of unsystematic subjects for meditation and in a host of details on the symbolism of the numbers 15, 50, and 150.

Twenty-five pages of the text are devoted to explicating the number symbolism of the prayer while three of the exempla emphasize the importance of observing the rule of 150 repetitions. In two of these stories, variations on the tale "The Monk and Our Lady's Sleeves" (nos. 2 and 19), the Virgin Mary appears wearing a dress without sleeves. The explanation is that her dress is incomplete because the monk, to whom she appears, has prayed an insufficient number of Hail Marys. After he begins to pray a complete psalter of 150 Aves, however, the Virgin comes to him again, this time in a complete dress and a happy mood.[85] The agenda of these tales is to stress the difference between Alanus's Ave-psalter and the "truncated" Carthusian devotion of just fifty Aves.

Instead of focusing on the spiritual purpose of meditations to accompany Ave-repetitions, attention is directed via popular songs and exempla toward the numbers of repetitions, toward indulgences to be gained, and toward guarantees of Mary's active intercession on behalf of members of her brotherhood. In this atmosphere, the devotion develops into a vehicle for stockpiling indulgences—spiritual insurance for oneself and one's friends. Because Protestant reformers of the early sixteenth century were not loath to poke fun at the church's charms and incantations, this kind of mathematical piety associated with the rosary constituted a particularly inviting target.

The Rosary and Spiritual Devotion

Keith Thomas accuses the medieval church of having severely weakened what he calls "the fundamental distinction between a prayer and a charm" and of having encouraged the idea "that there was virtue in the mere repetition of holy words." Not surprisingly, opponents ridiculed the rosary as sheer superstition.[86] One of the strongest critics of the rosary and its brotherhood was Martin Luther, and it is ironic coincidence that the copy of Marcus von Weida's rosary handbook that Luther himself read and wrote comments in has survived in the holdings of the library of the University of Jena. The comments that Luther jotted in the margins of the book scathingly mock the authenticity, the antiquity, and the efficacy of the rosary. At one point Luther exclaims, "Where in the Devil do so many and various lies come from?" In the margin next to a story about a wayward youth who is reformed by praying the rosary, Luther comments: "And thus through a stupid work he merited justification." Later, reacting to the tale of a nobleman saved from condemnation through the rosary-psalter and Mary's intercession, Luther writes, "not through Christ, but by works."[87]

Here one can see firsthand Luther's reaction to the mentality of the marketing of the rosary. It is not simply the hundreds of years of indulgences advertised in Weida's handbook that Luther opposes, but, more fundamentally, the very idea that one could achieve salvation by rituals or by good works at all. He categorically rejects any imputation of merit to such works and, most categorically of all, the intimation that it was possible to "pay" God.[88]

The Protestants repudiated the doctrine of purgatory as "an affront to the power and mercy of God," calling it "nothing but an invention of the devil."[89] With this change in doctrine, one of the primary reasons for praying the rosary was suddenly gone and, along with it one of what Stephen Ozment calls the "psychologically and socially burdensome" aspects of late-medieval piety.[90]

While Ozment's view is disputed by John Bossy, Eamon Duffy, and others, it does seem that the opportunity offered by the rosary brotherhood to enroll dead friends and family members and to lessen their pains in purgatory by saying a complete psalter on their behalf each week required a considerable time investment.[91] A. N. Galpern has characterized late-medieval religion as "in large part a cult of the living in service of the dead."[92] Who could know how many years of pardon a person (or one's friends) might really need. Although there was a minimum weekly quota of prayers to be met, there was no satisfiable upper limit. Attempts to stockpile indulgences forced Marcus von Weida to announce in his handbook a limit to the number of rosary indulgences that could be accumulated in one day.[93] Wealthy people hiring others to recite the rosary for them represents what is arguably the low point in the prayer's development.[94]

Yet, as seen, stockpiling insurance against purgatory had not always been the chief reason for praying the rosary. Earlier in the fifteenth century, when Dominic of Prussia and his Carthusian brothers promoted their new life-of-Christ rosary as part of the Observant monastic reform, the devotion was thought of primarily as a way of improving spiritual life. The exempla that Dominic and his fellow Carthusians circulated stressed the way that the prayer rehearsed the steps of the Savior's redemption of mankind. They emphasized how the practice fostered pious devotion. Exemplum no. 17 in Dominic's "Zwanzig-Exempel-Schrift" explains the rationale for the new rosary, saying that it is not a small thing to meditate on the life of Jesus while reciting the Hail Mary:

> One reads in many pious books that Our Lord is more pleased by the remembrance of his works of love on earth and his redemption of mankind than by any other spiritual exercise, [and] that a person should contemplate all the works of his divine love which he revealed to the human race on earth, how he truly redeemed us from eternal death by his holy suffering and his bitter death, and one should thank, praise and bless him because of it, for he is eternally worthy of all praise, and this we do to the best of our ability in the rosary. . . . Thus do we revere Christ our Savior in the stations of his holy life according to the Holy Gospels.[95]

As a new devotional practice, the Carthusian rosary had resonated with the growing need in lay society for greater religious participation and for new exercises of personal piety to supplement public observance of the corporate offices of the church. So congenial was this new practice that it quickly reached beyond the cloisters and was taken up enthusiastically by the lay populace. Its rapid dissemination among houses of other orders and among laypersons makes it no surprise that the new rosary was soon being promoted enthusiastically by Johannes Herolt, a Dominican of Basle, in his collection of Marian exempla, *Promptuarium Discipuli de Miraculis Beate Marie Virginis*, (Disciple's collection of miracles of the Blessed Virgin Mary, 1435/40). This text documents the devotion's spread to a wider populace, as Herolt urges the propagation of this new meditational practice "both among clerics and lay persons." In an exemplum that recounts how even the saints in heaven delight in reciting the new life-of-Christ rosary, Herolt concludes:

> We most earnestly beseech the lovers of God and his Mother that, like as the saints in heaven take delight in so doing, they should use this devout exercise of the rosary, teach it to others, and spread the knowledge of it among men learned and lay alike, in Latin or the vulgar tongue: that in like measure as they resolve so to do, so much may the peace of God and the joy of the Saints be increased, when this is more widely known by men of piety.[96]

Here, as in Dominic's Carthusian exempla, the emphasis is on achieving deeper spirituality and on the moral betterment worked by the exercise. Dominic himself remarks, "Anyone would have to be a very bad man to say the rosary for a year and not be improved by it."[97] Certainly, over the course of the 100 years from 1420 to 1520, efforts to promote the rosary had undergone a significant transition.

What had begun as a modest exercise in private devotion, an impulse connected to the Observant Reform movement that spread out to a larger lay audience, was overtaken twice: first by popular demand for quantitative guarantees of the welfare of the soul after death—assurances mediated by a lay association that bypassed the agency of the parish priest—and, again, by the more radical reforms of the Protestants that purported to make such works unnecessary and the individual believer his *own* priest.

6

Rosaries and the Language of Spirituality

In a recent essay on New Historicism, Anton Kaes has described texts not only as patchworks of other texts, but as "exchanges and negotiations."[1] To Protestants, the "negotiations" that the rosary was involved in in the late Middle Ages seemed decidedly "monetary" and were harshly condemned. To the degree that all language can be regarded as a medium of negotiation and exchange, the medieval rosary constitutes an interesting example of how words functioned as spiritual capital. In addition to the value of the words of the prayer themselves, indulgences that were attached to them constituted a "commodity" with far greater material implications. The purchasing of indulgences—with both hard and verbal currencies—to pay spiritual debts fuelled an inflationary spiral that could only end in a crash.

But in what ways did indulgences themselves affect piety? How, after all, are we to assess late-medieval spirituality and to understand its sensibilities and archaic idiom? Do the rosaries and Marian psalters that fill three volumes of the collected hymns of the Middle Ages express what R. N. Swanson terms "vital spirituality," or what he calls "mere convention?" Are such categories mutually exclusive in medieval terms? Swanson cautions that the "quantitative and qualitative inaccessibility of much medieval religious activity means that any assessment . . . is only impressionistic."[2] These limitations not withstanding, it will be argued here that in "telling tales upon their beads" medieval Christians were exercising a different kind of piety, but not necessarily so lacking in spirituality as has often been assumed.

Clearly, the issue of spirituality needs to be seen in the context of the larger, collective medieval conversation. Here categories like sacred and secular, spiritual and mechanical, qualitative and quantitative are not so sharply drawn but, rather, overlapping. The language of spirituality is more "instrumental" and more inclusive than we have perceived it to be.

Joseph Lortz has described the difficulty of trying to draw a precise picture of late-medieval popular religion as that of confronting "a deluge of antitheses, shading into sheer contradictions."[3] For every example of "externalism" or "decline" that one can cite, an opposing example of "interior spirituality" and "revival" can be produced.[4] While scholars like Jacques Toussaert and Etienne Delaruelle find in late-medieval piety only superficiality and externalized ritual that is utterly mechanical, "even heartless," other scholars point to a fifteenth-century rise in religious fervor that is evidenced "by every measure."[5] This groundswell of spirituality is to be seen not only in the spread of monastic reform movements such as the Observant reform and in lay initiatives like the Modern Devotion and the Friends of God, but also in increased endowments, greater participation in pilgrimages, intensified veneration of relics, and the growth of religious confraternities that permitted lay members to live as "semireligious."[6] While Lortz asserts that Luther's criticisms of the spirituality of the late-medieval church were widely held views that expressed the true feelings of sensitive Christians, Thomas Tentler contests this claim on the grounds that it "ignores too many sensitive Christians."[7] Clearly, spirituality and superstition, depth and superficiality, faith and calculation are contradictions that run to the core of any description of the spiritual climate on the eve of the Reformation. Indeed, they may be the best way of characterizing it.

At the turn of the century in 1500, three-fourths of the population of German-speaking areas were peasants and literacy was rare.[8] The principal means of teaching religious doctrine were the confessional, the vernacular Sunday sermon, and pictorial texts like narrative altarpieces, devotional paintings, and printed intructional woodcuts.[9] In the cities, where larger numbers of craftsmen and merchants could read, vernacular translations of the Bible and devotional works for private use were beginning to become available. Heinrich Hoffmann von Fallersleben relates the case of Augustinian provost Johannes Busch (d. 1471), who reported that he himself dutifully burned German copies of the canon whenever he discovered them in the possession of nuns. But he argued that vernacular devotional books, works on the life of Christ, saints' lives, and sermons should be permitted to both religious and the laity.[10]

Rosary books were among the earliest vernacular devotional writings to be printed, publications that participated in defining the role of print as a way of shaping and reflecting religious awareness and in preparing the way for the explosion of pamphleteering that was to occur in the sixteenth century. These were books that Luther himself read both before and after he became a monk, and Marcus von Weida's rosary manual was one of the works against which Luther reacted most strongly. As artifacts of popular piety, such rosary handbooks express the religious mentality of the lay milieu of Luther's time. Looking at these and other works about the practice can thus provide a contemporary perspective on how users regarded ritual performance and on their attitudes toward the relationship between quality and quantity in religious practice.

Clearly, medieval concepts of spirituality must be judged on their own terms, that is, as John Toews suggests, in terms of the options available at the time; they only have meaning within the system that generated them.[11] In the development of the rosary these options underwent a fundamental change with the granting of special indulgences for reciting the prayer, and particularly after indulgences were broadened to apply to souls already suffering in purgatory. How was the rosary practiced prior to this time and how did the change affect attitudes toward the prayer?

In its earliest form the Marian Ave-psalter had grown out of the desire to imitate the liturgy of the Divine Office—the chanting of the psalms, which were sung as a literal response to the biblical admonition to "pray without ceasing." This substitute "psalter" of 150 Ave-salutations was recited as a gesture of devotion, aimed at bringing delight to the Virgin but also in the hope that a courteous service (an extended greeting) would not go unacknowledged. Surely the Virgin would not neglect traditional forms of politeness or fail to reciprocate devoted service. Already at this earliest stage the tension between ritualism and meaningful spirituality—the divide between literacy and illiteracy—was felt. Although the psalms themselves formed a beautiful and meaningful liturgy for chanting, the 150 Aves of the "illiterate man's psalter" tended toward monotony.

This tension can be seen in the early Marian exempla that record Ave Marias (without meditations) being recited as an affectionate service to the Virgin, but one that could indeed be problematic. Some tales describe, for example, "dresses" or "robes"—created for the Virgin by reciting Aves—that lack sleeves or a head covering as, for example, in the story "The Monk and Our Lady's Sleeves."[12] The worshipers who have woven these incomplete garments with their prayers are reproved for failing to chant a complete "psalter" of 150 Aves or for failing to maintain a spiritual focus. One well-known tale, the story of the nun Eulalia, pointedly acknowledges the difficulty of trying to sustain concentration during this kind of exercise. In this exemplum the Virgin admonishes Eulalia for rushing through a set of mumbled Hail Marys and advises her to say instead just one-third of the Ave-psalter at a time, but to do it with better concentration.[13] These exempla underscore both the difficulty and the importance of maintaining a devotional attitude. Here sheer mechanical repetition is not condoned.

Attempts to alleviate the monotony by adding meditations to the prayer were a welcome innovation, and the chronological life-of-Christ narrative the most welcome innovation of all. After the early experiments around 1300 and Dominic of Prussia's highly successful version in the early fifteenth century, the prayer shows a shift away from emphasis on forms of courtesy and ritual service toward a more meaningful spiritual exercise that reviewed the progressive stations of the story of redemption.[14] The exempla written and adapted to promote this new Carthusian rosary around 1440 stress the salutary effects that the prayer should have on behavior and spirituality. These Carthusian exempla feature accounts of the visions and experiences of spiritually devout persons. They urge that less attention be paid to the words and more attention to the meaning of the devotion, and they admonish that whoever says the prayer to honor the pure Virgin Mary must himself be pure and lead a chaste life.[15]

Out of concerned opposition to the growing success of this new "truncated" *vita Christi* rosary of fifty Ave Marias, Alanus de Rupe had launched his campaign to repopularize the old Ave-psalter form of 150 repetitions. In the process he merged the *vita Christi* meditations with other sets—alphabetical acrostics, lists of parts of Christ's Body, one's own sins, or the duties of office—in which, however, meaningfulness suffered. Promotional writings for the new brotherhood Alanus founded to revive the Psalter of Our Lady marketed the devotion as a way to reduce or avoid time in purgatory and as a talisman to protect users against all manner of evil in this present life. The statutes of the Douai brotherhood already advertise very generous (but unauthenticated) indulgences of up to 30,000 years for saying the prayer.[16]

Five years later the rosary confraternity that was established by Jakob Sprenger at Cologne likewise offered an indulgence—a modest but at least "official" one—of forty days for each rosary (one hundred on feast days). Sprenger explained that his purpose in founding the brotherhood was to provide help for the souls of the poor by starting a confraternity without any membership fees, one that would be open to all. His German statutes from the year 1476 declare that in this way the poor can become "the equals of the rich." To attract members Sprenger advertised the brotherhood as an investment that would reap dividends; and he pragmatically applied the principle of self-interest ("aigner nutz"), which, Sprenger unabashedly asserted, "engages men more than does the common good."[17] But his underlying purpose in all this was clearly to induce people to pray a salutary devotion that, he felt, would encourage spirituality and truly benefit their souls. Ironically, the founding of Sprenger's organization was to coincide fatefully with another event that proved to be a bonanza for it. This was an official declaration by Pope Sixtus IV in 1476 that indulgences could apply to souls already languishing in purgatory, a move that made the confraternity's primary attraction—the guarantee that prayers would be said for one's soul after death—all the more efficacious.

With increasing confidence promoters now guaranteed help in the final moment from Mary, protectess of her brotherhood and the intermediary who moves Christ, the judge, to mercy. Mary's active role in rescuing souls from purgatory in response to rosary prayers is depicted in a woodcut from the year 1510 by Wolf Traut (Fig. 32). Here the enthroned Virgin is shown extending a rose chaplet (as ballast) to a naked soul that is being weighed against his sins in a balance. Above her hovers God the Father, while below angels are shown pulling other souls from the fires of purgatory. A banderole coming from the mouth of Saint Dominic reads: "Recite a rosary for all the faithful in purgatory."[18] A similar woodcut in Marcus von Weida's 1515 handbook shows Mary in heaven wearing a

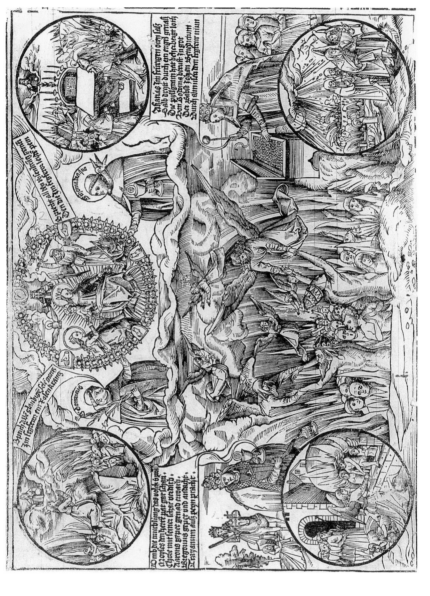

FIG. 32. Wolf Traut, woodcut, 1510. Karlsruhe, Badische Landesbibliothek

FIG. 33. *Der Spiegel hochloblicher Bruderschafft des Rosenkrantz Marie*
(Leipzig, 1515), fol. 107v. Reproduced by permission of the Bayerische
Staatsbibliothek

rose chaplet[19] (Fig. 33). In her arms she holds the infant Jesus and looks
on while a host of worshipers prays the rosary. At right is a flaming pit
filled with sufferers, some of whom are being rescued by angels and
transported upward toward God who holds a large sling filled with
hundreds of tiny souls.

By 1520 the amassing of all kinds of indulgences as insurance against purgatory had reached monumental proportions. Johann Eck criticized the Holy Ghost order for having acquired for its members a million years and forty-two plenary indulgences; even Frederick the Wise, elector of Saxony, himself could boast a total of nearly two million years attached to his collection of relics.[20] Marcus von Weida's handbook uncritically endorses the practice of hiring the rosary said by proxy.

Amid all of this maneuvering, the devotional narrative reviewing Christ's acts of redemption, which had been an essential part of the earlier Carthusian version of the devotion became lost in the headlong rush to acquire more and more insurance against purgatory and in the resulting inflation of the verbal currency. That many Christians besides Luther doubted the validity of indulgences, denied that grace could be achieved in this way, and criticized the brotherhood can be seen in rosary handbooks themselves by the number of defenses against detractors. Marcus von Weida reports, for example, the case of a woman who said she did not believe that the brotherhood had been granted either grace or indulgences, or that the rosary was "appreciated by God and his mother and useful to mankind." (Shortly after making this statement, the woman was afflicted by an ear infection so severe that she suffered constant pain and partial deafness. In great distress, she went to church and admitted her error, whereupon the illness vanished almost immediately.)[21] As the most vociferous critic of the practice, Luther denounced the reciting of such prayers as nothing but "sheer fraud." Confraternities he dismissed as societies for "gluttony and drinking."[22]

In one of his *Tabletalk* discussions, Luther himself tells the popular story of how the rosary began, recounting the tale of the monk who stops in a wood to recite fifty Aves and is saved from robbers by the Virgin's appearance. Luther ends his account with the exclamation: "Oh, dear God, what were we not expected to believe?"[23] This story is also contained in the rosary book by Marcus von Weida into which Luther wrote scathing comments in the margins. But the rosary that Luther so vigorously rejected in Weida's handbook was not the narrative life-of-Christ rosary. Indeed, Weida's manual contains neither the fifteen narrative mysteries—in picture or in written form—nor Dominic's popular life-of-Christ text. Instead, Weida's users are instructed simply to recite 150 Hail Marys, divided into three sets according to Alanus de Rupe's three themes. Those who could read might consult a long set of 150 meditational points (covering more than ninety pages in Weida's book) that forms more of a sermon than a narrative; but very few people would have had the time or the desire to read through ninety-two pages of Weida's text every time they performed the devotion.[24]

Yet despite being submerged for a time, the *vita Christi* meditations would soon resurface. Even though the fifteen narrative mysteries are not present in Weida's manual, they can be found at this time in altarpieces, wall paintings, and woodcuts in many parts of Germany. Sixt Buchsbaum's rosary song of 1492, which is based on these illustrations, is further evidence that they were alive and well. For a growing number of worshipers the scenes reviewing Christ's acts of redemption were becoming an integral part of the prayer.

Even though indulgences were an attractive selling point, they were not always the chief justification for performing the prayer cited in contemporary promotional writings. In fact, of five pre-Reformation popular tunes about the rosary in Wackernagel's survey of German religious song, *Das deutsche Kirchenlied von der ältesten Zeit bis zu Anfang des 17. Jahrhunderts*, two do not mention indulgences at all.[25] Sixt Buchsbaum's, for example, actively promotes membership in the confraternity, but is strangely silent about indulgences. Rather, Buchsbaum's song explains the fifteen images of the picture rosary in order to help users review "what Jesus Christ suffered on earth."[26] With similar emphasis, a sermon from 1497 asserts that the rosary is "nothing more nor less than the Gospel of Christ."[27] Such comments indicate that for many users the "condensed gospel" of the fifteen *vita Christi* scenes constituted not only an essential part but the true character of the devotion.

A third text, a song printed in 1525, likewise says nothing about indulgences and, surprisingly, even contains no mention of the brotherhood. Instead, this song instructs auditors that they should make confession of their sins, receive penance, and then pray the rosary joyfully to praise Christ's Blood that was shed for us all. The text goes on to review the events of Christ's Passion, which he suffered "in knightly fashion." It recounts the Incarnation and Christ's sacrificial death for man's sins, and ends with a call for true penance.[28] The rosary described here is directed to Mary's son, but enlists her support in enabling users to "do penance better here on earth." What this text shows is that, despite arguments to the contrary, penitential spirituality was for many a significant aspect of the devotion.

This is not to say that indulgences were rejected by all good Christians.

On the contrary, there were many sincere believers who accepted them. Members of the Modern Devotion movement, for example, who were avowedly committed to constant meditation on the life of Christ and to "conscious inner devotion," did not reject the rosary, but embraced it and collected its indulgences.[29] Thomas à Kempis (d. 1471) himself earlier had praised the Hail Mary as "sweeter to the angels than anything."[30] Johannes Mombaer (d. 1501) used the practice as the model for numerous spiritual exercises in his *Rosetum exercitiorum* (Rose garden of spiritual exercises, 1494).[31] Similarly, while the statutes of Sprenger's brotherhood on the one hand cite indulgences as inducements for people to join, on the other they clearly stipulate that members are expected to be "obedient to God's commandments." They hold out the hope that through meditating on the Passion of Christ members will ultimately attain justification of sins.[32] Although Sprenger's statutes did not spell out what the exact meditations on the Passion were to be, the statutes of Johannes of Erfurt's chapter at Venice went an important step further in combining the best of both the qualitative and quantitative aspects of the prayer. By finally putting together fifteen specific *vita Christi* meditations in writing, Johannes's statutes improved on Sprenger's formula and thereby created a more spiritually meaningful way for members of the confraternity to go about earning the indulgences that were available. In this most congenial pairing—the one that would go on to become the church's standard—the language of self-help and that of spirituality are cojoined. Here there is no hint that the two are perceived as mutually exclusive.

In contrast to the commonly held view that indulgences were always detrimental to spirituality, Nikolaus Paulus has argued that they sometimes had a positive effect. He cites examples of special short-term grants of indulgences that were offered in certain places and that had the effect of producing a kind of revival atmosphere. Often a charismatic preacher was engaged for a series of revival sermons, and people who had failed to appear for confession for a long time would be induced by the offer of a special dispensation to come and get right with God. Paulus reports, for example, that in the city of Bern in 1478 when a special indulgence was granted for Michelmas, Johannes Heynlin, a well-known preacher and professor of theology from Tübingen, was engaged to preach a special series of sermons in the cathedral once or twice every day. Paulus cites the account of one woman's change of heart that is recorded in Diebold Schilling's chronicle of the event, saying:

"Many people came to Berne from Germany and Italy." Confessors were employed "by the hundred." More than twelve hundred public penitents, men and women, took part in the procession. One of these women, who was separated from her husband, came from Zürich in order to share in the jubilee's grace. When she returned the Bernese Council gave her a letter to the Magistrate at Zürich beseeching him "kindly to help the woman, that she might come again to her husband; for she has here in the Romfahrt [jubilee pilgrimage] confessed and done penance and is willing in the future to conduct herself in a proper wifely manner."[33]

When another indulgence was issued in Lent of 1480, Heynlin was again engaged, for the citizens of Bern sought "an expounder of God's word who through wholesome teaching knew how to summon piety to their souls."[34] Far from being concerned about the sincerity of such penances, Observant reformer Johannes of Paltz argued confidently in 1518 that however paltry or partial a sinner's repentance might be, it was a starting point from which Christ could make up the difference.[35]

The issue of indulgences is, of course, not the same as that of repetitive prayer. Although both involve terminology of quantification, neither was necessarily incompatible with spirituality in the medieval way of thinking. Joseph Lortz has called the idea a "Protestant fallacy" that repetitive prayer is necessarily inconsistent with or constitutes a decay of Christian piety.[36] Certainly no one would assert that nuns who elected to pray one thousand repetitions of the Ave-prayer while prostrated on the ground were lacking in devotion. What is quite clear, however, is that the saying of prayers *solely* for the purpose of gaining indulgences was not condoned.

Even Dominic of Prussia's collection of twenty rosary exempla ("Zwanzig-Exempel"), which predates both Alanus de Rupe's and Jakob Sprenger's brotherhoods by more than thirty years, points out that an indulgence of thirty days for saying the name "Jesus Christ" had been granted by Urban IV (1261–64) and could, accordingly, be acquired if it were used in reciting the rosary.[37] Like the Modern Devotionalists, the Carthusians of Trier and those active in the Observant Reform movement did not see any incompatibility in the acquisition of indulgences for reciting the rosary. Clearly, "sincere Christians" might be on both sides of the issue.

Part of the excesses associated with the practice stemmed rather from the failure to distinguish between remission of the guilt of sin (*culpa*) and remission of the temporal penalty for sin (*poena*). Many people were unaware that although the temporal penalty for venial sins could be reduced by indulgences, the guilt of sin still required confession and priestly absolution. Exempla promoting Dominic of Prussia's Carthusian rosary had indeed promised forgiveness of sins to those who said the prayer. Johannes Herolt, in his collection of exempla, the *Promptuarium discipuli de miraculis Beate Marie Virginis* (Disciple's collection of miracles of the Blessed Virgin Mary, 1435/40), relates the popular story of a Carthusian monk of Trier who had a vision of heaven, and reported that he was told "in clear and plain speech that as often as anyone has repeated that rosary with its added meditations, so often would he receive full remission of his sins."[38] But another version of this same story, adds a very important qualification, namely, that one must first have received absolution. This version states, "Anyone who devoutly prays this rosary, to him all sins will be forgiven, that is, *if he is in a state of grace.*"[39] Confession was thus necessary before one could receive forgiveness. But if combined with confession and prayed in a spiritual way, the rosary here can aid in the remission of (venial) sins with or without indulgences.

Protestants like Martin Luther denounced as fraud all ritual reciting of prayers by "sinners of all kinds."[40] Moreover, Protestants saw the reliance on a treasury of collective credits, such as that generated by the confraternity, as inimical to the very idea of individual priesthood. Despite Protestant prognostications to the contrary, however, the self-help alliance constituted by the brotherhood represented a step in the direction of greater individual control and empowerment in religious practice. Christopher Black describes the early phases of the rosary confraternity as part of a reform movement "designed to foster greater religious participation by all sectors of lay society."[41] André Vauchez comments that the lay faithful tended to see harsh penance and meritorious practices as allowing them to establish "a direct relationship with the supernatural and thereby dispense with clerical mediation."[42] In this respect also the confraternity offered a way to escape the control of the parish priest—at least, in locations where members of the sponsoring Dominican order served as chaplains and confessors. Johan Huizinga asserts that much of the opposition to the rosary confraternity actually stemmed from the fear that parish churches would be emptied by competition from the lay confraternities established at Dominican chapels.[43] Such conflicts caused the rosary brotherhood actually to be banned in Breslau in 1481.[44]

In general, Catholics saw works of piety, including praying for the dying and for souls in purgatory, as useful to the spiritual life. They believed "good works not only *could* increase justification, but almost certainly *would*."[45] Luther, however, objected to what he saw as the legalistic quantification of "righteousness"—the sheer accumulation of spiritual capital—and denied that any one could be justified by such acts. Ironically, Luther, who himself had long sought personal affective certainty of salvation, found it only by giving up on the whole system of quantifiable assets and instead by undertaking a "leap of faith." For others, however, especially in the Counter-Reformation period, the life-of-Christ rosary constituted a very satisfying way to rehearse Christ's acts of redemption.

Yet at the same time that the *vita Christi* rosary was regaining ground, even prior to the Reformation, it was continuing to change. As has been shown, by the 1570s the final meditation had been replaced almost universally by the coronation of the Virgin. This substitution registered the Virgin's more prominent role as foundress and protectress of the organization. By the seventeenth century the words "pray for us sinners now and at the hour of our death" had become a standard part of the text.

The image of the coronation stems from a passage in the Song of Songs in which the bridegroom summons his bride, saying in the Vulgate text, "Veni de Líbano, sponsa mea, veni de Líbano, veni, coronáberis" (Come from Lebanon, my Bride, come from Lebanon, come, you shall be crowned, 4:7–8).[46] Medieval garden allegories like *Our Lady Mary's Rose Garden* and other devotional works created narratives in which Mary is cast as heroine and bride to Christ the Bridegroom. Ann Astell calls these characters "Mother-Bride" and "Christ-Knight" figures and explains the schema as an outgrowth of Mariological interpretations of the Old Testament Song.[47] It is a story that ends, as in the rosary, with the bride's coronation.

While allegorically the bride of the Song of Songs represents the church, tropologically she is the soul of the individual believer.[48] The familiar phrase "Veni in hortum meum" (5:1)—often translated in German texts as "Kumm in minen garten"—begins many mystical devotional works in which the soul communes with the bridegroom in a garden setting. In these extremely popular spiritual garden allegories, the roses represent Christ's wounds of love, the virtues of the soul, or of Mary—the first bride of Christ and herself a type of the church. Similarly, the red and white roses of the rosary stand not only for Christ's wounds but also for the Virgin's purity and her suffering along with his.[49] In the third section of the prayer these earthly red and white roses are elevated to supernatural, golden roses that represent Christ's heavenly triumph and his glorification together with that of Mary. Thus the narrative becomes a dual story recounting Mary's joy, suffering, and triumph as well as Christ's. As part of the larger, evolving discourse on justification and salvation, the narrative of the rose explains the special role of the Virgin Mary in the process of redemption. The language used is the idiom of the Song of Songs.

It would be difficult to overestimate the influence of the Old Testament canticle on late medieval devotional literature. As the most frequently quoted book of the fourteenth century, the language and images of the Song of Songs pervaded all aspects of religious writing, and served as the standard emotive idiom for mystical, devotional expression throughout the Middle Ages. In translating the Song of Songs to German, Luther changed all of the lilies of the Vulgate to roses. His reason for this, no doubt, had to do with his determination not to shape the language to the text but to fit the text into the vernacular language in a way that the average "man on the street" would recognize as the real thing. To this end Luther chose the rose as the blossom most closely linked to both divine and human love in the popular imagination.

The importance of language itself as spiritual capital and the influence of the powerfully emotive idiom of the Song of Songs in shaping devotional images and practices points up the larger role of language generally in the religious ferment of the Reformation period. The extent to which language played a "generative" role in the changes that took place in the sixteenth century is an unanswered question. Yet part of the reason why medieval Christians were willing to join Luther and the Protestants certainly had to do with the vernacular language—the means by which control of the dominant discourse was wrenched out of the hands of the established church. In addition to Luther's own superb use of the vernacular, his translation of the Bible and the liturgy into an eminently accessible and vivid German brought into the discussion a new and much larger group of informed participants. Most of all, Luther's masterful fixing of Early New High German—his successful undertaking to catch the "real" language of people in the text of his vernacular Bible—was probably the most profound change worked by the new discourse. Luther's translations and interpretations of words like "grace" and "justification" affected how these terms were conceived in German. In the same way that "Schuld" differs from "culpa" or "Strafe" from "poena," by virtue of the linguistic code-structure of the vernacular, so did perceptions of these terms differ. The old language of credits, the treasury of merits, and indulgences gave way before a redefined language of faith, justification, and individual priesthood. Terms like "works," "faith," and "grace" assimilated meanings that were gleaned from rereadings of the biblical text according to a different understanding of mankind's relationship to God and to the church. In the post-Reformation period the older discourse of devotion that had centered on the passion and on the joys of the Virgin would be refocused to include Christ as teacher and model for living, a theme that would emerge in the work of the Jesuits who promoted the rosary meditations as an exercise to teach virtue and to conform the lives of the faithful to that of Christ.

That all of these discourses are interrelated parts of a larger cultural conversation can be seen in the connections of the rosary to other works of literature—or rather, what are often called "literary" works, to contrast them with "religious" texts. Yet while the latter are generally thought of as belonging more to the separate field of religious studies and treated accordingly, "religious works" need to be looked at from a broader perspective. Indeed, medieval sources themselves do not observe these categories. A song of praise to the Virgin could be inserted within a courtly epic: for example, the "Marienlob" of forty-two stanzas found in some manuscripts of Albrecht von Scharfenberg's Arthurian tale, *Der jüngere Titurel* (The Titurel sequel, late thirteenth century).[50] The same medieval authors who wrote the works of the secular literary canon also composed religious ones. And these works were copied side by side into manuscripts that hold the most diverse collections of texts.

A case in point is the manuscript that contains the German Marian psalter discussed in Chapter 1 (the first vernacular psalter to experiment with a *vita Christi* narrative). Copied together with this psalter are Marian songs by well-known Minnesinger Walther von der Vogelweide (c. 1170–c. 1230) and Reinmar von Zweter (c. 1200–c. 1260), as well as a long Marian poem of two thousand lines by Konrad von Würzburg, the *Goldene Schmiede* (Golden ornament), plus three "secular" works by him. In all the manuscript contains thirty-five "religious" texts bound together with 178 secular ones.[51]

The fruitful aspect of looking at some of these works together is that they cast light on one another and on forms, images, and meanings that would otherwise be obscure. A good example is the *Goldene Schmiede*, a work said to have been written to rally support for a new phase of construction on the cathedral of Notre Dame at Strasbourg. (The Strasbourg cathedral formerly had on its facade a relief sculpture of Mary with the rosetree.) For a long time the shape of Konrad's *Goldene Schmiede* has been seen as formless and problematic. Peter Ganz calls it "an undifferentiated whole," Ute Schwab asserts that it "follows no logical plan," Jakob Baechthold judged it "tasteless," and Friedrich Ranke labeled it "Konrad's most gothic work."[52] Yet seen in the context of the Marian psalter form, the images and shape become less strange. What appears to be a random listing of epithets to the Virgin is essentially the technique we have seen employed in the Marian litany type of psalter, which consisted of a chain of 150 titles of the Virgin, many of them the same as those in the *Goldene Schmiede*. It has been shown that in Marian psalters these titles originally were not random, but were based on key words in the antiphons that introduced each of the psalms and interpreted them as references to the Virgin. Gradually, as the antiphons that made up the first Marian psalters came to be replaced by other verses, the connection to the Psalms was lost. Since the epithets enumerated in a Marian psalter formed a litany substituting for the 150 Psalms, there was no necessity for them to be arranged in a logical sequence.

The connection between the *Goldene Schmiede* and the Marian psalter-form in the medieval mind can be seen in a fifteenth-century Netherlandish adaptation of it called *Marien Voerspan of Sapeel* (Mary's necklace or chaplet, c. 1450).[53] Here Konrad's poem is arranged as a chaplet ("sapeel") with the epithets in the form of a rosary. In the prologue the anonymous redactor says, "If only my words could take flight, so that I could approach with my thoughts [Mary's] high honor and sweet renown and could fly up to the heavenly May garden, there to pick the flowers that my heart desires to weave into a worthy chaplet, shining like the sun."[54] Although Konrad's *Goldene Schmiede* does not have the stanza form of a rosary or psalter, but rather a chainlike structure, Konrad too speaks in the prologue of his wish to weave a properly worthy "chaplet" of verbal "flowers" for the Virgin, one "that would blossom with rosy phrases."[55] Thus when regarded from a medieval perspective as a kind of chaplet, Konrad's *Goldene Schmiede* should not frustrate readers with its apparent lack of logical sequence; it should be regarded as a devotional chain of symbolic blossoms, gold, and gems.

The interconnectedness and "patchwork" quality of texts can also be seen by looking again at the German Marian psalter mentioned above (the first one to have *vita Christi* meditations), also located in this same manuscript. This psalter has inserted within it a well-known miracle story, the tale of "The Priest Who Only Knew One Mass."[56] It is included here as a kind of intermission to provide "a breather" between the second and third rounds of the psalter and to entertain, but also to encourage the user to go on and complete the last third of the exercise. The author explains that he wants to tell this anecdote in order to show how Mary rewards those who serve her. Also in this same large manuscript are found twenty-four other Marian legends, from the *Passional* (including the rosary legend of the monk and the robbers). The references from one to another in these works and to sources held in common underscore the degree to which these texts are all overlapping. Accordingly, rosaries and psalters ought not to be marginalized or thought of as mere "religious" exercises, but rather seen and heard as participating voices in a larger and very lively common devotional discourse.

It is a discourse that frequently crosses disciplinary boundaries as seen, for example, in paintings of rosary exempla like the one made by Geertgen tot Sint Jans (d. 1495) for the brotherhood established at Haarlem in 1478, now preserved in two copies (see Fig. 34). This painting depicts the story of Blanche of Castile, Queen of France who, thanks to the collective efforts of those who prayed the rosary with her, conceived a son who would later become the sainted King Louis IX.[57] Besides this exemplum, a painting and several woodcuts of the rosary story of the monk and the robbers have been identified by Augusta von Oertzen.[58]

In addition to works of the visual arts, garden texts like *Our Lady Mary's Rose Garden* themselves cross boundaries with those of the medical genre by including exempla that describe the use of "rosenkuchen" (a rose-cake poultice) for treating ailments such as toothache.[59] All of this should remind us of the extremely "practical" uses to which all of these works were put as instruments of comfort and protection against the distresses of daily life. As Lynn Hunt and Anton Kaes assert, texts are neither innocent nor transparent but instruments, interventions, strategies, and mechanisms for shaping reality.[60]

Finally, from a literary theoretical point of view, the rosary, which is itself not one text but many, illustrates particularly well not only the interdisciplinary communality of medieval devotional writings and art-

FIG. 34. From the Legend of the Rosary of Saint Dominic, a copy after a lost painting by Geertgen tot Sint Jans (d. 1495). Leipzig, Museum der bildenden Künste

works but also the nature of religious discourse as collective conversation. Kaes cites Roland Barthes's "The Death of the Author" (1968), in which Barthes radically redefines texts as nothing but "a tissue of quotations drawn from the innumerable centres of culture." Kaes qualifies Barthes's statement by pointing out that it is, after all, the author who himself "picks and chooses the quotations."[61] In the case of the rosary, this collectivity inheres not so much in the act of an author's choosing among quotations generated by a contextual cultural community, but rather that of a community experimenting with multiple versions of similar works by different authors—in effect, choosing an author. The background is not to be perceived as "located" somewhere outside of the text; rather, the "text" is the community's collective enactment of multiple versions of the devotion.

The "documents" that surround the rosary—its songs, statutes, picture series, stories, handbooks—are themselves experiments that contest and affirm the spiritual reality that the performance invokes. Gabrielle Spiegel cautions that "documents" should not be thought of as more reliable than other written evidence from the past;[62] that is to say, they are not less "fictional" than other works. Indeed, one may ask, in what way a statute explaining rules, ideals, and rationale for the founding of a spiritual brotherhood should be less fictional than a "literary" work? Like other texts, "documents" are composed of patchworks of "social and discursive formations" that, while expressing the dominant discourse, simultaneously "resist, contest, or seek to transform" it.[63] Just as it is no longer possible to write a history of past "events" that is unconscious of deconstructionist theories of language, so too can one no longer be unaware that documents and histories about them are themselves stories that are "made" as instruments, interventions, strategies, and political mechanisms.

These textual formulations of communal concerns, needs, and desires both shape and are shaped by the collective conversation. The communal utterance contains many voices speaking "on behalf of those who have no voice."[64] In *Renaissance Self-Fashioning*, Stephen Greenblatt characterizes the mood of the early sixteenth century as one of grave spiritual anxiety and attributes the success of Luther's writings to the fact that they "spoke so powerfully to the psychological and spiritual state already in existence."[65] By the same token, the rosary also spoke to the needs of large numbers of people. Nor was its appeal extinguished by the Protestant Reformation; it increased in the Counter-Reformation period following the reforms of the Council of Trent.

Always controversial, the rosary has a surprisingly "political" and economic aspect, not just with respect to the Observant reformers' outreach to the laity or in the rise of self-help associations like confraternities, but even in the long-running conflict between the mendicant friars and the local priests of the secular clergy over rights to hear confessions, to offer services to the laity, and to bury the dead. Far from being simply a self-contained, private spiritual exercise, the rosary was an active agent in the complex struggle for spiritual renewal and reform on the eve of the Reformation.

Appendix

Three exempla from the rosary handbook,
*Von dem psalter vnnd Rosenkrancz vnser
lieben frauen* (Augsburg: Anton Sorg,
1492).

Exemplum 8
A Young Woman Named Alexandra[1]

We read of a noble young lady named Alexandra who was moved by the preaching of Saint Dominic in the kingdom of Arrogonia (Aragon) to join the brotherhood of Mary's psalter. And although this Alexandra had been a member of Mary's brotherhood for several years, she had prayed the psalter [of Our Lady] only seldom because of her frivolous way of life. In the mornings she would devote more than an hour to dressing herself and making herself ready.

For the love of this Alexandra many men competed against each other in great and expensive jousting tournaments. Thus it happened that one of those who desired to wed Alexandra arranged a grand tournament which she attended in all her finery and haughtiness. And when this same young lord had unhorsed many opponents with his great strength and the power of his lance, he gloried in his success with extreme and pretentious arrogance and cried in a loud voice "Mark you, Alexandra, I undertake this joust for the sake of your love."

Now this was heard by another man who likewise wanted to sue for Alexandra's hand and said to the first man, "I will ride against you in a joust for her love." And thus it happened that the horses of the two impetuous opponents ran so hard at each other that the two impaled one another. And amid the most violent curses and swearing both of them gave up the ghost and died in the sight of all that were present.

When the friends of the two men saw how shamefully they both had died, their anger was kindled against Alexandra and they lay in wait for her as she went out of her house and fell on her and stabbed her and also those who accompanied her. But when Alexandra and her retinue had been sorely wounded and lay about on the ground, Alexandra fended off death crying out in a loud voice for a confessor and seeking to make her confession. Fearing they would be discovered due to Alexandra's continuous loud shouting for a confessor they cut off her head, threw it into a nearby well, and then rode away.

But Saint Dominic knew all of these things in his heart where he was in a city called Oxoma (Osuna). And after 150 days Saint Dominic came to the well where Alexandra's head was and called her up out of it. And forthwith Alexandra appeared, all bloody as if her head had only just been severed and she shouted and sought to make confession. And after Alexandra had confessed and had taken the holy sacrament, she thanked Saint Dominic earnestly and said she positively would have been damned had it not been for the merits of the brothers and sisters of Mary's psalter. For she said that a host of devils had tried to take her soul and would have succeeded in bringing it to hell had not the excellent Virgin Mary been present and protected her from these devils for 150 days until Saint Dominic came to the well.

Then Alexandra said that she was to be sentenced to 200 years in the pains of purgatory because of the two men who had run each other through in the joust over her, and she was sentenced to another 400 years because her vanity, haughtiness, and self-adornment had enticed great numbers of people into sin. In all Alexandra was to spend 700 [sic] years in purgatory. But she said that she hoped nevertheless to be released soon through the help of the brothers and sisters (of Mary's psalter). So Saint Dominic buried the head and went away.

Fifteen days later Alexandra appeared again to Saint Dominic in the form of a bright and shining star and bearing three messages. The first was a message from all the believers in purgatory asking and beseeching their friends and fathers and mothers to enroll themselves in the brotherhood of Mary's psalter so that they might be shareholders in the merits of the brothers and sisters of Mary's psalter. The second was her profuse gratitude to Saint Dominic because she had been released so quickly. Third, she wished it to be known that the saints and angels rejoiced exceedingly over the brotherhood of Mary's psalter and that the saints and angels called [its members] brothers and sisters, and God the Almighty called himself their father and Mary their mother. After Alexandra had spoken these words she departed from Saint Dominic and ascended to eternal glory and joy with Mary as her guide and after this life was granted the life eternal.

Exemplum 12
Mary, the Charcoaler's Daughter

A learned master of Holy Writ named Master Johannes von Berg tells in his *Marial* of a charcoaler's daughter named Mary who had an exceedingly honorable and pious mother.[2] From her earliest youth the girl had been instructed and taught by her mother to pray Mary's Psalter. The daughter was a hard worker and early or late she was always the first one to start and the last one to finish collecting wood or preparing the pit for her father. At every task she worked tirelessly. Often she drove loads of charcoal with the horses from the forest into the city of Paris and sold them. And always she had her beads affixed to her belt or carried them in her hands and prayed her psalter constantly. After each task she would recite an Our Father and ten Ave Marias and thus could accommodate her prayer to all the things that she did. For she had been taught and instructed by God through the Mother of our Lord in all the circumstances in this world both good and evil to have recourse to the Ave Maria. As Anselm writes, in this way Mary is not only a mother and queen of good things, but a healing salve and a help against all the evils and bad things of this world.

Thus it happened that the prince, the future king, noticed Mary the charcoaler's daughter—all black as a devil—when she came once or twice a week to the court with a load of charcoal. In her hands she held her psalter beads which she prayed continually. Thus one day, as God and His Dear Mother would have it, he was moved to speak with her and asked her name, her status, and what prayer she was saying. The girl answered all his questions in a proper manner. After that, whenever she came to court the king would stop whatever he was doing and converse with her piously and with tender affection. The king freely bought great quantities of charcoal with no regard for the cost and urged her often and intently that she should enjoy herself with his sisters. But Mary always refused the offer for she was loath to lose a single hour that she might never retrieve.

Finally, one day after the still unmarried prince had assumed full powers as king, Mary came to the court as was her habit and the king spoke to her saying, "Oh Mary, dear daughter, tell me where your father's house is. For I plan to go hunting and wish to lodge there for the night." Then Mary said to the king, "Oh most worthy Lord King I have no lodging other than a charcoaler's cottage." The king said, "Indeed, that is just what I am seeking."

Thus it was that the king rode into the forest to hunt and came upon a deer that took flight and ran hard straight to the charcoaler's cottage. When Mary the charcoaler's daughter saw the deer in distress, she mercifully opened the gate of the garden for it and then shut it in front of the hunting dogs that were in pursuit. Thus the dogs ran about, filling the forest with their baying. But the king intended to go on with the hunt and to catch Mary the charcoaler's daughter for his bride with the consent of her father and mother.

And thus when he came to the charcoaler's cottage he left off hunting and went inside with all his men to have a meal. But in the cottage there was neither carpet nor bench, chair nor silverware, nor any thing in the house but sacks of black coal lying about. The father came at a run just like a black devil, and the mother like a mooress and nearly frightened the king and his retinue to death. But Mary hid herself away like a shamefaced sweetheart.

The king ordered her to be fetched, but she could not be found anywhere in the house. Presently, a hunting dog began to bark and bay in front of the garden, for the dog had scented her hidden there behind the fence. A hunter ran to the spot and saw Mary the charcoaler's daughter standing behind the fence in prayer. And beside her he saw the most beautiful queen with a tiny child in her arms who was even more beautiful. There could be no doubt that they were the most blessed queen and mother Mary with her son Jesus. And because of that the dogs could not enter the garden nor harm the daughter.

In this way Mary was found and brought before the king who stood up and said to her, "Oh Mary, what have you done to us?" And the king spoke thus to all his men, saying, "You have urged me that I should take to wife whomsoever I wish and most desire. Is that not true, my lords?" The men answered that it was so. Then said the king, "I swear to you by my scepter and my crown that I shall wed no other woman than this Mary, the charcoaler's daughter. And certainly what the king and his men have spoken shall come to pass and not be changed."

Immediately the servants arrived and laid cloaks under Mary's feet and decorated the cottage as well as they could and made ready for the marriage of the king and the charcoaler's daughter. They placed the queen in a royal wagon and drove her to the city of Paris. And there she was crowned in a joyful and glorious ceremony. But the father kept his daughter's old clothes, saying to himself, "Well do I know that my daughter will need these again." And the king was wed on a feast day of Our Lady.

And when Mary the charcoaler's daughter had become queen of France, she rid the land of war and distress through her wisdom and goodness. The poor she freed from the clutches of the unjust nobles, for truly she was a mother to the poor. And she removed the corrupt officials and replaced them with honest and pious ones. Thus through her wisdom and excellent guidance the land increased greatly in goods and prosperity.

But the devil and the evil ones who serve him could not tolerate this and incited the princes and lords to rise up against the king and threatened to kill him if he did not depose this rough and crude charcoal woman and renounce her. And when the king saw this he sent for the queen and for her three small sons to come before him, and he stripped her of her dress down to her shift and commanded that she leave his house and return to her father's house whence she had come. Thus Mary came almost naked to the door of her father's house with her three sons. And the father ran to meet her saying, "Oh, my dear daughter. Because I foresaw that this would happen I kept your dress." And he brought out her old clothes. Mary put them back on and stayed with her father and served him as before without sadness or sorrow just as though she had never been queen. And her father too was humble and upright, not wishing to elevate himself or raise his station in the realm by taking so much as a heller or a penny.

Now after all of the princes had gained back their goods and positions of power, they began to squabble, quarrel, and to make war amongst themselves in foolish strife and enmity. At last, the king prayed to God for an end to the strife in his land and Mary the Mother of God appeared to him and told him that until he again took unto him Mary the charcoaler's daughter, there would never be peace in France. When the king heard that, he sent for Mary and returned her to her former station with great honor. And when this had come to pass the war ceased, strife throughout the realm was laid to rest, and peace returned to the land. And afterward the queen became a special patroness to the clergy, of monasteries, hospitals, and churches, and a protector of the poor. To anyone who wished to pray Mary's psalter she gave a set of beads and instructed all her serving men and maids to pray it as well.

Now, after the queen had attained great honor and glory in the eyes of both God and men, and her life had reached its end, Mary the mother of

God appeared unto her and conducted her into the joy of eternal blessedness. Yet all the time that the queen had lived and reigned there was
never sadness or discord in France but only the most profound peace and
blessing in all good things.

Exemplum 14
Eleodorus the Infidel[3]

In the days of Saint Dominic there was in the kingdom of Spain a great
war between the Christians and the infidels. In this war the Christians
took captive along with many others an infidel, his wife, and his son and
brought them to a place in the Christian lands where they were to be sold.
And when this happened, the twenty-year-old son, who was captive with
them, became exceedingly sad and dejected. First, he was despondent over
his captivity and became so distraught that he often considered killing
himself. Second, he suffered miserably because he had lost the use of all
his limbs. Third, he had little more than bread and water to eat and only
the meanest of clothing to wear—he who as a free man had before been a
leader among the infidels and was brought up as the respected son of one
of the greatest and mightiest of knights. Fourth, he had become possessed
by devils and was plagued by fits of madness and raving. Fifth, he suffered
because the wounds that he had sustained in the war had begun to rot and
stink. So bad were the stench and the awful worms breeding in the
wounds that he could hardly endure it. Thus he constantly invoked the
devil and cursed Christ and Mary with all his might. Sixth, he developed
the foolish notion that he could see hell and claimed that he would not
escape being sent there.

   Now, when Saint Dominic was traveling and preaching in this kingdom,
he heard in the city where he was staying of the great wretchedness and
misery of this infidel and went to speak with him, saying "Son, do you
wish to be healed?" The infidel answered back straightway that indeed, he
desired to be healed. Saint Dominic said, "as soon as you become a
Christian you will immediately be well." Then the infidel shouted in a
loud voice "That I will not do, for anything in the world, for it would be
abandoning the laws of my parents."

   So Saint Dominic saw that he could achieve nothing and spoke to him
again, saying, "Son, I know two beautiful charms that have the greatest

power. If you would say them 150 times every day you would be healed in a short time. And when the infidel heard that he said, "I would gladly do that as long as the words are not against my law." Saint Dominic said to him, "Oh, dear son, these phrases are not against the laws of God and thus they are not adverse to you but rather will help you."

Eleodorus replied to Saint Dominic, "Now I would like to say these charms if I can and as long as they are not about your Christ and your Mary." Saint Dominic said, "The words that I will disclose to you are exceedingly joyful, pleasant, effective and useful against all misfortune. And they are not only effective when spoken by the Christian sinner but are also powerful when recited by non-Christians and Jews." Thus did Saint Dominic amicably deceive this wretched man so that he agreed to do as he wished.

And Saint Dominic began to recite the Our Father and the Ave Maria, but did not say the names Jesus Christ and Mary aloud. And when Saint Dominic had finished the Our Father and the Hail Mary the infidel said he could not learn or remember the words. So Saint Dominic entreated God secretly in his heart. And immediately Eleodorus could recite the Paternoster and the Ave Maria perfectly. And Saint Dominic said to him, "Dear Son, by this you can see and understand how powerful these words are that you could learn them in an instant and retain them."

So Eleodorus began to pray the psalter after Saint Dominic had left him, not in a Christian way but with an entirely opposing view and in a profane manner desiring rather to heal his body and spirit. And when he had prayed this psalter of Mary through to the end, he began to pray in the heathen fashion and felt a great bliss and delight in his heart as though he were experiencing the joy and pleasure of paradise. And on the next day as soon as he had prayed Mary's psalter through, his strength and the use of his limbs returned to him through the power of God.

And on the third day he found buried under the spot where he lay an immense treasure with which he purchased his freedom and afterward made many gifts to churches and poorhouses. For in this treasure he found a thousand ancient gold coins. Now this hidden treasure had once belonged to a heathen king and each gold coin was worth seven Rhenish guldens. And there was also a great deal of silver and other items besides in a buried coffin. All of this Eleodorus found when he was cleaning his cell under the place where he slept. And this treasure later supported many campaigns against the infidels under the direction of Saint Dominic.

On the fourth day after Eleodorus had prayed his psalter through, the devils departed from him amid curses, howling, and shrieking. And on the fifth day a very beautiful lady appeared to him with a small child in her arms and applied a fragrant salve to all his sores. She told him that if he wished to be completely healed, he must bathe himself in the fountain of life. On the sixth day when he had prayed his psalter he was transported in a vision to heaven where he saw Christ and the glory of the saints. And there he saw how Christ was judging men and many were being sentenced to eternal damnation but only a few to the glory of eternal joy.

And he too received a sentence and was judged worthy of eternal damnation. But then a beautiful and lovely young woman appeared and entreated the judge on his behalf. And the judge said to her, "In all his life he has done nothing good." And the young woman said, "Lord, he prayed six psalters to me and to you." At this moment he came to himself and went out and had himself baptized. Thus Eleodorus became a pious Christian, serving Mary devotedly with her psalter and ended his days well.

Notes

Introduction

1. *Unser Jungfrauwen Mariae Rosengertlin,* in *Adolf von Essen und seine Werke. Der Rosenkranz in der geschichtlichen Situation seiner Entstehung und in seinem bleibenden Anliegen,* ed. Karl-Josef Klinkhammer, Frankfurter Theologische Studien 13 (Frankfurt: Knecht, 1972), 141, 143–44.

2. Klinkhammer, ed., *Adolf von Essen,* 141.

3. Hans-Joachim Schmidt, "Die Trierer Erzbischöfe und die Reform von Kloster und Stift im 15. Jahrhundert," in *Reformbemühungen und Observanzbestrebungen im spätmittelalterlichen Ordenswesen,* ed. Kaspar Elm, Berliner Historische Studien 14, Ordensstudien 6 (Berlin: Duncker and Humblot, 1989), 472, 474–75; and Heinrich Rüthing, "Die Kartäuser und die spätmittelalterlichen Ordensreformen," in *Reformbemühungen,* ed. Elm, 40.

4. Andreas Heinz, "Eine spätmittelalterliche Exempelsammlung zur Propagierung des Trierer Karthäuser-Rosenkranzes," *Trierer Theologische Zeitschrift* 92 (1983): 307–8; Klinkhammer, *Adolf von Essen,* 54–56, 111; and Petrus Becker, "Erstrebte und erreichte Ziele benediktinischer Reformen im Spätmittelalter," in *Reformbemühungen,* ed. Elm, 23–34, here 26.

5. Willy Andreas, *Deutschland vor der Reformation: Eine Zeitwende,* 5th ed. (Stuttgart: Deutsche Verlagsanstalt, 1948), 172.

6. Luke 1:28 combined with Luke 1:42. Herbert Thurston, *Familiar Prayers: Their Origin and History* (Westminster, Md.: Newman, 1953), 103–6; Rainer Scherschel, *Der Rosenkranz: Das Jesusgebet des Westens,* Freiburger Theologische Studien 116 (Freiburg: Herder, 1979), 58. For the early history of the prayer see also Thurston, "Our Popular Devotions: II. The Rosary," *The Month* 96 (1900): 403–18; and Thomas Esser, "Geschichte des englischen Grußes," *Historisches Jahrbuch der Görres-Gesellschaft* 5 (1884): 88–116.

7. See Jakob Hubert Schütz, ed., *Die Geschichte des Rosenkranzes: Unter Berücksichtigung der Rosenkranz-Geheimnisse und der Marien Litaneien* (Paderborn: Junfermann, 1909), ix–xviii. Dominic of Prussia himself comments in this "Zwanzig-Exempel-Schrift" that in his childhood in Cracow the name Jesus was not part of the prayer. See Klinkhammer, *Adolf von Essen,* 182. For a summary tracing the addition of the name Jesus to the prayer see Scherschel, *Der Rosenkranz,* 68–90. The creed appears already in some fifteenth-century versions such as that used at Colmar in 1485.

8. John J. Keating, *Outlines of Catholic Teaching* (New York: Paulist, 1955), 183.

9. Andreas Heinz, "Die Zisterzienser und die Anfänge des Rosenkranzes," *Analecta Cisterciensia* 33 (1977): 262–309.

10. Peter Ochsenbein, *Das Große Gebet der Eidgenossen* (Bern: Francke, 1989), 155.

11. Steven Ozment, *The Age of Reform, 1250–1550* (New Haven: Yale University Press, 1980), 220.

12. Richard Kieckhefer groups the rosary together with meditations on the Passion and Books of Hours, designating them as imitations for lay persons of the monastic hours. See "Major Currents in Late Medieval Devotion," in *Christian Spirituality: High Middle Ages and Reformation,* ed. Jill Raitt, World Spirituality 17 (New York: Crossroad, 1989), 100. Likewise Thomas Esser, *Unserer lieben Frauen Rosenkranz* (Paderborn: Schöningh, 1889), terms the rosary "the breviary of the laity"(23); and Josef Stadlhuber, "Das Laienstundengebet vom Leiden Christi in seinem mittelalterlichen Fortleben," *Zeitschrift für katholische Theologie* 67 (1950), refers to it as "the simple man's Hours," here 319–20.

13. Stephanus Axters, *Geschiedenis van de vroomheid in de Nederlanden,* 3 vols. (Antwerp: De Sikkel, 1950–56), 3:407 n. 5, cited in Sixten Ringbom, *Icon to Narrative: The Rise of the Dramatic Close-up in Fifteenth-Century Devotional Painting.* Acta Academiae Aboensis, ser. A, Humaniora 31, no. 2 (Åbo: Åbo Akademi, 1965), 27.

14. See Francis Oakley, *The Western Church in the Later Middle Ages* (Ithaca: Cornell University Press, 1979), 118; and Kathleen Wood-Legh in *Perpetual Chantries in Britain* (Cambridge: Cambridge University Press, 1965), 312.

15. Joseph H. Lynch, *The Medieval Church: A Brief History* (London: Longman, 1992), 338.

16. Bernd Moeller, "Piety in Germany around 1500," in *The Reformation in Medieval Perspective,* ed. Steven Ozment (Chicago: Quadrangle, 1971), 50–75, here 51; Joseph Lortz, *The Reformation in Germany,* 2 vols., trans. Ronald Walls (New York: Herder, 1968), 1:110.

17. Moeller, "Piety," 51, 60, 64.

18. Steven Ozment, *The Reformation in the Cities* (New Haven: Yale University Press, 1975), p. 21.

19. Oakley, *Western Church,* 128.

20. Cited in Ernst Schubert, *Einführung in die Grundprobleme der deutschen Geschichte im Mittelalter* (Darmstadt: Wissenschaftliche Buchgesellschaft, 1992), 276.

21. Ibid.

22. Anne Middleton, "Medieval Studies," in *Redrawing the Boundaries: The Transformation of English and American Literary Studies,* ed. Stephen Greenblatt and Giles Gunn (New York: Modern Language Association, 1992), 28.

23. Eamon Duffy, *The Stripping of the Altars: Traditional Religion in England c. 1400–c.1580* (New Haven: Yale University Press, 1992), 5.

24. See Thurston, *Familiar Prayers,* 90; and Thomas Esser, "Beitrag zur Geschichte des Rosenkranzes: Die ersten Spuren von Betrachtungen beim Rosenkranz," *Der Katholik* 77 (1897): 346–60, 409–22, 515–28.

25. Herbert Thurston, "Our Popular Devotions: II. The Rosary," *The Month* 96 (1900): 403–18, 513–27; 97 (1901), 67–79, 172–88. See also, for example, Denys Mézard, *Etude sur les origines du rosaire: Réponse aux articles du P. Thurston, . . . parus dans le Month 1900 et 1901* (Caluire: Couvent de la Visitation, 1912).

26. Stephan Beissel, *Geschichte der Verehrung Marias in Deutschland I: Während des Mittelalters* and *II: im 16. und 17. Jahrhundert,* 2 vols. (Freiburg: Herder, 1909–10), 1:228–50; Wilhelm Schmitz, *Das Rosenkranzgebet im 15. und im Anfange des 16. Jahrhunderts* (Freiburg: Herder, 1903); and Jakob Hubert Schütz, ed., *Die Geschichte des Rosenkranzes.*

27. Franz M. Willam, *Die Geschichte und Gebetsschule des Rosenkranzes* (Vienna: Herder, 1948); Willibald Kirfel, *Der Rosenkranz, Ursprung und Ausbreitung,* Beiträge zur Sprach- und Kulturgeschichte des Orients 1 (Walldorf, Hessen: Verlag für Orientkunde H. Vorndran, 1949). See also James G. Shaw, *The Story of the Rosary* (Milwaukee, Wis.: Bruce, 1954); and Maxime Gorce, *Le Rosaire et ses antécédents historiques d'après le manuscrit 12483 fond français de la Bibliothèque Nationale* (Paris: Picard, 1931).

28. Stefano Orlandi, ed. *Libro del Rosario della Gloriosa Vergine Maria* (Rome: Centro Internationale Domenicano Rosariano, 1965).

29. Jean-Claude Schmitt, "Apostolat mendiant et société: Une confrérie dominicaine à la veille de la réforme," *Annales: E. S. C.* (1971): 83–104.

30. Scherschel, *Jesusgebet*, 137–47.

31. *500 Jahre Rosenkranz, 1475–1975: Kunst und Frömmigkeit im Spätmittelalter und ihr Weiterleben* (Cologne: Bachem, 1975).

32. Heinz, "Zisterzienser," 262–309.

33. André Duval, "Rosaire," in *Dictionnaire de spiritualité*, ed. Joseph de Guibert, Marcel Viller, and Ferdinand Cavallera (Paris: Beauchesne, 1988), 13:cols. 937–80.

34. *Vnser lieben Frauen Psalter* (Ulm: Dinckmut, 1483).

35. See Dietrich Schmidtke, *Studien zur dingallegorischen Erbauungsliteratur des Spätmittelalters: Am Beispiel der Gartenallegorie.* Hermaea 43 (Tübingen: Niemeyer, 1982).

36. Ann W. Astell, *The Song of Songs in the Middle Ages* (Ithaca: Cornell University Press, 1990), 61, 68–69.

37. See Peter Dronke, "The Song of Songs and the Medieval Love-Lyric," in *The Bible and Medieval Culture*, ed. W. Lourdaux and D. Verhelst, Mediaevalia Lovanensia Ser. 1, no. 7 (Louvain: Louvain University Press, 1979), 236–62; and Arnold Oppel, *Das Hohelied Salomonis und die deutsche religiöse Liebeslyrik*, Abhandlungen zur Mittleren und Neueren Geschichte 32 (Berlin and Leipzig: Rothschild, 1911), 21–36.

38. Mary Juliana Schroeder, *Mary-Verse in "Meistergesang,"* Catholic University Studies in German 16 (Washington, D.C., 1942), 145–48, 267.

39. Ohly, *Hohelied-Studien*, 212. Ohly's term "Liebesleidenschaft" translates as "passion of love."

40. Rosemarie Herde, "Das Hohelied in der lateinischen Literatur des Mittelalters bis zum 12. Jahrhundert," *Studi medievali*, 3d ser., 8 (1967): 982. In Peter Eckel von Haselbach's "Predigt auf die hl. Barbara," for instance, the "pure, virginal heart" is described as a garden and Mary is identified as the "first garden." The "Meffreth" first sermon on Saint Barbara contains a similar passage. Both sermons are printed in the appendix to Schmidtke, *Erbauungsliteratur*, 516–29, here 518 and 526.

41. A passage in *Unser Jungfrauwen Mariae Rosengertlin* states that "each of us has in his heart a garden where we go daily to pluck roses and to make a chaplet for Mary," (Klinkhammer, *Adolf von Essen*, 137).

42. Jacques Le Goff, *The Birth of Purgatory*, trans. Arthur Goldhammer (Chicago: University of Chicago Press, 1984), 298.

43. Oakley, *Western Church*, 113, and Aron Gurevich, *Medieval Popular Culture: Problems of Belief and Perception*, trans. János Bak and Paula Hollingsworth (Cambridge: Cambridge University Press, 1988), xiv.

44. Gurevich, *Popular Culture*, 2–3, 218.

45. Ibid., 4–6, 31–32.

46. In a typical example Caesarius begins by stating, "This story I heard from a priest of our Order, a reliable witness, who knew the whole affair"; Caesarius of Heisterbach, *The Dialogues on Miracles*, 2 vols., trans. H. von E. Scott and C. C. Swinton Bland (London: Routledge, 1929), 1:5.16, p. 336.

47. Johannes Herolt, *Miracles of the Blessed Virgin Mary*, ed. G. G. Coulton and Eileen Power, trans. C. C. Swinton Bland (London: Routledge, 1928), xix.

48. Caesarius of Heisterbach, *Dialogues*, 2:9.1, p. 108.

49. Ibid., 1.

50. Oakley, *Western Church*, 236.

51. Stephen Greenblatt, *Shakespearean Negotiations: The Circulation of Social Energy in Renaissance England* (Berkeley and Los Angeles: University of California Press, 1988), 4–5.

Chapter 1. Early Rosaries

1. Guido Dreves and Clemens Blume, eds., *Analecta hymnica medii aevi*, (1886–1922; repr. Frankfurt am Main: Minerva, 1961), vols. 6, 35, 36, but also 3:22–24, 38:239–44.

2. For the origin of the seventh-century antiphon see Scherschel, *Der Rosenkranz*, 53–54. For a history of the Hail Mary see Esser, "Geschichte des englischen Grußes"; Beissel, *Geschichte der Verehrung Marias in Deutschland*, 228–50; Thurston, "Our Popular Devotions," 96:403–18, 513–27, 97:67–79; and idem, *Familiar Prayers*, 90–114.

3. See, for example, Caesarius of Heisterbach, *Dialogues on Miracles*, book 7, no. 49, 1:533; Thurston, *Familiar Prayers*, 103; Scherschel, *Jesusgebet*, 57; Harry L. D. Ward and John A. Herbert, eds., *Catalogue of Romances in the Department of Manuscripts of the British Museum*, 3 vols. (1893, repr. London: British Museum, 1962) 2:634, 668; Adolfo Mussafia, *Studien zu den mittelalterlichen Marienlegenden*, Sitzungsberichte der kaiserlichen Akademie der Wissenschaften in Wien, Phil.-hist. Klasse, 113 (1886), 927, 942, 115 (1887), 61, 62.

4. Thurston, "Our Popular Devotions," 96:406.

5. Willibald Kirfel, *Der Rosenkranz*, 16–18; Eithne Wilkins, *The Rose-Garden Game: The Symbolic Background to the European Prayer-Beads* (London: Victor Gollancz, 1969), 31–32, Wilfred Cantwell Smith, *Towards a World Theology: Faith and the Comparative History of Religion* (Philadelphia: Westminster, 1981), 12–13.

6. Thomas Esser, *Zur Archäologie der Paternoster-Schnur* (Fribourg: Paulus, 1898), 10–12; Wilkins, *Rose-Garden Game*, 25.

7. Wilkins, *Rose-Garden Game*, 33–34; Esser, *Archäologie*, 9.

8. Thurston, "Our Popular Devotions," 96:407.

9. Caesarius of Heisterbach, *Dialogues*, book 7, no. 49, 1:533.

10. Mussafia, *Marienlegenden* 115 (1887), 60; Thomas Frederick Crane, *The Exempla or Illustrative Stories from the "Sermones vulgares" of Jacques de Vitry*, Folk-lore Society London 26 (London: Nutt, 1890), 223. The mistress, who prays the Hail Marys, becomes convicted of her sin when the wife confronts her and resolves to lead a chaste life thereafter.

11. See, for example, the stories of Eulalia and the young man of Brabant, in Mussafia, *Marienlegenden* 113 (1886), 942, 115 (1887), 62; and "The Monk and Our Lady's Sleeves," in *The Middle English Miracles of the Virgin*, ed. Beverly Boyd (San Marino, Calif.: Huntington Library, 1964), 50–55, 119–22.

12. Cited in Beissel, *Geschichte*, 239. The *Sachsenspiegel* 1.24.3 states that a widow may keep "rings and bracelets, chaplets, psalters, and all books that pertain to the divine service," ed. Karl A. Eckhardt, *Monumenta Germaniae Historica, Fontes Iuris Germanici Antiqui*, n.s., 2d ed. (Göttingen: Musterschmidt, 1955), 1:91. By the middle of the twelfth century, "chaplet" can be found referring to prayer beads or to the spiritual exercise of reciting chains of Aves. "Rosarium" appears to be a translation from the German Rosenkranz (rose wreath) used in German versions of the widely distributed exemplum "Aves Seen as Roses." See Ward and Herbert, *Catalogue of Romances*, 2:668. This legend, called "Marien Rosenkranz" in the Middle High German *Passional* (1280/1300), describes the reciting of chains of Aves as the act of creating a symbolic wreath for the Virgin. In this tale, fifty Ave-salutations chanted by a monk miraculously turn into roses and form a chaplet, which is called a "rosen crantz." Originally, the Latin term *rosarium* had been used to designate a garden or an anthology of texts. By the fourteenth century it had come to refer popularly to fifty salutations to the Virgin. See legend 21 in Hans-Georg Richert, ed., *Marienlegenden aus dem Alten Passional*, Altdeutsche Textbibliothek 64 (Tübingen: Niemeyer, 1965), 115–30. A thorough investigation tracing the origins and distribution of the tale, "Aves seen as roses," can be found in Joseph Dobner, *Die mittelhochdeutsche Versnovelle Marien Rosenkranz* (Borna-Leipzig: Noske, 1928). Werner Ross dates the first

appearances of flower chaplets in romances, troubadour lyrics, and Minnesang about the year 1200; see his "Rose und Nachtigall," *Romanische Forschungen* 67 (1956), 77.

13. Gilles Gérard Meersseman, "Etudes sur les anciennes confréries dominicaines, III. Les congrégations de la Vierge," *Archivum Fratrum Praedicatorum* 22 (1952): 5–176, at 43–44.

14. Esser, *Archäologie*, 8. Eugène Honée offers an interesting perspective on this practice, "Image and Imagination in the Medieval Culture of Prayer: A Historical Perspective," in *The Art of Devotion in the Late Middle Ages in Europe, 1300–1500*, edited by Henk van Os (Princeton: Princeton University Press, 1994), 171–72.

15. Gilles Gérard Meersseman, *Der Hymnos Akathistos im Abendland*, 2 vols., Spicilegium Friburgense 2–3 (Fribourg: Universitätsverlag, 1958–60), 2:3–28.

16. Willam, *Geschichte und Gebetsschule des Rosenkranzes*, 23–44.

17. The *Analecta hymnica* contains eight Marian and Jesus psalters that date from before 1300. See 35:137–52, 153–71, 189–99, 254–62, 263–73; 36:11–26, 42–56, 57–70. In these works the meditations are keyed to the Psalms, and none of them contains a sequenced life-of-Christ narrative similar to that in the Cistercian rosary or Dominic's. Additional psalters and rosaries dating from the fourteenth ceutury and later can be found in volumes 3, 6, 35, 36, and 38. See also Meersseman, *Hymnos Akathistos*, 2:79–159; Franz Josef Mone, ed., *Lateinische Hymnen des Mittelalters*, 3 vols. (Freiburg, 1853–55), vol. 2; and Josef Szövérffy, *Die Annalen der lateinischen Hymnendichtung: Ein Handbuch*, 2 vols. (Berlin: Erich Schmidt, 1964–65), vol. 2.

18. Sr. Mary Immaculate Bodenstedt, *Praying the Life of Christ: First English Translation of the Prayers Concluding the 181 Chapters of the "Vita Christi" of Ludophus the Carthusian*, Analecta Cartusiana 15 (Salzburg: Institut für Englische Sprache und Literatur, Universität Salzburg, 1973), iii; and Richard Kieckhefer, *Unquiet Souls: Fourteenth-Century Saints and Their Religious Milieu* (Chicago: University of Chicago Press, 1984), 90–91, 99.

19. Stadlhuber, "Laienstundengebet," 282, 309.

20. Duffy, *The Stripping of the Altars*, 19.

21. Esser, "Beitrag," 346–60, 409–22, 515–28. See also Thurston, "Our Popular Devotions," 96: 513–27, 97:67–79.

22. Esser, "Beitrag," 410.

23. Andreas Heinz, "Zisterzienser," 262–309.

24. Scherschel, *Rosenkranz*, 144. Klinkhammer dates Dominic's earliest version 1409; see Klinkhammer, *Adolf von Essen*, 220.

25. Dominic writes in the nineteenth exemplum of his "Zwanzig-Exempel-Schrift," printed in Klinkhammer, *Adolf von Essen*, 173–87, "That the life of our Lord Jesus Christ should be set to Ave Marias in the rosary was shown by the Lord himself, as one reads in the 'Book of Spiritual Grace' when he showed Mechtild a beautiful tree with many leaves on which was written: 'Jesus Christ, born of a virgin; Jesus Christ, circumcised on the eighth day; Jesus Christ, whom the three kings worshiped; Jesus Christ, who was presented in the Temple; Jesus Christ, whom John baptized,' etc. And in this manner his life was described point by point in the leaves" (186). Klinkhammer mistakenly attributes this text to Adolf of Essen. See Scherschel, *Rosenkranz*, 134–47, for a critical evaluation of attributions to Adolf. For Mechtild's vision, see *Revelationes Gertrudianae ac Mechthildiane*, ed. Ludwig Paquelin, 2 vols. (Paris: Oudin, 1875–77), 2:30.

26. Heinz, "Zisterzienser," 266, 270, cites the work of three investigators who place the manuscript and the hand that copied the rosary devotion at the beginning of the fourteenth century.

27. For a summary of edited Middle High German rosaries and psalters, see Peter Appelhans, *Untersuchungen zur spätmittelalterlichen Mariendichtung: Die rhythmischen mittelhochdeutschen Mariengrüße*, Germanische Bibliothek, ser. 3: *Untersuchungen* (Heidelberg: Winter, 1970), 35–40.

28. Ibid, 73.

29. Klinkhammer, *Adolf von Essen*, 278.

30. In German they occur in the thirteenth century as "Gegruezet sîstu, Maria, genâden vol. Got ist mit dir. Gesegent bistu ob allen frouwen, und gesegent ist die fruht dînes lîbes (Iesus)." See Appelhans, *Untersuchungen*, 81.

31. The older text (Wrocław, Biblioteka Uniwersytecka, MS I. qu. 269, fol. 59r–v) appears in Josef Klapper, ed., "Miszellen: Mitteldeutsche Texte aus Breslauer Handschriften," *Zeitschrift für deutsche Philologie* 47 (1918): 83–87. The later one (Berlin, Deutsche Staatsbibliothek, MS Germ. qu. 494, fols. 1r–7r) is printed in Philipp Wackernagel, ed., *Das deutsche Kirchenlied von der ältesten Zeit bis zu Anfang des 17. Jahrhunderts*, 5 vols (1864–77; repr. Hildesheim: Olms, 1964), 2:614–17. For a comparison of the two versions and a reconstructed archetype, see Appelhans, *Untersuchungen*, 35–36. The fragmentary early version, in Bavarian dialect, preserves only twenty-five stanzas. The later version consists of sixty-three (rather than fifty) four-line stanzas, each beginning with "Ave Maria." Although Wackernagel in his edition of the Berlin manuscript reduced the number of stanzas to fifty (in order to reveal its character as a rosary), sixty-three is not an unusual number of stanzas for a rosary. Many similar works have sixty-three in honor of the supposed number of years in the life of the Virgin.

32. "a. ma'ya roze ane dorn. / du bist m' zcu troste geborn. / En kunegîne hoch . geborn. / hilf m' daz ich icht w'de vorlorn." Klapper, "Miszellen," 83.

33. This text, in Bavarian dialect, was discovered in the private Brenner zu Grafenegg archive near Krems, Austria. Although the resemblance to Latin texts is strong, comparisons with extant Latin Marian psalters and rosaries yield no work from which this vernacular text might have been translated. It is printed in Anton E. Schönbach, ed., "Aus einem Marienpsalter," *Zeitschrift für deutsches Altertum* 48 (1906): 365–70. For more information on the manuscript see Appelhans, *Untersuchungen*, 37–38.

34. "Ave Maria, von Yesse ein stam, / Von dir chom der edel sam, / Dein chind Jesus, dez suzzer nam / Uns alle unser sunde benam."

35. The earliest manuscript (Nuremberg, Stadtbibliothek, MS Cent. VI, 43v, destroyed during the war) is printed in Karl Bartsch, ed., *Die Erlösung: Mit einer Auswahl geistlicher Dichtungen*, Bibliothek der gesamten deutschen National-Literatur 37 (Quedlinburg and Leipzig: G. Basse, 1858), 284–90, and in Wackernagel, *Kirchenlied*, 2:320–23 (from the Bartsch edition). It also survives in an unedited sixteenth-century version, Berlin, Deutsche Staatsbibliothek MS Germ. oct. 573, fols. 155r–59v. See Appelhans, *Untersuchungen*, 38–39, for a brief description of this manuscript. The Nuremberg text, in Middle German dialect, is prefaced by the rubric: "These are fifty noble salutations to our dear Lady, which are called 'Mary's Rose Garden.' This, you spiritually devout sisters, should like to read in praise of Mary, the esteemed virgin. I also desire from each devout sister a sincere 'Ave Maria' for God's sake" (lvi). Citations are from Bartsch, *Die Erlösung*, 285–90.

36. "Ich grûze dich Marjâ frouwe mîn, / entphâch dit rôsenkrenzelîn, / daz ich dir hûte gesprochen hân."

37. "Ich grûz dich des hemels rôsengarte, / die ûzerwelte reine zarte, / du edel sûze rôsenblûte, / bit got vor mich durch dîne gûte."

38. It is preserved whole or in part in six manuscripts from the fourteenth and the fifteenth centuries. Early-fourteenth-century manuscripts (listed in Appelhans, *Untersuchungen*, 36–37) include Vienna, Nationalbibliothek, MS Vind. 2677, no. 31, fols. 56v–58r; Heidelberg, Universitätsbibliothek, MS Pal germ. 341, fols. 16r–22r; and Geneva, Bibliotheca Bodmeriana, MS I, fols. 18v–24v (formerly Kalocsa Codex). The text in the Kalocsa Codex is printed in Franz Pfeiffer, ed., "Mariengrüsse," *Zeitschrift für deutsches Altertum* 8 (1851): 274–98, and in Wackernagel, *Kirchenlied*, 2:107–14. Rosenhagen hypothesizes that there must have been a still older manuscript of Marian devotional works from which the Heidelberg, Kalocsa, and Vienna manuscripts all copied directly. See Gustav Rosenhagen, ed., *Die Heidelberger Handschrift cod.*

Pal. germ. 341, Deutsche Texte des Mittelalters 17 (Berlin: Weidmann, 1909), xvii. The prayer appears to have originated in a Bavarian- or Middle German-speaking region, possibly Bohemia. Citations are from the Pfeiffer edition.

39. Many psalters and rosaries of the traditional, Marian litany type also vary the salutation in the manner of Konrad von Haimburg's (d. 1360) "Crinale B.M.V.," which uses five different salutations ("ave," "salve," "vale," "gaude," "O Maria"). See *Analecta hymnica,* 3:22–25. For further examples see *Analecta hymnica,* 6:156–59, 160–63; 35:11–25, 172–88, 218–38; 38:239–42.

40. "Wis gegrüezet, Jessê künne, / lop der engel, vröude, wünne, / fürstenkint ûz küneges stamme, / gotes tohter, Kristes amme."

41. "Hilf uns durch die kristes blicke, / die er tet an dich vil dicke / als ein kint an sîne muoter: / swaz dû wilt, durch dich daz tuoter. // Hilf uns, vrouwe, durch die vorhte / die Herôdes der verworhte / mit den kindern an dir mahte. / diu er sluoc unt dich erschrahte. // Hif uns durch daz reine vliehen / nâch Egypten: durch das ziehen / got dû züge an dînen brüsten, / des dich mohte wol gelüsten."

42. "Hilf uns durch daz werde enphâhen / mit den palmen, dô Krist nâhen / Jerusalem der stete wolde, / dâ we lêrte daz er solde." "Hilf uns, vrouwe, durch die vreise / die Krist hêt ûf tôdes reise, / dô Pilâtus twuoc die hende, / daz uns vinde rehter ende."

43. *Analecta hymnica,* 35:79–90, 123–36.

44. The "Rosarium series altera," ibid., 6:163–202.

45. Klinkhammer, *Adolf von Essen,* 111.

46. Ibid., 225–37.

47. Cited from Esser, "Beitrag," 413–16. Besides her assumption and coronation in clause 48, Mary is mentioned in clauses 1–5, 9, 34, 40, and 44.

48. Patrick S. Diehl, *The Medieval European Religious Lyric: An Ars Poetica* (Berkeley and Los Angeles: University of California Press, 1985), 22.

49. Klinkhammer, *Adolf von Essen,* 182.

50. Klinkhammer, *Adolf von Essen,* 93. Alanus states in his *Apologia,* of 1475 (which, according to Meersseman, *Der Hymnos Akathistos,* 2:27, is the only work that reliably can be attributed to Alanus), "in ista sociatione devota nullum est votum, nullum statutum, nulla penitus obligatio ad quodcumque peccatum sive mortale sive veniale, sed tantum ibi est obligatio ad poenam privationis meritorum aliorum iam dictam." Cited in Klinkhammer, *Adolf von Essen,* 345, from Kiel, Universitätsbibliothek, MS Bordesholm 58A, fol. 32.

51. Sprenger's instructions in German are printed in Schütz, *Geschichte des Rosenkranzes,* 25–29. Excerpts from the 1476 and 1480 editions of Michael Francisci's *Quodlibet,* which also describes the brotherhood and its regulations, are printed in Heribert Christian Scheeben, "Michael Francisci ab Insulis O. P., 'Quodlibet de veritate fraternitatis rosarii,' " *Archiv der deutschen Dominikaner* 4 (1951): 97–162. Alanus suggests various methods including: (a) 50 Ave Marias to the Incarnation, 50 to the Passion, and 50 to the honor of all saints; (b) 50 to Mary's physical attributes, 50 to Christ on the Cross, and 50 to the altars in the church; (c) 150 to the virtues of the Blessed Virgin; (d) 150 Aves recited while reviewing one's sins; (e) enumeration of relatives and benefactors, beginning with the pope; (f) listing of the various duties of one's office. See Klinkhammer, *Adolf von Essen,* 92.

52. Esser, "Beitrag," 526–27.

53. See Klinkhammer, *Adolf von Essen,* 347 n. 168; and Esser, "Beitrag," 527.

54. The earliest edition, [. . .] *es ist vnser lieben frowen Rosenkrantz* was published in Basel by Flach in 1475. Two other editions were printed by Knoblochtzer in Strassburg c. 1484 and by Johann and Conrad Hist in Speyer c. 1485. See also Thurston, "Our Popular Devotions," 96: 519 and 416; and *500 Jahre Rosenkranz,* 157.

55. Printed in Ulm by Konrad Dinckmut (1483, 1489, and 1492), in Augsburg by Anton Sorg

(1490 and 1492) and by Lukas Zeissenmair (1495 and 1502). Because the manual cites material from "Maister Alanus" it is usually listed under Alanus de Rupe with the title *Vnser lieben frauen Psalter*.

56. Sorg edition (1492), fol. B7r.

57. Schmitz, *Das Rosenkranzgebet*, 105. See also *Analecta hymnica*, 36:236. Dominic, too, calls it: "dat Rosenkrenztge geziert mit gedechtnisse des leuens vnd lydēs christi" (The rosary, decorated with meditations on the life and suffering of Christ), Esser, "Beitrag," 515.

58. Wilkins, *Rose Garden Game*, has discussed at length the salutary effects of repetitive prayer and the aesthetic qualities of devotional beads.

59. Klinkhammer, *Adolf von Essen*, 278; and idem, "Die Entstehung des Rosenkranzes und seine ursprüngliche Geistigkeit," in *500 Jahre Rosenkranz*, 30–50, at 38. Scherschel, *Rosenkranz*, 137, asserts that there is no basis for Klinkhammer's claims that Adolf practiced this kind of meditation and that he suggested it to Dominic.

60. The legend of Eulalia is quoted in Thurston, "Our Popular Devotions," 96:410–12.

61. Shaw, *Story*, 94.

62. Shaw, *Story*, 127–28, with a translation of de Montfort's formulae.

63. Wackernagel, *Kirchenlied*, 2:860. Another asserts, "Whoever prays three rosaries each week, to him all sins are forgiven, twice, I tell you, once at death and once in life, so help me Mary" (st. 5.1, 5–8), "Ein schon lyet von Marie Rosenkrantz," Wackernagel, *Kirchenlied*, 2:853.

64. A typical example of the testimonial assurances used in popularizing the rosary is found in the fifteenth-century tract of the Sankt Anna-Bruderschaft, edited by Schütz, *Geschichte des Rosenkranzes*, 162–72, which relates the anecdote of a woman's early release from purgatory, saying: "Doctor Alamis [Alanus] writes of the great indulgence and many lovely exempla and wonders in the book that he made about the brotherhood that is called Mary's psalter. In it he tells of the great blessedness and usefulness of this psalter and of how many people have been protected by the Virgin from eternal damnation and quickly released from purgatory, as one reads of a woman named Alexandra who was supposed to suffer 600 years in purgatory but was released in 15 days" (here 168).

65. Dominic advises Benedicta, "Enroll yourself in the brotherhood so that the Mother of all Grace will have mercy on you and come to your aid because of the merits of the other brothers and sisters of the psalter." The text of the story of Benedicta can be found in the statutes of the Colmar brotherhood edited by Schmitt, "La Confrérie," 97–124, here 117.

66. Schütz, *Geschichte des Rosenkranzes*, 26.

67. Jean-Claude Schmitt, "Apostolat mendiant." The fifteenth-century tract of the Sankt Anna-Bruderschaft, edited by Schütz, *Geschichte des Rosenkranzes*, 162–72, contains an invitation to women to join that states: "The brotherhood accepts everyone for God's sake with no fee, [whether] rich or poor, man or woman, layperson or religious" (here 164). In addition, a popular song from 1500 by Sixt Buchsbaum, called "Unser lieben frawen Rosenkrantz," welcomes women into the confraternity, saying: "Mary has chosen / those who pray her psalter, / has gathered them in her brotherhood / and will represent them before God. / Be they woman or man / whoever calls upon her / she will stand by faithfully." Wackernagel, *Kirchenlied*, 2:854, st. 1.7–13.

68. Diehl, *Religious Lyric*, 42.

69. Duffy stresses the "vitality" of traditional religion and asserts that "the laity were able to appropriate, develop, and use the repertoire of interited ritual" to meet their spiritual needs, *Altars*, 2, 5, and 7.

70. Paul Zumthor, "The Text and the Voice," *New Literary History* 16, no. 1 (1984): 67–92, at 67.

71. See Suzanne Fleischmann, "Philology, Linguistics, and the Discourse of the Medieval Text," *Speculum* 65 (1990): 19–37, at 22; and David R. Olsen, "From Utterance to Text: The Bias of Language in Speech and Writing," *Harvard Educational Review* 47 (1977): 257–81, at 258.

Chapter 2. The Picture Text and Its "Readers"

1. Estimates are clearly uncertain but Rolf Engelsing judges literacy to have been no higher than 5 percent, *Analphabetentum und Lektüre: Zur Sozialgeschichte des Lesens in Deutschland zwischen feudaler und industrieller Gesellschaft* (Stuttgart: Metzler, 1973), 6–38; and Robert W. Scribner, *For the Sake of Simple Folk: Popular Propaganda for the German Reformation*, Cambridge Studies in Oral Literature and Culture 2 (Cambridge: Cambridge University Press, 1981), 1–9.

2. Scribner, *Simple Folk*, 1, and idem, *Popular Culture and Popular Movements in Reformation Germany* (London: Hambledon, 1987), 49–69.

3. Surviving copies of the 1483 and 1489 Dinckmut editions lack a title page, but Dinckmut's 1492 edition (Hain 14041) bears the name, *Vnser lieben frauen Psalter*. See Amelung, *Frühdruck*, 1:236–43.

4. Thomas Esser, "Über die allmähliche Einfrührung der jetzt beim Rosenkranz üblichen Betrachtungspunkte," *Der Katholik* 30 (1904): 114. Jakob Schütz gives examples of twenty-five different kinds of rosaries in *Geschichte des Rosenkranzes*, 88–238. See also Kirfel, *Rosenkranz*, 9–10; and Willam, *Geschichte und Gebetsschule*, 41–44. A good impression of how many varieties of rosaries were included in prayer books of the sixteenth century can be had by examining the inventory of prayer-book contents in Gerard Achten, *Das christliche Gebetbuch im Mittelalter: Andachts- und Stundenbücher in Handschrift und Frühdruck*, Staatsbibliothek Preußischer Kulturbesitz, exh. cat. 13 (Wiesbaden: Reichert, 1980).

5. The earliest edition, [. . .] *es ist vnser lieben frowen Rosenkrantz* was published in Basel by Flach in 1475. Two other editions were printed by Knoblochtzer in Strasbourg c. 1484 and by Johann and Conrad Hist in Speyer c. 1485.

6. Because the manual cites material from "maister alanus," it is usually listed under Alanus de Rupe. For the seven editions published by Dinckmut and Sorg between 1483 and 1496 see Amelung, *Frühdruck*, 1:237, 242–43. Two further editions were printed by Zeissenmair in Augsburg in 1495 and 1502.

7. Sixten Ringbom, *Icon to Narrative: The Rise of the Dramatic Close-up in Fifteenth-Century Devotional Painting*, Humaniora 31, no. 2 (Åbo: Åbo Akademi, 1965), 16 and 19; and idem, "Devotional Images and Imaginative Devotions. Notes on the Place of Art in late Medieval Private Piety," *Gazette des Beaux-Arts* 73 (1969): 159.

8. Cited by Herbert Thurston, "Our Popular Devotions," 96:524, from the 1488 edition of the *Compendium psalterii beatissimae Trinitatis*, fol. C7r. The most accessible edition of the *Compendium* is the 1505 Italian text printed in Stefano Orlandi, *Libro del Rosario*, 181–214, here 205.

9. Bertilo de Boer, "De Souter van Alanus de Rupe," *Ons Geestelijk Erf* 33 (1959): 153.

10. Esser, "Über die allmähliche Einführung," 33:66.

11. Robert Calkins, *Illuminated Books of the Middle Ages* (Ithaca: Cornell University Press, 1983), 246–48; James Snyder, *Northern Renaissance Art: Painting, Sculpture, the Graphic Arts from 1350–1575* (New York: Abrams, 1985), 21; and Flóris Szabó and Elisabeth Soltész, *Horae Beatae Mariae Virginis: Zwei Aufsätze über den Kodex der Erzabtei Pannonhalma* (Budapest: Kossuth, 1985), 25–26.

12. Cf. *Biblia pauperum*, ed. Avril Henry (Ithaca: Cornell University Press, 1987): and *The Mirour of Mans Saluacioune: A Middle Enlgish Translation of "Speculum humanae salvationis,"* ed. Avril Henry (Philadelphia: University of Pennsylvania Press, 1987).

13. See Christian Heße and Martina Schlagenhaufer, *Wallraf-Richartz-Museum Köln: Vollständiges Verzeichnis der Gemäldesammlung* (Cologne and Milan: DuMont/Electa, 1986), 116–176, esp. pls. 071, 078a–e, 081a–c, 082, 148a–149b, 153a–h, 189–191a–1, 217a, 250a–c, 253.

14. In their earliest form, meditations on the five joys of the Virgin date back to the seventh

century. Later versions expand the list to seven joys (perhaps by association with the seven gifts of the Holy Spirit), then to twelve, and finally to fifteen or more joys. See Gilles Gérard Meersseman, *Hymnos Akathistos*, 2:37–43; Stephan Beissel, *Geschichte der Verehrung Marias in Deutschland*, 632–34. French books of hours typically include a meditation on the fifteen joys of the Virgin, which is not part of most Dutch Books of Hours; see Calkins, *Illuminated*, 245. In England a meditation on the fifteen joys was popular among Cistercian nuns as early as the thirteenth century. See André Wilmart, "Les Méditations d'Etienne de Salley sur les joies de la Vierge Marie," in *Auteurs spirituels et textes dévots du moyen âge latin* (Paris: Bloud and Gay, 1932), 317–60.

15. *Blockbücher des Mittelalters: Bilderfolgen als Lektüre*, Gutenberg-Gesellschaft and Gutenberg Museum, exh. cat. (Mainz: von Zabern, 1991), 56, 187.

16. Beissel, *Geschichte der Verehrung Marias in Deutschland*, 632.

17. Erwin Vischer, *Formschnitte des fünfzehnten Jahrhunderts in der großherzoglichen Hof- und Landesbibliothek zu Karlsruhe* (Strasbourg: Heitz, 1912), 15.

18. See Meersseman, *Akathistos*, 3:39; Beissel, *Geschichte der Verehrung Marias in Deutschland*, 408; and Georg Söll, "Maria in der Geschichte von Theologie und Frömmigkeit," in *Handbuch der Marienkunde*, ed. Wolfgang Beinert and Heinrich Petri (Regensburg: Pustet, 1984), 164. A survey of devotions on the joys of Mary listed by Beissel (*Geschichte der Verehrung Marias in Deutschland*, 632–34) and contained in the *Analecta hymnica* shows that early meditations on the five joys divide attention between Christ's infancy and praise of Mary as the God-bearer and intercessor. The seven joys typically add Christ's Resurrection, Ascension, the Pentecost outpouring of the Holy Spirit, and the Assumption of the Virgin. Longer lists from the fourteenth century introduce the heavenly joys, recounting Mary's honors as Queen of Heaven, while fifteenth-century examples of fourteen or fifteen meditations focus on earthly joys, giving more space to a detailed portrayal of earthly life of Mary, particularly the infancy of Christ. They expand the events of the infancy from three to nine scenes, add brief coverage of Christ's ministry (usually three scenes), and keep the same post-Resurrection series.

19. Wilhelm L. Schreiber, *Handbuch der Holz- und Metallschnitte des XV. Jahrhunderts*, 2d ed., 8 vols. (Leipzig: Hiersemann, 1926–30), 2:153.

20. Another print with very similar images and text now in the Rosenwald collection of the National Gallery of Art bears the date 1485. See Schreiber, *Handbuch*, 2:153 (see Fig. 6).

21. See Ferdinand Geldner, *Die deutschen Inkunabeldrucker des XV. Jahrhunderts*, 2 vols. (Stuttgart: Hiersemann, 1968), 1:292–93. Both pictures and text are reproduced on microfilm in Bildarchiv Foto Marburg, *Marburger Index: Bilddokumentation zur Kunst in Deutschland* (Munich: Verlag Dokumentation, 1976–), no. 2418E10-G9. Other likely candidates include some of the narrative altarpieces composed of scenes of the Passion that end with the same Last Judgment scene depicted in the picture rosary. See, for example, Heße and Schlagenhaufer, *Wallraf*, plates 071, 078e, 081b, and 253.

22. The joys depicted include: (1) the Annunciation, (2) the Visitation, (3) the Nativity, (4) the Magi, (5) the Presentation, (6) Finding the Child Jesus in the Temple, (7) Mary's Assumption and the Coronation. Immediately following are nineteen illustrations of the Passion including: (1) the Entry into Jerusalem, (2) the Mount of Olives, (3) the Arrest, (4) Christ before Caiaphas, (5) the Flagellation, (6) the Crowning with Thorns, (7) Herod and Pilate, (8) Veronica, (9) Carrying the Cross, (10) Nailing on the Cross, (11) Crucifixion and Death, (12) the Lamentation, (13) the Entombment, (14) the Harrowing of Hell, (15) the Resurrection, (16) the Appearance to Mary Magdalene, (17) the Ascension, (18) Pentecost, and (19) the Last Judgment.

23. See Emile Mâle, *Religious Art in France: The Thirteenth Century. A Study of Medieval Iconography and Its Sources*, trans. Marthiel Mathews, Bollingen Series 90, no. 3 (Princeton: Princeton University Press, 1984), 184; Johannes Beer, *Die Illustration des Lebens Jesu in den deutschen Frühdrucken (c. 1460–1500)*, Archiv für Schreib- und Buchwesen, Sonderheft 3 (Wolfenbüttel: Heckner, 1929), 8 and 17.

24. Stadlhuber, "Laienstundengebet," 318, 322; and Kieckhefer, *Unquiet Souls*, 89–121.

25. Stadlhuber, "Laienstundengebet," 288.

26. Ernst Schubert, *Einführung*, 274.

27. Richard Kieckhefer has pointed this out in his "Major Currents," 100.

28. Thomas Cramer, ed., *Die kleineren Liederdichter des 14. und 15. Jahrhunderts*, 4 vols. (Munich: W. Fink, 1977–85), 1:86–103, 428–38; and Philipp Wackernagel, ed., *Das deutsche Kirchenlied*, 2:854–59; and Frieder Schanze, "Sixt Buchsbaum," in *Die deutsche Literatur des Mittelalters, Verfasserlexikon* (Berlin: de Gruyter, 1978), 1:cols. 1109–10.

29. Cramer, *Liederdichter*, 427.

30. Marcus von Weida, *Der Spiegel hochloblicher Bruderschafft des Rosenkrantz Marie*, ed. Anthonÿ van der Lee, Quellen und Forschungen zur Erbauungsliteratur des späten Mittelalters und der frühen Neuzeit 3. (Amsterdam: Rodopi, 1978).

31. Heinz, "Zisterzienser," 281, 303.

32. See Dominic's "Zwanzig-Exempel" in Klinkhammer, *Adolf von Essen*, 185.

33. Natalie Z. Davis, *Society and Culture in Early Modern France: Eight Essays* (Stanford: Stanford University Press, 1975), 210.

34. Tessa Watt, *Cheap Print and Popular Piety, 1550–1640* (Cambridge: Cambridge University Press, 1991), 6–7, 12–13, 131.

35. See Stephen G. Nichols, "Introduction: Philology in a Manuscript Culture," *Speculum* 65 (1990): 8.

36. Johannes Lambsheym, *Libellus perutilis de fraternitate sanctissima et Rosario Marie virginis* (Mainz: Peter von Friedberg, 1495), pars. 2, c. 7.

37. See Esser, "Über die allmähliche Einführung," 30:358; and Thurston, "Our Popular Devotions," 96:631. That sequencing of illustrations in the Middle Ages was not so standard as it is today has been shown by Marilyn Aronberg Lavin, *The Place of Narrative: Mural Decoration in Italian Churches, 431–1600* (Chicago: University of Chicago Press, 1990).

38. Nichols, "Philology," 8–9, refers to the "manuscript matrix."

39. Esser, "Über die allmähliche Einführung," 32:201–16, 252–66, 332–50.

40. For picture rosaries see Esser, "Über die allmähliche Einführung," 32:252–66; Beissel, *Geschichte der Verehrung Marias in Deutschland*, 557–67; Augusta van Oertzen, *Maria, die Königin des Rosenkranzes: Eine Ikonographie des Rosenkranzgebetes durch zwei Jahrhunderte deutscher Kunst* (Augsburg: Filser, 1925); and Frances H. A. van den Oudendijk-Pieterse, *Dürers Rosenkranzfest en de ikonografie der Duitse rozenkransgroepen van de XV en het begin der XVI eew* (Amsterdam and Antwerp: Spiegel, 1939).

41. The instructions indicate only that the first round should be recited "in honor of the incarnation and Mary's motherly love, the second in honor of Christ's suffering and that of Mary, the third in praise of the glory of Christ and Mary. See Oertzen, *Maria, die Königin*, 28. The meditations begin in the inner circle at lower left and move clockwise. Here the Visitation (usually no. 2) is missing and the Raising of Lazarus has been included as no. 5. In the middle ring, beginning bottom center, Christ before Pilate has been inserted before the Flagellation (usually no. 2) and the Carrying of the Cross (usually no. 4) has been left out.

42. See Esser, "Über die allmähliche Einführung," 32:213–16.

43. See Arthur M. Hind, *Early Italian Engravings: A Critical Catalogue with Complete Reproduction of all the Prints Described*, 7 vols. in 4 (1938–48; repr. Nendeln, Liechtenstein: Kraus, 1970), 1:119–20, 3:pls. 172–87.

44. Herolt, *Miracles*, xxix.

45. The painting is now held by the Kurpfälzisches Museum in Heidelberg. See Oertzen, *Maria, die Königin*, 34–35.

46. Alberto da Castello, *Rosario della gloriosa vergine Maria* (Venice: Ravani, 1521). For a summary of the editions, see Esser, "Über die allmähliche Einführung," 32:337.

47. Andrea Gianetti da Salo, *Rosario della sacratissima Vergine Maria raccolto dall' opere del R.P.F. Luigi di Granata* (Rome: Angeli, 1573), 56, 104, and 160.

48. Gaspare Loarte, *Instrvctions and Advertisements: How to Meditate on the Misteries of the Rosarie of the Most Holy Virgin Mary*, trans. J. Fenne (Rouen: n.p., 1600?), fol. 104r.

49. Adam Walasser, *Von der gnadenreichen, hochberümpten . . . Bruderschaft des Psalters oder Rosenkrantz Marie* (Dillingen: Sebaldus Mayer, 1572).

50. Ibid., fol. 33.

51. Willam, *Geschichte und Gebetsschule*, 79.

52. Nichols, "Philology," 8.

Chapter 3. One for Sorrow, Two for Joy

1. Esser, "Über die allmähliche Einführung," 30:98–114, 192–217, 280–301, 351–73; 32:201–16, 252–66, 323–50; 33:49–66.

2. Ibid., 32:208–11; 30:284–91, 296, 297–99.

3. Thurston, "Our Popular Devotions," 96:628.

4. "Dans les textes du 15e siècle ni le *Livre et ordonnance* de Douai (1475), ni le *Quodlibet* de Michel François, ni le légat Malatesta (10 mai 1476), ni l'évêque de Sibenik (30 nov. 1478), ni les bulles *Pastoris aeterni* (30 mai 1478) ou *Ea quae* (17 mai 1479) de Sixte IV, ni le chapitre général dominicain de 1484 ne font allusion à la manière de réciter les Ave Maria sinon pour en fixer le nombre." Duval, "Rosaire," in *Dictionnaire de spiritualité*, 13:col. 955.

5. Gilles Gérard Meersseman, *Ordo Fraternitatis*, 3:1157–58, 1164–65; Esser, "Über die allmähliche Einführung," 30:284.

6. Thurston, "Our Popular Devotions," 96:417 and 515; and Carl Horstmann, ed., *Altenglische Legenden: Neue Folge* (1881; repr. Hildesheim: Olms, 1969), 220–24.

7. Gilles G. Meersseman, *Ordo Fraternitatis*, 3:1164; also printed in André Wilmart, "Comment Alain de la Roche prêchait le rosaire ou psautier de la Vierge," *La Vie et les arts liturgiques* 11 (1924–25): 108–15. Specifically, the Douai instructions state that members should pray each day, 150 salutations "in remembrance of the 150 prophecies that were spoken of [Mary's] blessed son Jesus and likewise of her; and also in remembrance of the 150 joys that she had with her blessed child before his sorrowful Passion; and, also in honor of the 150 pains that she suffered in her child's blessed death and Passion."

8. Meersseman, *Ordo Fraternitatis*, 3:1165. Although Heinrich Egher of Kalkar (d. 1408) is often credited with having been the first to divide the Ave psalter into fifteen decades, Thurston disputes this claim, "Our Popular Devotions," 96:416–17.

9. Meersseman warns that the *Liber apologeticus* is reliable only in the earliest editions, *Hymnos Akathistos*, 3:27. This cautionary note, no doubt, refers to Johann Andreas Coppenstein's *Beatus Alanus de Rupe redivivus de Psalterio seu Rosario Christi ac Mariae* (Cologne: P. Henning, 1624), an edition of Alanus's works that have been largely rewritten. The 1498 edition of *Magister Alanus de Rupe, sponsus novellus beatissime virginis Marie . . . de immensa et ineffabili dignitate et utilitate psalterii precelse ac intemerate semper virginis Marie*, published by the Monastery of Mariefred (Gripsholm, 1498), contains an early version of the "Liber Apologeticus," fols. R6r–X3v. Klinkhammer quotes from the Kiel MSS, Bordesholm 58A and 58B; see Klinkhammer, *Adolf von Essen*, 92 and 344 n. 100.

10. Scheeben, "Michael Francisci ab Insulis," 106–7.

11. Ibid., 97–98.

12. Michael's recommendation is to meditate on "the 150 joys that the Virgin had on earth with her son, an equal number of sorrows she endured at the Passion, and an equivalent number of joys that she now enjoys in heaven above all the saints." Scheeben, "Michael Francisci ab

Insulis," 154–55. Fifteen Paternosters to the Passion of Christ are present as well among the many meditations offered in Alanus's *Liber apologeticus* that is contained in *Magister Alanus de Rupe*, fols. R8v–Sr. In addition, the *Compendium psalterii beatissime Trinitatis*, compiled from Alanus's works by his followers, c. 1478, describes the Psalter of Our Lady as consisting of 150 Aves that correspond to the psalms of David plus fifteen Paternosters that commemorate Christ's Passion. An Italian translation of the *Compendium* is printed in Orlandi, *Libro del Rosario*, 181–214, here 183.

13. See the text of Sprenger's German statutes printed in Schütz, *Geschichte des Rosenkranzes*, 26. The reference to white and red is also already present in Alan's account of his vision in which the Virgin charged him to preach her psalter. The vision is recounted in *Magister Alanus de Rupe*, fol. A3v, cited by Thurston, "Our Popular Devotions," 96:623. Here Alan refers to fifty Aves to the incarnation as "white" and fifty Aves to the passion as "red." In Sprenger's version, however, red refers to Paternosters rather than Aves.

14. This copy (Hain 14962), printed by Johannes Bämler in Augsburg, is held by the Staatsbibliothek in Bamberg.

15. The written text of this prayer as outlined in the Colmar statutes states:

Whoever wants to pray a rosary to the praise and honor of Our Dear Lady, let him first pray the creed, which represents the circlet on which he shall bind the roses. After that let him pray ten Ave Marias in praise of Our Lady when she received the greeting of the angel Gabriel. Then say the first Pater Noster to the sufferings of Christ that he received on the Mount of Olives where he sweat drops of blood. Then again pray ten Ave Marias in praise of Our Lady when she went over the mountains to her cousin Elisabeth. Then say the second Pater Noster to the sufferings of Christ that he received in the flagellation. Then again ten Ave Marias in praise of Our Dear Lady to the joy that she experienced when she gave birth to Our Lord. After that say the third Pater Noster to the suffering that Christ endured when he was crowned with thorns. Then another ten Ave Marias in praise of Our Dear Lady for the joy that she felt when she saw our Lord sitting in the Temple in the midst of the learned doctors. After that say the fourth Pater Noster in praise of the sufferings of Christ that he experienced on the way to the crucifixion. Then say ten Ave Marias in praise of the joy that Our Lady had at her death and assumption to heaven. Then say the fifth Pater Noster to the suffering, the pain, and the bitter death that he [Christ] endured on the cross.

Schmitt, "La Confrérie," 106.

16. See the text of this handbook printed in Schütz, *Geschichte des Rosenkranzes*, 109–22, at 112.

17. This pamphlet lists the "seven great joys that [Mary] had on earth" as: (1) when she conceived the Son of God, (2) when she visited her cousin Elisabeth, (3) when she gave birth, (4) when the three kings came, (5) when she presented her child [at the temple], (6) when Christ arose, and (7) when he ascended into heaven. The second rosary recounts the five "heartaches" (*herzlaid*) that Mary suffered for her son: (1) Simeon's prophecy, (2) when Jesus was lost [at age 12], (3) when Mary heard of his arrest, (4) when she saw her son crucified, (5) when she saw him buried. The third rosary recounts Mary's seven great joys in heaven: (1) her glory and honor surpass that of all the saints, (2) she sits transfigured in body by the Trinity, (3) all the heavenly host honor and obey her as mother of the Highest King, (4) like the sun she illuminates the Heavenly Host, (5) the wishes of the Trinity are united with hers, (6) the Trinity will reward those who serve her according to her wishes, (7) she has the certainty that her joys will last for eternity. See *Ein GAR nützlich Büchlein von dem Psalter oder Rosenkranz Marie* (Ulm: Schäffer, 1501), fols. B1r–B2v.

18. Orlandi, *Libro del Rosario*, 215–25.

19. Meersseman, *Ordo Fraternitatis*, 3:1214–18.

20. Meersseman, *Ordo Fraternitatis*, 3:1177–83; Orlandi, *Libro del Rosario*, 130 n. 1; and *Acta Sanctae Sedis necnon magistrorum et capitulorum generalium Sacri Ordinis Praedicatorum pro Societate Ss. Rosarii*, 2 vols. in 4, ed. Josephi Mariae Larroca (Lyon: Jevain, 1890–91), 2:1260. The *Acta Sanctae Sedis pro societate SS. Rosarii* lists 1481 as the year of his death, which, Meersseman states, is probably incorrect.

21. Oudendijk-Pieterse, *Dürers Rosenkranzfest.*

22. The Venice statutes, printed in Meersseman, *Ordo Fraternitatis*, 3:1215–18, are an adaptation of Sprenger's German statutes printed in Augsburg in 1476 and 1477. See also pp. 1183–84.

23. Mary Juliana Schroeder, *Mary-verse in "Meistergesang,"* Catholic University of America Studies in German 16 (1942; repr. New York: AMS Press, 1970), 217 n. 127; and Wackernagel, *Das deutsche Kirchenlied*, 2:324n.

24. Scheeben, "Michael Francisci ab Insulis," 154.

25. Alanus de Rupe, "Liber apologeticus," in *Magister Alanus de Rupe*, chap. 14.

26. See Thurston, "Our Popular Devotions," 96:517, 526–27; 97:67–79, 287. Thurston relates Alanus's account of a Carthusian monk of Trier who saw in a vision Mary's psalter being recited. The story was earlier related by Dominic of Prussia as a vision that had been reported by Adolf of Essen. The account Thurston cites is from *Magister Alanus de Rupe*, fol. Z4v.

27. Alanus's personal vision of the Virgin is related in Herbert Thurston, "Alanus de Rupe and his Indulgence of 60,000 Years," *The Month* 100 (1902): 290–91, and cited from *Magister Alanus de Rupe*, chap. 10, fols. S6v and S8r. Alan's report of the Virgin's charge to "Saint Dominic" is found in the *Compendium psalterii beatissime Trinitatis*. See Esser, "Über die allmähliche Einführung," 30:284; or the 1505 Italian edition printed in Orlandi's *Libro del Rosario*, 181–214, at 184.

28. This method is the first one listed in section 5, "How to Pray the Psalter." After describing three ways to say the prayer, the handbook states: "[B]ut the first method is the one that was taught by St. Dominic," *Von dem psalter vnnd Rosen krancz vnser lieben frauen* (Augsburg: Anton Sorg, 1492), fols. B5r and B6r.

29. Oddly, the version of Dominic's fifty clausulae from the *Liber experientiarum* printed by Esser in "Beitrag zur Geschichte," 413–16, mentions the Last Judgment only indirectly; whereas the overwhelming majority of sets of the fifty clausulae both in Latin and German and including those attributed to Dominic of Prussia do contain it. See Klinkhammer, *Adolf von Essen*, 222–23, 238–40, 241–46, 246–50; Karl Euling, ed., *Kleinere mittelhochdeutsche Erzählungen, Fabeln und Lehrgedichte II: Die Wolfenbüttler Handschrift 2. 4. Aug. 2°*, Deutsche Texte des Mittelalters 14 (Berlin: Weidmann, 1908), 184–95; Schütz, *Geschichte*, 155–57, 158–61; Dreves and Blume, eds., *Analecta hymnica*, 36:220–22, 223–37, 228–30, 233–35; and *Dis ist Unser lyeben frowen Rosenkrantz und wie er von ersten ist uffkummen* (Speyer: Johannes and Conrad Hist, 1485), fols. 2v–4v.

30. Landsberg suggests a three-part schema of 20, 20, and 10, organizing the meditations so that the first two decades encompass "the 20 principal joys that the Virgin experienced in the incarnation, birth, and childhood of Jesus." The next two decades, 20–39, contain "the pain and sorrows that she endured during the bitter suffering of her son"; and the fifth decade includes "the joy that she had at the Resurrection, Ascension, Sending of the Holy Spirit, and in her own Glorification." See Esser, "Über die allmähliche Einführung," 30:210.

31. Sprenger's statute begins with the explanation, "To the honor of the esteemed mother and unblemished Virgin Mary I, brother Jakob Sprenger, doctor of the Holy Scriptures and prior of the great Dominican convent of Cologne have in the year [14]75 on the day of our Lady's birth revived and reestablished the traditional, old prayer of the rosary of Our Lady." See Schütz, *Geschichte des Rosenkranzes*, 25–26.

32. See Francis Xavier Martin, "The Augustinian Observant Movement," in *Reformbemühungen und Observanzbestrebungen im spätmittelalterlichen Ordenswesen*, ed. Kaspar Elm, Berliner Historische Studien 14, Ordensstudien 6 (Berlin: Duncker and Humblot, 1989), 333, 336–38; and Johannes Meyer, *Buch der Reformacio Predigerordens*, ed. Benedictus Maria Reichert, Quellen und Forschungen zur Geschichte des Dominikanerordens in Deutschland 2, no. 3 (Leipzig: Harrassowitz, 1908–9), 3:ii–v, 7–9.

33. Meyer, *Reformacio*, 3:9.

34. Ibid., 7–11.

35. Gabriel M. Löhr, *Die Teutonia im 15. Jahrhundert: Studien und Texte vornehmlich zur Geschichte ihrer Reform*, Quellen und Forschungen zur Geschichte des Dominikanerordens in Deutschland 19 (Leipzig: Harrassowitz, 1924), 2–6; and Meyer, *Reformacio*, 2:xiv–xv.

36. Meyer, *Reformacio*, 2:x.

37. Eugen Hillenbrand, "Die Observantenbewegung in der deutschen Ordensprovinz der Dominikaner" in *Reformbemühungen und Observanzbestrebungen*, ed. Elm, 235; and Bernt Hamm, *Frömmigkeitstheologie am Anfang des 16. Jahrhunderts: Studien zu Johannes von Paltz und seinem Umkreis*, Beiträge zur Historischen Theologie 65 (Tübingen: Mohr, 1982), 296.

38. Martin, "Augustinian," 338, 339.

39. Löhr, *Teutonia*, 17–18.

40. Hans-Joachim Schmidt, "Die Trierer Erzbischöfe und die Reform von Kloster und Stift im 15. Jahrhundert," in *Reformbemühungen*, ed. Elm, 472, 474–75; and Heinrich Rüthing, "Die Karthäuser und die spätmittelalterlichen Ordensreformen," in *Reformbemühungen*, ed. Elm, 40.

41. Heinz, "Eine spätmittelalterliche Exempelsammlung," 307–8; Klinkhammer, *Adolf von Essen*, 54–56; and Petrus Becker, "Erstrebte und erreichte Ziele benediktinischer Reformen im Spätmittelalter," in *Reformbemühungen*, ed. Elm, 23–34, here 26.

42. Paulus von Loë, *Statistisches über die Ordensprovinz Saxonia*, Quellen und Forschungen zur Geschichte des Dominikanerordens in Deutschland 4 (Leipzig: Harrassowitz, 1910), 39; and Albert de Meyer, *La Congrégation de Hollande ou la réforme dominicaine en territoire bourguignon (1465–1515)* (Liege: Soledi, 1946), 433.

43. De Meyer, *Congrégation*, 433; and Thomas Kaeppeli, *Scriptores ordinis Praedicatorum medii aevi*, 3 vols. (Rome: Vatican, 1970–80), 1:21.

44. De Meyer, *Congrégation*, lxxxi.

45. *Von dem psalter vnnd Rosenkrancz vnser lieben frauen*, fols. A3r, and B8 r–v.

46. Heinrich Hubert Koch, *Das Dominikanerkloster zu Frankfurt am Main (13. bis 16. Jahrhundert)* (Freiburg: Herder, 1892), 61; and Wolfgang Kliem, *Die spätmittelalterliche Frankfurter Rosenkranzbruderschaft als volkstümliche Form der Gebetsverbrüderung* (Ph.D. diss., University of Frankfurt, 1962), 92.

47. Meyer, *Reformacio*, 3:42–53, 148–50. See also Annette Barthelmé, *La Réforme dominicaine au XVe siècle en Alsace et dans l'ensemble de la province de Teutonie*, Collection d'études sur l'histoire du droit et des institutions de l'Alsace 7 (Strasbourg: Heitz, 1931), 150.

48. Médard Barth, "Die Rosenkranzbruderschaften des Elsass geschichtlich gewürdigt," *Archives de l'église d'Alsace* 16 (1967–68): 61.

49. Paul Ruf, "Der Augsburger Pfarrer Molitoris und sein Holzschnittsiegel," *Zeitschrift für bayerische Landesgeschichte* 3 (1930): 404–5; Kliem, *Frankfurter*, 68; Benedictus Maria Reichert, ed., *Registrum litterarum: Raymundi de Capua, 1386–1399, Leonardi de Mansuetis, 1474–1480*, Quellen und Forschungen zur Geschichte des Dominikanerordens in Deutschland 6 (Leipzig: Harrassowitz, 1911), 50.

50. Ruf, "Augsburger," 393.

51. Barth, "Rosenkranzbruderschaften," 64.

52. See Martin, "Augustinian," 339; and Denys Hay, *The Church in Italy in the Fifteenth Century* (Cambridge: Cambridge University Press, 1977), 68.

53. Gabriel M. Löhr, ed., *Registrum litterarum pro provincia Saxoniae*, Quellen und Forschungen zur Geschichte des Dominikanerordens in Deutschland 37 (Leipzig: Harrassowitz, 1939), 52, 66, 72. Servatius Petrus Wolfs mentions that three vicars of the Congregation of Holland, Adrianus van der Meer, Michael Francisci, and Cornelius van Sneek, themselves wrote works about the rosary. See Wolfs, "Dominikanische Observanzbestrebungen: Die Congregatio Hollandiae (1464–1517), in *Reformbemühungen*, ed. Elm, 291. In addition, Observantist preachers such as Clemens Lossow and Guillaume Pepin published sermons and other works on the rosary. See Theodor Rensing, "Die Reformbewegung in den westfälischen Dominikanerklöstern" *Westfalen* 17 (1932): 95; Larissa Taylor, *Soldiers of Christ: Preaching in Late Medieval and Reformation France* (Oxford: Oxford University Press, 1992), 48; and Marcus von Weida, *Der Spiegel*, 29.

54. Carl Blasel, "Studien zur Geschichte der Rosenkranzbruderschaft bei St. Adalbert in Breslau," *Schlesisches Pastoralblatt* 33 (1912): 24–25.

55. Löhr, *Registrum*, 58; Wolfs, "Congregatio," 286; and Meersseman, *Ordo Fraternitatis*, 3:1176, 1180.

56. Meersseman, *Ordo Fraternitatis*, 3:1185–89.

57. Schütz, *Geschichte des Rosenkranzes*, 26–27.

58. Ibid., 28.

59. Ibid., 28.

60. Meersseman, *Ordo Fraternitatis*, 3:1163–64.

61. *Ein GAR nützlich Büchlein*, fol. B3v.

62. Blasel, "Studien," 3.

63. André Vauchez, *The Laity in the Middle Ages: Religious Beliefs and Devotional Practices*, ed. Daniel E. Bornstein, trans. Margery J. Schneider (Notre Dame: University of Notre Dame Press, 1993), 111, 114.

64. Kieckhefer, "Major Currents," 100.

65. Steven Ozment, *Reformation in the Cities*, 21; and idem, *Age of Reform*, 219.

66. See the 1476 edition printed in Schütz, *Geschichte des Rosenkranzes*, 28; and Jacob Sprenger, *In spiritu penses hoc opus* . . . (Augsburg: Bämler, 1477), fol. 6r.

Chapter 4. Secular Love Gardens

1. See Thomas Esser, "Beitrag," 515. For Alan's objections see note 2.

2. See chapter 3 of Alanus's "Liber apologeticus" in *Magister Alanus de Rupe*, fol. R8r.

3. Ernst Fehrle, *Garten, Rose und Rosengarten im deutschen Mittelalter* (Ph.D. diss., University of Heidelberg, 1924), 49–50.

4. Charles Joret, *La Rose dans l'antiquité et au moyen âge: Histoire, légendes et symbolisme* (Paris, 1892), 413; cited in Mâle, *Religious Art*, 196 n. 196. See also Wilkins, *Rose-Garden Game*, 151–63; Ross, "Rose und Nachtigall," 77–78.

5. Ross, "Rose und Nachtigall," 58–59.

6. Dieter Hennebo, *Gärten des Mittelalters* (Munich: Artemis, 1987), 119.

7. Frank Crisp, *Mediaeval Gardens. "Flowery Medes" and Other Arrangements of Herbs, Flowers and Shrubs Grown in the Middle Ages, with Some Account of Tudor, Elizabethan and Stuart Gardens*, ed. Catherine Childs Paterson, 2 vols. (1924; repr. New York: Hacker, 1966), 1:23. For secular love gardens see Roberta Smith Favis, "The Garden of Love in Fifteenth-Century Netherlandish and German Engravings: Some Studies in Secular Iconography in the Late Middle Ages and Early Renaissance" (Ph.D. diss., University of Pennsylvania, 1974); and Paul F. Watson, *The Garden of Love in Tuscan Art of the Early Renaissance* (Philadelphia: Art Alliance Press, 1979).

8. *Die Gedichte vom Rosengarten zu Worms*, ed. Georg Holz (Halle: Niemeyer, 1893); *Laurin und der kleine Rosengarten*, ed. Georg Holz (Halle: Niemeyer, 1897).

9. In actual practice the term "Rosengartenspiel" (rose garden pageant) was used to designate tournaments that were held as part of festivals of the May. A document from 1311, for example, describes such a knightly pageant being held in Rostock. Several others are recorded in the fourteenth and fifteenth centuries. See Eckehard Simon, "Rosengartenspiele: Zu Schauspiel und Turnier im Spätmittelalter," in *Entzauberung der Welt: Deutsche Literatur, 1200–1500*, ed. James F. Poag and Thomas C. Fox (Tübingen: Francke, 1989), 197–209. Eithne Wilkins reports such a pageant in the city of Worms in 1495 in which Emperor Maximillian himself participated; see Wilkins, *Rose-Garden Game*, 168.

10. Der Pleier, *Garel von dem Blüenden Tal: Ein höfischer Roman aus dem Artussagenkreise von dem Pleier*, ed. M. Walz (Freiburg: Wagner, 1892), lines 3181–3268, 3837–3915.

11. Fehrle, "Rosengarten," 48.

12. Jakob Grimm and Wilhelm Grimm, et al., *Deutsches Wörterbuch*, 16 vols. (Leipzig: Hirzel, 1854–1954), 8:cols. 1197–98.

13. Friedrich Heinrich von der Hagen, *Gesamtabenteuer: Hundert altdeutsche Erzählungen*, 3 vols. (1850; repr. Darmstadt: Wissenschaftliche Buchgesellschaft, 1961), 3:114, lines 133, 137.

14. See Friedrich Heinrich von der Hagen, *Minnesinger: Deutsche Liederdichter des zwölften, dreizehnten und vierzehnten Jahrhunderts*, 5 vols. (1838–61; repr. Aalen: Zeller, 1962), 3:206, no. 19, stanza 4.1–4.

15. Guillaume de Lorris and Jean de Meun, *The Romance of the Rose*, ed. Charles W. Dunn, trans. Harry W. Robbins (New York: Dutton, 1962).

16. Pierre d'Ailly (or Jean Gerson), "Le jardin amoureux de l'âme dévote," in *Jean Gerson: Oeuvres complètes*, ed., Palémon Glorieux (Paris: Desclée, 1966), 7:144–54.

17. Jacques Paul Migne, ed. *Patrologia cursus completus . . . Series Latina*, 221 vols. (Paris: Migne, 1844–80), 16:col. 212; 19:col. 595. Cited in Ross, "Nachtigall," 66–67. See also Anselm Salzer, *Die Sinnbilder und Beiworte Mariens in der deutschen Literatur und lateinischen Hymnenpoesie des Mittelalters* (1893; repr. Darmstadt: Wissenschaftliche Buchgesellschaft, 1967), 183–92. "Rose among thorns" is apparently an adaptation of the phrase "lily among thorns" found in Song of Songs 2:2. See Ross, "Nachtigall," 67.

18. See, for example, the twelfth-century litany printed in Gilles Gérard Meersseman, *Hymnos Akathistos*, 3:223, line 35.

19. Dreves and Blume, eds., *Analecta hymnica*, 8:57. See also Salzer, *Sinnbilder*, 186–87; and Renate Wolfgarten, *Die Ikonographie der Madonna im Rosenhag* (Ph.D. diss., University of Bonn, 1953), 3, 15–26.

20. See Salzer, *Sinnbilder*, 183–85. For the Marienlied of Melk, see Friedrich Maurer, ed., *Die religiösen Dichtungen des 11. und 12. Jahrhunderts*, 3 vols. (Tübingen: Niemeyer, 1964–70), 1:363.

21. Dreves and Blume, eds., *Analecta hymnica*, 17:23; 52:41. Cited in Wolfgarten, "Ikonographie," 21.

22. Ludwig Pfannmüller, ed., *Frauenlobs Marienleich* (Strasbourg: Trübner, 1913), 60.

23. *The "Divine Comedy" of Dante Alighieri: A Verse Translation*, trans. Allen Mandelbaum, 3 vols. (New York: Bantam, 1982–84), 3:209.

24. See Wilhelm Bäumker, ed., *Das katholische deutsche Kirchenlied in seinen Singweisen*, 4 vols. (1883–1911; repr. Hildesheim: Olms, 1962), 1:339.

25. Wackernagel, *Das deutsche Kirchenlied*, 2:278–79.

26. See Gertrud Schiller, *Ikonographie der christlichen Kunst*, 5 vols. (Gütersloh: Mohn, 1966–90), 4.2:206; Ewald Vetter, *Maria im Rosenhag* (Düsseldorf: Schwann, 1956); and Wilkins, *Rose-Garden Game*, 116 and plate 23.

27. Saint Ambrose (d. 347) is the first to interpret the bride in a threefold way as the

church, the soul, and Mary. Friedrich Ohly, *Hohelied-Studien: Grundzüge einer Geschichte der Hoheliedauslegungen des Abendlandes bis um 1200* (Wiesbaden: Franz Steiner, 1958), 35.

28. See Herde, "Das Hohelied," 958–60, 982; Ohly, *Hohelied-Studien*, 19–20, 34–35, 50, 125, 304–5; Peter Eckel von Haselbach's "Predigt auf die hl. Barbara" and the Meffreth first sermon on Saint Barbara printed in Schmidtke, *Studien*, 516–29, at 518 and 526; E. Ann Matter, *"The Voice of My Beloved": The Song of Songs in Western Medieval Christianity* (Philadelphia: University of Pennsylvania Press, 1990), 163–70; and Astell, *Song of Songs*, 60–71; and Stanley Stewart, *The Enclosed Garden: The Tradition and the Image in Seventeenth-Century Poetry* (Madison: University of Wisconsin Press, 1966), 169.

29. See, for example, *Mirour of Mans Saluacioune*, ed. Henry, 52, and 53, lines 570–71.

30. *Das St. Trudperter Hohe Lied*, ed. Hermann Menhardt, 2 vols. (Halle: Niemeyer, 1934), 1:194, lines 10–11.

31. *Der Harder: Texte und Studien*, ed. Tilo Brandis, Quellen und Studien zur Sprach- und Kulturgeschichte der germanischen Völker, n.s., 13. (Berlin: de Gruyter, 1964), 147–48, st. 4.2, 7–8.

32. Cited in Heimo Reinitzer, *Der verschlossene Garten: Der Garten Marias im Mittelalter*, Wolfenbüttler Hefte 12 (Wolfenbüttel: Herzog August Bibliothek, 1982), 14.

33. Klinkhammer, *Adolf von Essen*, 139. The oft-cited chiasmic connection Ave—Eva can be found, for example, in the ninth-century hymn "Ave maris stella." See Hilda Graef, *The Devotion to Our Lady* (New York: Hawthorn, 1963), 40–41; and Beissel, *Geschichte der Verehrung Marias in Deutschland*, 127.

34. Stewart, *Enclosed Garden*, 38.

35. Konrad von Megenberg, *Das Buch der Natur von Konrad von Megenberg*, ed. Franz Pfeiffer (1861; repr. Hildesheim: Olms, 1962), 161–62.

36. Konrad von Würzburg, *Die goldene Schmiede*, ed. Wilhelm Grimm (Berlin: Klemann, 1840), 8–9, sts. 256–65.

37. This image is found in a fifteenth-century herbal, *Le livre des simples médecines*, of M. Platéarius, MS français 12322, fol. 188.

38. Wackernagel, *Kirchenlied*, 2:914.

39 Klinkhammer, *Adolf von Essen*, 142–43.

40. Schmidtke, *Erbauungsliteratur*, 484.

41. Ibid., 56, 112, 405–6.

42. Origen states in the prologue to his commentary on the Song of Songs that the soul "falls in love with [God's] splendor and by this receives from Him some dart and wound of love. . . . And he will receive from Him the saving wound and will burn with the blessed fire of His love"; *Origen*, trans. Rowan A. Greer (New York: Paulist, 1979), 223. For the *Vitis mystica* (formerly attributed to Saint Bernard) see Migne, *Patrologia Latina*, 184:636–740, at cols. 711–14; cited by Mâle, *Late Middle Ages*, 104 n. 91. For the *Nürnberger Garten* see Schmidtke, *Erbauungsliteratur*, 482–91, at 484.

43. Migne, *Patrologia Latina*, 184:col. 1020.

44. Henry Suso, *The Exemplar, with Two German Sermons*, trans. Frank Tobin (New York: Paulist, 1989), 106.

45. Saint Jerome, Epistola IX, *De Assumptione Beatae Mariae Virginis*, in Migne, *Patrologia Latina*, 30:col. 132; cited in Derek Pearsall and Elizabeth Salter, *Landscapes and Seasons of the Medieval World* (Toronto: University of Toronto Press, 1973), 69.

46. Dreves, *Analecta hymnica*, 3:30–32.

47. Wackernagel, *Kirchenlied*, 2:657–59.

48. Schmidtke, *Erbauungsliteratur*, 484–86.

49. See George H. Williams, *Wilderness and Paradise in Christian Thought* (New York: Harper, 1962), 31, 40, 44; Pearsall and Salter, *Landscapes*, 59 and 62; and Schmidtke, *Erbauungsliteratur*, 395–97.

50. *Der sogenannte St. Georgener Prediger*, ed. Karl Rieder, Deutsche Texte des Mittelalters 10 (Berlin: Weidmann, 1908), 160–62. See Wolfgang Stammler, "Der allegorische Garten," in *"Hart, warr nich mööd": Festschrift für Christian Boeck*, ed. Gustav Hoffmann and Gustav Jürgensen (Hamburg: Wellingsbüttel, 1960), 261.

51. See Sermon no. 46, *The Works of Bernard of Clairvaux*, vol. 3, *On the Song of Songs*, 4 vols., trans. Kilian Walsh and Irene Edmonds (Kalamazoo, Mich.: Cistercian Publications, 1971–80), 2:244, 246.

52. For a comprehensive list of German and Middle Netherlandish garden allegories dating from the twelfth through the sixteenth centuries, see Schmidtke, *Erbauungsliteratur*, 12–17, 23–73.

53. Klinkhammer, *Adolf von Essen*, 173–74. For other versions of this widely circulated story see Dobner, *Mittelhochdeutsche Versnovelle*, 1–4, 28–57, 60–68. See also *Marienlegenden*, ed. Richert, 115–30; and Mussafia, *Studien*, 113:985, 119:50.

54. Cited in Esser, *Unserer lieben Frauen Rosenkranz*, 129, from the tragedy *The Passion of Christ* in the Venice edition of Gregory's works (1752), 2:252.

55. Meersseman, "Etudes," 5–176, at 43–44.

56. Alfonso X, *Cantigas de Santa Maria*, 3 vols., ed. Walter Mettmann (Coimbra: University of Coimbra Press, 1959–64), 2:59.

57. See Hans-Georg Richert, "Rosenkranz," *Zeitschrift für deutsche Sprache* 21 (1965): 155; Dobner, *Mittelhochdeutsche Versnovelle*, 47–48; and Herbert Thurston, "The Name of the Rosary," *The Month* 111 (1908): 518–29, 610–23.

58. Dreves and Blume, eds., *Analecta hymnica*, 35:123–34.

59. See, for example, the tale "The Monk and Our Lady's Sleeves" in Boyd, ed., *The Middle English Miracles*, 8–9, 50–55.

60. Konrad von Würzburg, *Die goldene Schmiede*, 1–3. In lines 892–93 Konrad also speaks of weaving a dress ("ein rîchez êren kleit") of words. See also *Albrechts von Scharfenberg Jüngerer Titurel*, 3 vols. in 4 pts., ed. Werner Wolf and Kurt Nyholm, Deutsche Texte des Mittelalters 45, 55, 61, 73 (Berlin: Akademie, 1955–84), 1:111–17. The forty-two verses of the "Marienlob" are inserted between stanzas 439 and 440. Further interesting examples are the garlands made for Saint Barbara by nuns in Alsace and the cloak woven for the Virgin by the nuns of Saint Nikolaus in Undis in Strasbourg. See Eugène Honée, "Image and Imagination in the Medieval Culture of Prayer: A Historical Perspective," in *Art of Devotion*, ed. van Os, 170–72.

61. The vision, found in Dominic's "Zwanzig-Exempel," is printed in Klinkhammer, *Adolf von Essen*, 184–85.

62. See Andreas Heinz, "Eine Spätmittelalterliche Exempelsammlung," 311–12.

63. Ulrich Pinder, *Der beschlossen Gart des Rosenkrantz Marie*, 2 vols. (Nuremberg: Pinder, 1489–1505); Schmidtke, *Erbauungsliteratur*, 286 n. 39.

64. The text of the *Rostocker Gartengebet* is printed in Schmidtke, *Erbauungsliteratur*, 492–95, at 494.

65. Schroeder, *Mary-Verse in "Meistergesang,"* 267.

66. In Suso's *Büchlein der ewigen Weisheit*, for example, Wisdom refers to the Servant's soul as a "spice garden." See *The Exemplar*, trans. Frank Tobin, 214. See *Hadewijch: The Complete Works*, trans. Columba Hart (New York: Paulist, 1980), 270–71. The text of the *Münchner Minnegarten* is printed in the appendix to Schmidtke, *Erbauungsliteratur*, 495–99, at 497.

67. See Dronke, "Song of Songs," 242–43 and 251–52.

68. Kurt Schmidt, *"Der lüstliche Würtzgarte": Ein Beitrag zur Geschichte der deutschen Mystik im Spätmittelalter* (Ph.D. diss., University of Greifswald, 1932), 62–63.

69. Scheeben, "Michael Francisci ab Insulis," 117.

70. Ibid., 144–45.

71. Ibid., 145.

72. Ibid., 117–18.
73. Walasser, *Von der gnadenreichen, hochberümpten . . . Bruderschaft.*
74. See Sprenger's German statutes printed in Schütz, ed., *Geschichte des Rosenkranzes,* 26.
75. Ibid., 29. This passage follows the "Sterbebüchlein" that is printed together with the statutes in this edition.
76. See Dominic's "Zwanzig-Exempel" printed in Klinkhammer, *Adolf von Essen,* 173–87, at 177.

Chapter 5. Popular Promotion and Reception

1. Gislind Ritz, "Der Rosenkranz," in *500 Jahre Rosenkranz,* 51–101, at 76.
2. Thomas Esser, *Zur Archäologie,* 53.
3. Ibid., 53.
4. Ibid., 48–49. See Etienne Boileau, *Les Métiers et corporations de la ville de Paris* (Paris: Lespinasse and Bonnardot, 1879), 57–61.
5. Konrad D. Hassler, ed., *Ott Rulands Handlungsbuch,* Bibliothek des Literarischen Vereins in Stuttgart 1 (Stuttgart, 1843), vii and 29; cited in Esser, *Zur Archäologie,* 50–51.
6. Ritz, "Rosenkranz," in *500 Jahre Rosenkranz,* 77.
7. *Vnser lieben frauen Psalter* (Ulm: Dinckmut, 1483), fols. G3v–G4r.
8. "Of smal coral aboute hir arm she bar / A paire [set] of bedes, gauded al with greene, / And theron heeng a brooch of gold ful sheene." *Chaucer's Poetry: An Anthology for the Modern Reader,* ed. E. T. Donaldson (New York: Ronald, 1958), 10. Herbert Thurston speculates that the term "gaudy" for the marker beads could be related to the Latin word "gaude" used in saluting the joys of the Virgin; see "Our Popular Devotions," 96:418.
9. Cited in Gislind Ritz, *Der Rosenkranz* (Munich: Don Bosco, 1962), 25. See Hans Folz, *Die Reimpaarsprüche,* ed. Hanns Fischer, Münchener Texte und Untersuchungen zur Literatur des Mittelalters 1 (Munich: Beck, 1961), 417–18.
10. Joseph Baader, ed., *Nürnberger Polizeiordnungen aus dem XIII. bis XV. Jahrhundert,* Bibliothek des Literarischen Vereins in Stuttgart 63 (Stuttgart: Literarischer Verein, 1861), 103. Cited in Esser, *Archäologie,* 42.
11. Baader, *Polizeiordnungen,* 66. Also cited in Esser, *Archäologie,* 42.
12. Michael Nielsen, *Tre danske Riimværker fra A. 1496: Om Jomfru Marie Rosenkrands, Om Skabelsen og Om det menneskelige Levnet,* ed. Christian Molbech (Copenhagen: Danske Literaturs Fremme, 1836), 112; cited in Schmitz, *Rosenkranzgebet,* 48.
13. The Douai statute is printed in Meersseman, *Ordo Fraternitatis,* 3:1163–69, at 1166.
14. Walasser, *Von der gnadenreichen, hochberümpten . . . Bruderschaft,* fol. 12v.
15. Nielsen, *Riimvaerker,* 21; cited in Schmitz, *Rosenkranzgebet,* 43–44.
16. Ritz, *Rosenkranz,* 64–65.
17. The rosary handbook from Giessen printed in Schütz, ed., *Geschichte des Rosenkranzes,* 108–22, recounts how the people have been healed of the plague by the rosary psalter, a man possessed by an evil spirit was released, and a raving maniac calmed by wearing the beads, at 115, 116, 117, and 118.
18. Esser, *Unserer lieben Frauen Rosenkranz,* 69; and Lortz, *Reformation in Germany,* 1:113.
19. The indulgence granted by Alexander is printed in Marcus von Weida's rosary handbook of 1515, *Der Spiegel hochloblicher Bruderschafft des Rosenkrantz Marie,* fols. 115v–116v. For some of the early confraternities see Stephan Beissel, *Geschichte der Verehrung Marias im 16. und 17. Jahrhundert* (Freiburg: Herder, 1910), 87. See also Willam, *Geschichte,* 50, and Hardo Hilg, "Marienmirakelsammlungen," in *Die deutsche Literatur des Mittelalters, Verfasserlexikon,* ed. Wolfgang Stammler and Karl Langosch (Berlin: de Gruyter, 1987), 6:col. 35.

20. See Sprenger's German regulations for members printed in Schütz, *Geschichte*, 26.

21. Amelung, *Frühdruck*, 1:237.

22. Weida, *Spiegel*, fol. 29r–30r.

23. Schütz, *Geschichte*, 26.

24. Christopher F. Black, *Italian Confraternities in the Sixteenth Century* (Cambridge: Cambridge University Press, 1989), 39.

25. Ibid., 38 and 103.

26. Ibid., 103.

27. Weida, *Spiegel*, fol. 28r.

28. *Ein GAR nützlich Büchlein*, fols. A4r–A4v.

29. Weida, *Spiegel*, fol. 106v.

30. Rodolfo Pallucchini, *La pittura veneziana del Seicento*, 2 vols., (Milan: Alfieri, 1981), 2:515 and pl. 191.

31. See Erwin Panofsky, *The Life and Art of Albrecht Dürer* (Princeton: Princeton University Press, 1955), fig. 148.

32. Black, *Confraternities*, 246.

33. For works of art donated by German rosary confraternities see Beissel, *Geschichte der Verehrung Marias in Deutschland*, 540–67.

34. *Vnser lieben frauen Psalter*, fols. A6r–A7r.

35. Schmitz, *Rosenkranzgebet*, 37–38.

36. Schütz, *Geschichte*, 171.

37. Ibid., 166 and 168.

38. Meersseman, *Ordo Fraternitatis*, 3:1167.

39. Nielsen, *Riimværker*, 94; cited in Schmitz, *Rosenkranzgebet*, 38–39.

40. *Büchlein*, fols. A3r–A4r. The vision of Saint Dominic is also found in the *Legenda aurea*. See Jacobus de Voragine, *The Golden Legend: Readings on the Saints*, 2 vols., trans. William Granger Ryan (Princeton: Princeton University Press, 1993), 2:47–48.

41. *Büchlein*, fol. B3v.

42. Schmitz, *Rosenkranzgebet*, 35.

43. Weida, *Spiegel*, fol. 107r.

44. See Schütz, *Geschichte*, 28. Those with sufficient means might endow personal chantries. See Wood-Legh, *Perpetual Chantries*. For those who could not afford their own, confraternities served as the equivalent of collective chantries.

45. *Büchlein*, fol. B4r.

46. See Schütz, *Geschichte*, 28.

47. *Bericht, Uhrkund, Gedenckzaichen, ewiges Rosenkrantz Gebetts, von der heiligen Ertzbruderschafft Rosarii für die sterbende im 1640 Jahr allhie auffgericht, und einverleibt* (Salzburg: n.p., c. 1640). The copy in the British Museum has a woman's name and a time filled in.

48. Black, *Confraternities*, 152.

49. Weida, *Spiegel*, 12–13, fols. 114r, 122r, 127r–129r. See also John Bossy, *Christianity in the West, 1400–1700* (New York: Oxford University Press, 1985), 55.

50. Richard W. Southern, *Western Society and the Church in the Middle Ages*, Pelican History of the Church 2 (London: Penguin, 1970), 290.

51. Weida, *Spiegel*, fols. 115v–129r. In the thirteenth and fourteenth centuries, Popes Urban IV (1261–64) and Johannes XXII (1316–1334) had granted indulgences for reciting the name Jesus Christ, which originally was not part of the Ave prayer but became attached to it in the course of the fourteenth century. See Scherschel, *Rosenkranz*, 84–85.

52. Weida, *Spiegel*, fols. 126r–127r, explains Alanus's claim by linking it to recitation of the prayers of St. Gregory. See also Emile Mâle, *Religious Art in France: Late Middle Ages;* and Herbert Thurston, "Alanus de Rupe," 281–99.

53. Mâle, *Religious Art in France: Late Middle Ages,* 96.

54. See Bossy, *Christianity,* 55.

55. Francisci distinguishes between deceased members of the brotherhood and persons who have been enrolled after their deaths. For the latter one must pray, but for those who were members during their lifetimes it is not necessary to pray since they automatically participate in the benefits of the brotherhood. See Jean-Claude Schmitt, "La Confrérie du rosaire de Colmar (1485): Textes de fondation, Exempla en allemand d'Alain de la Roche, listes des Prêcheurs et des Soeurs dominicaines," *Archivum Fratrum Praedicatorum* 40 (1970): 108. Weida's handbook quotes Francisci regarding the enrolling of deceased persons, *Spiegel,* fols. 24r–24v. For Sprenger's comments, see Schütz, *Geschichte,* 27–28.

56. See Weida, *Spiegel,* fol. 24r.

57. Schmitt, "Confrérie," 108.

58. *Büchlein,* fol. B5r.

59. See Thurston, "Our Popular Devotions," 97:290–91.

60. *Magister Alanus de Rupe.* The *Compendium psalterii beatissime Trinitatis* was usually printed bound together with Michael Francisci's *Quodlibet de veritate fraternitatis rosarii.*

61. Although Hilg, "Marienmirakelsammlungen," 6:col. 36, suggests that Alanus wrote all the tales himself, at least six of them can be traced to earlier collections of exempla. These include nos. 2 and 19, which are variations on the story "The Monk and Our Lady's Sleeves," described in Boyd, ed., *Middle English Miracles,* 119; no. 3, "The Clerk of Pisa," described in Ward and Herbert, eds., *Catalogue of Romances,* 2:609; no. 4, the story of the "Young Man of Brabant" who returns from the dead, described by Mussafia, *Studien,* 115:62; no. 5, the story "100 Aves a Day," listed by Ward and Herbert, *Catalogue of Romances,* 2:634; and no. 13, "The Nun Who Saw the World," Ward and Herbert, *Catalogue of Romances,* 2:659. Other sources that Alanus cites (e.g., Johannes de Monte) appear to be fictitious. See Scheeben, "Michael Francisci ab Insulis," 111–12. Those that Alanus did not write himself, he did revise to apply to his psalter and to the brotherhood.

62. While the Ulm handbook contains twenty-seven of these testimonial anecdotes, the rosary manual in MS 784 of the Giessen Universitätsbibliothek contains these same anecdotes plus a few additions; see Schütz, *Geschichte,* 115–20. The numbers used here refer to those in the Giessen text.

63. *Vnser lieben frauen Psalter,* fols. F1v–G3r.

64. See Schmitt, "Confrérie," 115–18.

65. *Vnser lieben frauen Psalter,* fols. E1v–E6r.

66. Ibid., fols. H2r–H7r.

67. Ibid., fols. E1v–E6r.

68. Ibid., fols. C8r–D1r.

69. Ibid., fols. G4v–G8v.

70. Ibid., fols. I1r–I4v. While Dinckmut's editions give the name as Eleodotus, Sorg's editions spell it Eleodorus.

71. Ibid., fols. I4v–K1v.

72. Ibid., fols. E6v–F1v.

73. Wackernagel, *Das deutsche Kirchenlied,* 2:860–61.

74. Schütz, *Geschichte,* 171. This song can also be found in Wackernagel, *Das deutsche Kirchenlied,* 2:853. The Donaueschingen copy has left out the important word "sooner" ("e").

75. Wackernagel, *Das deutsche Kirchenlied,* 2:853–65.

76. Ibid., 2:862, 864.

77. Ibid., 2:860, 861.

78. Ibid., 2:862.

79. Ibid., 2:864.

80. Ibid., 2:859.

81. Ibid., 2:861–62.

82. Herolt, *Miracles*, xxix.

83. See Wackernagel, *Das deutsche Kirchenlied*, 2:853–54, 862, 864.

84. *Vnser lieben frauen Psalter*, fol. D2r. This method resembles that recounted in the verse legend "Comment le sauter noustre dame fu primes cuntroue" printed in Horstmann, ed., *Altenglische Legenden*, 222. Exemplum 6 actually contains two recommended methods, the second of which advises praying the three sets of fifty Aves in order that one may live well, die well, and honor the holy sacraments, fols. E1v–E6r.

85. Ibid., fols. D1r–D3r and L6v–L8v. For "The Monk and Our Lady's Sleeves," see Boyd, *Miracles*, 50–55, 119.

86. Keith Thomas, *Religion and the Decline of Magic* (New York: Scribner's, 1971), 42. In his *Quodlibet*, Michael Francisci himself mentions "superstition" as an accusation made against the rosary by its critics, Scheeben, "Quodlibet," 158.

87. Weida, *Spiegel*, 22, 24, and 25. See also D. G. Kawerau, "Gedanken und Bemerkungen. Luthers Randglossen zum Marienpsalter 1515," *Theologische Studien und Kritiken* 80 (1917): 81–87.

88. Marc Lienhard, "Luther and the Beginnings of the Reformation," in *Christian Spirituality: High Middle Ages and Reformation*, ed. Jill Raitt, World Spirituality 17 (New York: Crossroad, 1989), 287.

89. Bossy, *Christianity*, 97; Ozment, *Reformation in the Cities*, 71.

90. Ozment, *Reformation in the Cities*, 50.

91. Bossy, *Christianity*, viii; Duffy, *Stripping of the Altars*, 7.

92. A. N. Galpern, "Late Medieval Piety in Sixteenth-Century Champagne," in *The Pursuit of Holiness in Late Medieval and Renaissance Religion*, ed. Charles Trinkaus and Heiko A. Oberman, Studies in Medieval and Reformation Thought 10 (Leyden: Brill, 1974), 149.

93. Weida, *Spiegel*, fol. 15r.

94. See Weida's provision for having the rosary said by paid proxy, *Spiegel*, fol. 26r.

95. Karl-Josef Klinkhammer, *Adolf von Essen*, 185.

96. Herolt, *Miracles*, 133.

97. See the "Zwanzig-Exempel-Schrift," Klinkhammer, *Adolf von Essen*, 174.

Chapter 6. Rosaries and the Language of Spirituality

1. Anton Kaes, "New Historicism and the Study of German Literature," *German Quarterly* 62, no. 2 (1989), 212.

2. R. N. Swanson, *Religion and Devotion in Europe, c. 1215–c. 1515* (Cambridge: Cambridge University Press, 1995), 226 and 234.

3. Lortz, *Reformation*, 1:110.

4. Ibid., 1:110, 123, 140–41.

5. See Ozment, *Reformation in the Cities*, 18–21; and Moeller, "Piety in Germany."

6. Lynch, *Medieval Church*, 338; and Angelika Dorfler-Dierken, *Vorreformatorische Bruderschaften der heiligen Anna*, Abhandlungen der Heidelberger Akademie der Wissenschaften, Phil.-hist. Klasse, Jahrgang 1992, 3 (Heidelberg: Winter, 1992), 10–11.

7. Lortz, *Reformation*, 1:14; and Thomas N. Tentler, *Sin and Confession on the Eve of the Reformation* (Princeton: Princeton University Press, 1977), 366.

8. Engelsing, *Analphabetentum und Lektüre*, 6–38; Moeller, *Deutschland im Zeitalter der Reformation*, Deutsche Geschichte 4 (Göttingen: Vandenhoeck, 1977), 36.

9. Scribner, *For the Sake of Simple Folk*, 1–2; and Lortz, *Reformation*, 1:51, 111–12.

10. See Heinrich Hoffmann von Fallersleben, *Geschichte des deutschen Kirchenlieds bis auf Luthers Zeit* (Wroclaw: Grass and Barth, 1832), 111–13.

11. John E. Toews, "Stories of Difference and Identity: New Historicism in Literature and History," *Monatshefte* 84 (1992):196.

12. Boyd, *Middle English Miracles*, 50–55, 119–22.

13. See Mussafia, *Studien*, 113:942; and Thurston, "Our Popular Devotions," 96:410–12.

14. Herbert Thurston comments that Dominic's version was the most widely used one in England before the break with Rome, "Our Popular Devotions," 96:631.

15. See exempla 7, 10, and 17 of Dominic's "Zwanzig-Exempel-Schrift" in Klinkhammer, *Adolf von Essen*, 178–80, 184–85.

16. Meersseman, *Ordo Fraternitatis*, 3:1166.

17. See Sprenger's statutes in Schütz, ed., *Geschichte des Rosenkranzes*, 25–28, at 26.

18. See Oertzen, *Maria, die Königin*, 45–46.

19. Weida, *Spiegel*, fol. 107v.

20. Lortz, *Reformation*, 1:120; and Roland Bainton, *Here I Stand: A Life of Martin Luther* (New York: Mentor, 1950), 53.

21. Weida, *Spiegel*, fols. 136r–136v.

22. *D. Martin Luthers Werke: Kritische Gesamtausgabe*, 90 vols. (Weimar: Böhlaus, 1883–), 6:211, 2:754.

23. *D. Martin Luthers Tischreden, 1531–46*, vol. 5: *Tischreden aus den Jahren, 1540–44*, ed. D. G. Kawerau and Karl Drescher (Weimer: Böhlaus, 1919), 683–84.

24. See Weida, *Spiegel*, fols. 57v–102v.

25. Wackernagel, ed., *Das deutsche Kirchenlied*, 2:853–65. The six texts Wackernagel reproduces include two different versions of one, 2:861–64.

26. Wackernagel, *Das deutsche Kirchenlied*, 2:855.

27. Cited in Thurston, "Our Popular Devotions," 97:301–2.

28. Wackernagel, *Das deutsche Kirchenlied*, 2:864–65.

29. See Regnerus Richardus Post, *The Modern Devotion: Confrontation with Reformation and Humanism*, Studies in Medieval and Reformation Thought 3 (Leiden: Brill, 1968), 400–401, 679–80; Oakley, *Western Church*, 107.

30. From chapter 5 of the *Enchiridion Monachorum*. Cited here by Thomas Esser, *Unserer lieben Frauen Rosenkranz*, 11.

31. See Oakley, *Western Church*, 107.

32. Schütz, *Geschichte*, 27.

33. Cited from Nikolaus Paulus, *Indulgences as a Social Factor in the Middle Ages*, trans. J. Elliot Ross (New York: Devin-Adair, 1922), 31.

34. Ibid., 32.

35. Hamm, *Frömmigkeitstheologie*, 280–83.

36. Lortz, *Reformation*, 1:136.

37. See Klinkhammer, *Adolf von Essen*, 182–83; and Esser, "Geschichte des englischen Grußes," 103. Dominic comments that in his childhood, Jesus' name was not yet part of the Hail Mary. Klinkhammer, *Adolf von Essen*, 182.

38. See Herolt, *Miracles*, 132–33.

39. My emphasis. See Heinz, "Eine spätmittelalterliche Exempelsammlung," 314. Technically, what this requires is absolution of mortal sins, in which case the indulgence could remit the punishment for venial sins.

40. Luther, *Werke*, 6:211.

41. Black, *Italian Confraternities*, 274.

42. Vauchez, *Laity in the Middle Ages*, 117.

43. Huizinga, *Herbst des Mittelalters*, 179. The commonly used English abridged edition does not include this statement. See Johan Huizinga, *The Waning of the Middle Ages*, trans. F. Hopman (New York: Doubleday Anchor, 1949). The new unabridged English translation identifies Alanus de Rupe here as Adamus de Ruper and the rosary brotherhood as the Rosicrucians; see *The Autum of the Middle Ages*, trans. Rodney J. Payton and Ulrich Mammitzsch (Chicago: University of Chicago Press, 1996), 176.

44. Blasel, "Studien," 26–27.

45. Black, *Italian Confraternities*, 11–17.

46. Heinrich Schmidt and Margarethe Schmidt, *Die vergessene Bildersprache christlicher Kunst* (Munich: Beck, 1984), 242.

47. Astell, *Song of Songs*, 16, 61, 68.

48. Matter, *"Voice of My Beloved,"* 14–15, 86, 123, 142, 168–70.

49. See Schmidtke, *Studien.*; and Anne Winston-Allen, " 'Minne' in Spiritual Gardens of the Fifteenth Century," in *Canon and Canon Transgression in Medieval German Literature*, ed. Albrecht Classen (Göppingen: Kümmerle, 1993).

50. See *Albrechts von Scharfenberg Jüngerer Titurel*, 1:111–17.

51. See Rosenhagen, ed., *Heidelberger Handschrift*, xxxvi–xli; and *Konrads von Würzburg Goldene Schmiede*, ed. Wilhelm Grimm (Berlin: Klemann, 1840).

52. See Joachim Moschall, ed., *"Marien Voerspan of Sapeel": Eine mittelniederländische Bearbeitung der "Goldenen Schmiede" des Konrad von Würzburg*, Erlanger Studien 40 (Erlangen: Palm und Enke, 1983), 134–35; and Rüdiger Brandt, *Konrad von Würzburg*, Erträge der Forschung 249 (Darmstadt: Wissenschaftliche Buchgesellschaft, 1987), 146.

53. Moschall, ed., *Marien Voerspan of Sapeel*. Here the word *Voerspan* means a piece of jewelry worn at the neck, on the forehead, or at the hairline (116). Many rosaries, like that of Chaucer's Madame Eglantine, were attached to a brooch.

54. Moschall, *Voerspan*, 11.

55. *Konrads von Würzburg Goldene Schmiede*, 3, lines 62–85.

56. This story can be found, for example, as exemplum 8 in the Middle High German *Passional* (1280/1300), a collection of verse legends. See *Marienlegenden*, ed. Richert, 43–46. See also Ward and Herbert, eds., *Catalogue of Romances*, 2:607.

57. Bernhard Ridderbos, "The Rotterdam-Edinburgh Diptych: 'Maria in Sole' and the Devotion of the Rosary," in *Art of Devotion*, ed. Os, 155. The painting is preserved in two anonymous copies held by the Museum der Bildenden Künste in Leipzig and in a private collection; see Grete Ring, "Attempt to Reconstruct a Lost Geertgen Composition," *The Burlington Magazine* 94 (1952), 147. Alanus's exemplum of Queen Blanche is included as number 11 in the Ulm rosary handbook of 1483, fols. G8v–H2r. Also shown in the diptych is Saint Dominic receiving the rosary from the Virgin Mary and her child.

58. See von Oertzen, *Maria, die Königin*, 66, 70–73, pls. 10 and 26.

59. Klinkhammer, *Adolf von Essen*, 155–156. In this story, however, a suffering monk refuses the rose-cake poultice, choosing, instead, to meditate on the Passion and on Christ's body, which was martyred ("baked") in "the fire of the Holy Spirit."

60. Hunt, *New Cultural History*, 14 and 17; Kaes, "New Historicism," 210, 212–13.

61. Anton Kaes, "New Historicism," 216, 219 n. 40.

62. See Gabrielle Spiegel, "History, Historicism, and the Social Logic of the Text in the Middle Ages," *Speculum* 65 (1990): 64.

63. Idem, 77.

64. Kaes, "New Historicism," 214.

65. Stephen Greenblatt, *Renaissance Self-Fashioning: From More to Shakespeare* (Chicago: University of Chicago Press, 1980), 52.

Appendix

1. A Latin version of this story can be found as exemplum 10 in the *Compendium psalterii beatissime Trinitatis . . .* (Bologna: 1500) compiled by followers of Alanus de Rupe. It also bears some resemblance to a story recounted by Thomas de Cantimpré (c. 1270) in his *Bonum universale de apibus* 2.29.18 in which the head of a robber who has been beheaded shouts for a confessor. See Mussafia, *Studien,* 115:63.

2. This is apparently a fictitious attribution; there is no evidence of such a collection of exempla by a Johannes von Berg, Iohannis de Monte, or anyone by a similar name. See Scheeben, "Michael Francisci ab Insulis," 112; and Jacques Quétif and Jacques Echard, *Scriptores ordinis praedicatorum,* 2 vols. (Paris: Ballard and Simart, 1719–21), 1:851.

3. The earliest edition of this handbook published by Dinckmut in Ulm in 1483 spells the protagonist's name "Eleodotus."

Selected Bibliography

Primary Sources

Acta Sanctorum Ordinis S. Benedicti. 9 vols. Edited by Luc d'Archery, Jean Mabillon, and Thierry Ruinart. Venice: Coleti and Bettinelli, 1733–38.

Albrechts von Scharfenberg Jüngerer Titurel. 3 vols. in 4 parts. Edited by Werner Wolf and Kurt Nyholm. Deutsche Texte des Mittelalters 45, 55, 61, 73. Berlin: Akademie, 1955–84.

Alfonso X. *Cantigas de Santa Maria.* 3 vols. edited by Walter Mettmann. Coimbra: University of Coimbra Press, 1959–64.

Baader, Joseph, ed. *Nürnberger Polizeiordnungen aus dem XIII. bis XV. Jahrhundert.* Bibliothek des Literarischen Vereins in Stuttgart 63. Stuttgart: Literarischer Verein, 1861.

Bartsch, Karl, ed. *Deutsche Liederdichter des zwölften bis vierzehnten Jahrhunderts: Eine Auswahl.* 1879. Reprint, Darmstadt: Wissenschaftliche Buchgesellschaft, 1966.

———. *Die Erlösung: Mit einer Auswahl geistlicher Dichtungen.* Bibliothek der gesamten deutschen National-Literatur 37. Quedlinburg and Leipzig: G. Basse, 1858.

Bäumker, Wilhelm, ed. *Das katholische deutsche Kirchenlied in seinen Singweisen.* 4 vols. 1883–1911. Reprint, Hildesheim: Olms, 1962.

Bericht, Uhrkund, Gedenckzaichen, ewiges Rosenkrantz Gebetts, von der heiligen Ertzbruderschafft Rosarii für die sterbende im 1640 Jahr allhie auffgericht, und einverleibt. Salzburg: n.p., c. 1640.

Bernard of Clairvaux. *The Works of Bernard of Clairvaux.* 4 vols. Vol. 3, *On the Song of Songs.* Translated by Kilian Walsh and Irene Edmonds. Kalamazoo, Mich.: Cistercian Publications, 1971–80.

Biblia pauperum. Edited by Avril Henry. Ithaca: Cornell University Press, 1987.

Biblia sacra: Vulgatae editionis Sixti V pontificis maximi. Rome: Editiones Paulinae, 1957.

Bodenstedt, Sister Mary Immaculate. *Praying the Life of Christ: First English*

*Translation of the Prayers Concluding the 181 Chapters of the "Vita Christi"
of Ludolphus the Carthusian.* Analecta cartusiana 15. Salzburg: Institut für
Englische Sprache und Literatur, Universität Salzburg, 1973.

Boileau, Etienne. *Les Métiers et corporations de la ville de Paris.* Paris: Lespinasse
and Bonnardot, 1879.

Bonaventure: *The Soul's Journey into God, The Tree of Life, the Life of St.
Francis.* Translated by Ewert Cousins. New York: Paulist, 1978.

Boyd, Beverly, ed. *The Middle English Miracles of the Virgin.* San Marino, Calif.:
Huntington Library, 1964.

Brandis, Tilo, ed. *Der Harder: Texte und Studien.* Quellen und Forschungen zur
Sprach- und Kulturgeschichte der germanischen Völker, n.s., 13. Berlin: de
Gruyter, 1964.

Budge, E. A. Wallis, ed. *One Hundred and Ten Miracles of Our Lady Mary,
Translated from Ethiopic Manuscripts.* London: Oxford University Press,
1933.

Caesarius of Heisterbach. *The Dialogues on Miracles.* 2 vols. Translated by
H. von E. Scott and C. C. Swinton Bland. London: Routledge, 1929.

Cantimpré, Thomas de. *Bonum universale de proprietatibus apum.* Cologne:
Koelhoff, 1473.

Castello, Alberto da. *Rosario della gloriosa vergine Maria.* Venice: Ravani, 1524.

Le Chapellet et psaultier de la confrairie Notre Dame. Lyon: Jacques Mailhet,
1495.

Chaucer, Geoffrey. *Chaucer's Poetry: An Anthology for the Modern Reader.*
Edited by E. T. Donaldson. New York: Ronald, 1958.

Cramer, Thomas, ed. *Die kleineren Liederdichter des 14. und 15. Jahrhunderts.* 4
vols. Munich: W. Fink, 1977–85.

Dis ist Unser lyeben frowen Rosenkrantz und wie er von ersten ist uffkummen.
Speyer: Johannes and Conrad Hist, 1485.

The Divine Comedy of Dante Alighieri. 3 vols. Translated by Allen Mandelbaum.
New York: Bantam, 1982–84.

Dreves, Guido, and Clemens Blume, eds. *Analecta hymnica medii aevi.* 55 vols.
1886–1922. Reprint, Frankfurt am Main: Minerva, 1961.

Euling, Karl, ed. *Kleinere mittelhochdeutsche Erzählungen, Fabeln und Lehrgedichte II: Die Wolfenbüttler Handschrift 2. 4. Aug. 2°.* Deutsche Texte
des Mittelalters 14. Berlin: Weidmann, 1908.

Folz, Hans. *Die Reimpaarsprüche.* Edited by Hanns Fischer. Münchener Texte
und Untersuchungen zur Literatur des Mittelalters 1. Munich: Beck, 1961.

Francisci, Michael. *Quodlibet de veritate fraternitatis rosarii.* Bologna: Joannes
Antonius de Benedictis, 1500.

Frauenlobs Marienleich. Edited by Ludwig Pfannmüller. Strasbourg: Trübner,
1913.

Ein GAR nützlich Büchlein von dem Psalter oder Rosenkranz Marie. Ulm:
Schäffer, 1501.

Gasquet, F. A. "An English Rosary Book of the Fifteenth Century." *Downside
Review* 12 (1893): 215–28.

Die Gedichte vom Rosengarten zu Worms. Edited by Georg Holz. Halle: Niemeyer, 1893.

Geisberg, Max. *The German Single-Leaf Woodcut, 1500–1550*, 4 vols. Edited and revised by Walter L. Strauss. New York: Hacker, 1974.

Gerson, Jean. *Oeuvres complètes*. 10 vols. Edited by Palémon Glorieux. Paris: Desclée, 1960–74.

Gianetti da Salò, Andrea. *Rosario della sacratissima Vergine Maria, raccolto dall' opere del R.P.F. Luigi di Granata*. Rome: Angeli, 1573.

Grignon de Montfort, St. Louis. *Le Secret admirable du très saint rosaire*. Tours: Oudin, 1912.

Guillaume de Lorris, and Jean de Meun. *The Romance of the Rose*. Edited by Charles W. Dunn. Translated by Harry W. Robbins. New York: Dutton, 1962.

Hadewijch: The Complete Works. Translated by Columba Hart. New York: Paulist, 1980.

Hagen, Friedrich Heinrich von der. *Gesamtabenteuer: Hundert altdeutsche Erzählungen*. 3 vols. 1850. Reprint, Darmstadt: Wissenschaftliche Buchgesellschaft, 1961.

———. *Minnesinger: Deutsche Liederdichter des zwölften, dreizehnten und vierzehnten Jahrhunderts*. 5 vols. 1838–61. Reprint, Aalen: Zeller, 1962.

Der Harder: Texte und Studien. Edited by Tilo Brandis. Quellen und Studien zur Sprach- und Kulturgeschichte der germanischen Völker, n.s., 13. Berlin: de Gruyter, 1964.

Hassler, Konrad D., ed. *Ott Rulands Handlungsbuch*. Bibliothek des Lit[t]erarischen Vereins in Stuttgart 1. Stuttgart: Lit[t]erarischer Verein, 1843.

Haupt, Moriz, and Heinrich Hoffman, eds. *Altdeutsche Blätter*. 2 vols. 1836–40. Reprint, Hildesheim: Olms, 1978.

Hensberg, Vincent. *Viridarium Marianum septemplici rosario, variis exercitiis, exemplis ut plantationibus peramoenum*. Antwerp: Gaspar Beller, 1615.

Herolt, Johannes. *Miracles of the Blessed Virgin Mary*. Edited by G. G. Coulton and Eileen Power. Translated by C. C. Swinton Bland. London: Routledge, 1928.

Horstmann, Carl, ed. *Altenglische Legenden: Neue Folge*. 1881. Reprint, Hildesheim: Olms, 1969.

Jacobus de Voragine. *The Golden Legend: Readings on the Saints*. 2 vols. Translated by William Granger Ryan. Princeton: Princeton University Press, 1993.

Kehrein, Joseph, ed. *Katholische Kirchenlieder, Hymnen, Psalmen*. 3 vols. 1859–65. Reprint, Hildesheim: Olms, 1965.

Klapper, Josef, ed. "Miszellen: Mitteldeutsche Texte aus Breslauer Handschriften." *Zeitschrift für deutsche Philologie* 47 (1918): 83–87.

Konrad von Megenberg. *Das Buch der Natur*. Edited by Franz Pfeiffer. Stuttgart: Aue, 1861. Reprint, Hildesheim: Olms, 1962.

Konrads von Würzburg Goldene Schmiede. Edited by Wilhelm Grimm. Berlin: Klemann, 1840.

Lambsheym, Johannes. *Libellus perutilis de fraternitate sanctissima et Rosario Marie virginis*. Mainz: Peter von Friedberg, 1495.

Larroca, Josephi Mariae, ed. *Acta Sanctae Sedis necnon magistrorum et capitu-*

lorum generalium Sacri Ordinis Praedicatorum pro Societate Ss. Rosarii. 2 vols. in 4. Lyon: Jevain, 1890–91.

Laurin und der kleine Rosengarten. Edited by Georg Holz. Halle: Niemeyer, 1897.

Le Livre et ordonnance [statutes of the brotherhood at Douai]. Paris: Michel Le Noir, c. 1500.

Loarte, Gaspare. *Instrvctions and Advertisements: How to Meditate on the Misteries of the Rosarie of the Most Holy Virgin Mary.* Translated by J. Fenne. Rouen: n.p., 1600?

Luther, Martin. *D. Martin Luthers Tischreden, 1531–46.* Vol. 5, *Tischreden aus den Jahren, 1540–44.* Edited by D. G. Kawerau and Karl Drescher. Weimar: Böhlaus, 1919.

———. *D. Martin Luthers Werke: Kritische Gesamtausgabe.* 90 vols. Weimar: Böhlaus, 1883–.

Marienlegenden aus dem alten Passional. Edited by Hans-Georg Richert. Altdeutsche Textbibliothek 64. Tübingen: Niemeyer, 1965.

Maurer, Friedrich, ed. *Die religiösen Dichtungen des 11. und 12. Jahrhunderts.* 3 vols. Tübingen: Niemeyer, 1964–70.

Mechthild of Hackeborn. *The Booke of gostlye grace of Mechthild of Hackeborn.* Edited by Theresa Halligan. Studies and Texts 46. Toronto: Pontifical Institute of Medieval Studies, 1979.

———. *Revelationes Gertrudianae ac Mechthildiane.* 2 vols. Edited by Ludwig Paquelin. Paris: H. Oudin, 1875–77.

Meyer, Johannes. *Buch der Reformacio Predigerordens.* Edited by Benedictus Maria Reichert. Quellen und Forschungen zur Geschichte des Dominikanerordens in Deutschland 2, no. 3. Leipzig: Harrassowitz, 1908–9.

Mielot, Jean. *Miracles de Notre Dame.* Edited by George F. Warner. Westminster: Nichols and Sons, 1885.

Migne, Jacques Paul, ed. *Patrologia cursus completus . . . Series Latina.* 221 vols. Paris: Migne, 1844–80.

The Mirour of Mans Saluacioune: A Middle English Translation of "Speculum humanae salvationis." Edited by Avril Henry. Philadelphia: University of Pennsylvania Press, 1987.

The Mirror of the Blessed Virgin Mary (Speculum Beatae Mariae Virginis) and the Psalter of Our Lady (Psalterium Beatae Mariae Virginis). Translated by Sister Mary Emmanuel. St. Louis, Mo.: Herder, 1932.

Mombaer, Johannes. *Rosetum exercitiorum spiritualium et sacrarum meditationum.* Zwolle: Pieter van Os, 1494.

Mone, Franz Josef, ed. *Lateinische Hymnen des Mittelalters.* 3 vols. 1853–55. Reprint, Aalen: Scientia, 1964.

Nielsen, Michael. *Tre danske Riimværker fra A. 1496: Om Jomfru Marie Rosenkrands, Om Skabelsen og Om det menneskelige Levnet.* Edited by Christian Molbech. Copenhagen: Danske Literaturs Fremme, 1836.

Origen: An Exhortation to Martyrdom, Prayer, First Principles: Book IV, Prologue to the Commentary on the Song of Songs, Homily 27 on Numbers. Translated by Rowan A. Greer. New York: Paulist, 1979.

Orlandi, Stefano. *Libro del Rosario della Gloriosa Vergine Maria.* Rome: Centro Internationale Domenicano Rosariano, 1965.

Pfeiffer, Franz, ed. "Mariengrüsse." *Zeitschrift für deutsches Altertum* 8 (1851): 274–98.

Pinder, Ulrich. *Der beschlossen Gart des Rosenkrantz Marie.* 2 vols. Nuremberg: Pinder, 1489–1505.

Pleier, der. *Garel von dem Blüenden Tal: Ein Höfischer Roman aus dem Artussagenkreise von dem Pleier.* Edited by M. Walz. Freiburg: Wagner, 1892.

Das Rheinische Marienlob: Eine deutsche Dichtung des 13. Jahrhunderts. Edited by Adolf Bach. Leipzig: Hiersemann, 1934.

Rosenhagen, Gustav, ed. *Die Heidelberger Handschrift cod. Pal. germ. 341.* Deutsche Texte des Mittelalters 17. Berlin: Weidmann, 1909.

Rupe, Alanus de. *Beatus Alanus de Rupe redivivus de Psalterio seu Rosario Christi ac Mariae.* Edited by Johann Andreas Coppenstein. Cologne: P. Henning, 1624.

———. *Compendium psalterii beatissime Trinitatis ad laudem Domini nostri Jesu Christi et beatissimae semper virginis matris. . . . See* Michael Francisci, *Quodlibet de veritate fraternitatis rosarii.*

———. *Jungfru Marie psaltare (rosenkrans) af Alanus de Rupe: öfversättning från latinet, efter den enda kända handskriften, från 1534.* Edited by Robert Geete. Uppsala: Almqvist and Wiksells, 1923–25.

———. *Magister Alanus de Rupe, sponsus novellus beatissime virginis Marie . . . de immensa et ineffabili dignitate et utilitate psalterii precelse ac intemerate semper virginis Marie.* Gripsholm: Monastery of Mariefred, 1498.

———. *Unser lieben Frawen Psalter vonn den dreien Rosenkrenntzen.* Augsburg: Zeissenmair, 1502.

———. *Vnser lieben frauen Psalter* [Psalterium Virginis Mariae]. Ulm: Conrad Dinckmut, 1483.

———. *Von dem psalter vnnd Rosenkrancz vnser lieben frauen.* Augsburg: Anton Sorg, 1492.

Sachsenspiegel: Landrecht. Edited by Karl A. Eckhardt. *Monumenta Germaniae Historica, Fontes Iuris Germanici Antiqui,* n.s., vol. 1:1, 2d rev. ed. Göttingen: Musterschmidt, 1955.

Schmitt, Jean-Claude. "La Confrérie du rosaire de Colmar (1485): Textes de fondation, Exempla en allemand d'Alain de la Roche, listes des Prêcheurs et des Soeurs dominicaines." *Archivum Fratrum Praedicatorum* 40 (1970): 97–124.

Schönbach, Anton E., ed. "Aus einem Marienpsalter." *Zeitschrift für deutsches Altertum* 48 (1906): 365–70.

Schütz, Jakob Hubert, ed. *Die Geschichte des Rosenkranzes: Unter Berücksichtigung der Rosenkranz-Geheimnisse und der Marien-Litaneien.* Paderborn: Junfermann, 1909.

Die sieben Freuden Mariae und die Leidensgeschichte Jesu. Bamberg: n.p., c. 1460.

Der sogenannte St. Georgener Prediger. Edited by Karl Rieder. Deutsche Texte des Mittelalters 10. Berlin: Weidmann, 1908.

Sprenger, Jacob. *In spiritu penses hoc opus* . . . [German statutes of the Brotherhood of the Rosary]. Augsburg: n.p., 1476.

———. *In spiritu penses hoc opus*. . . . Augsburg: Bämler, 1477.

Das St. Trudperter Hohe Lied. Edited by Hermann Menhardt. 2 vols. Halle: Niemeyer, 1934.

Suso, Henry. *The Exemplar, with Two German Sermons*. Translated by Frank Tobin. New York: Paulist, 1989.

Swanson, R. N., ed. and trans. *Catholic England: Faith, Religion and Observance before the Reformation*. Manchester: Manchester University Press, 1993.

Van Engen, John, ed. and trans. *Devotio Moderna: Basic Writings*. New York: Paulist, 1988.

Vnser lieben Frauen Psalter. Attributed to Alanus de Rupe. Ulm: Dinckmut, 1483.

Von dem psalter vnnd Rosen krancz vnser lieben frauen. Attributed to Alanus de Rupe. Augsburg: Anton Sorg, 1492.

von der Hagen, Friedrich Heinrich, ed. *Gesamtabenteuer: Hundert altdeutsche Erzählungen*. 3 vols. 1850. Reprint, Darmstadt: Wissenschaftliche Buchgesellschaft, 1961.

Wackernagel, Philipp, ed. *Das deutsche Kirchenlied von der ältesten Zeit bis zu Anfang des 17. Jahrhunderts*. 5 vols. 1864–77. Reprint, Hildesheim: Olms, 1964.

Walasser, Adam. *Von der gnadenreichen, hochberümpten . . . Bruderschaft des Psalters oder Rosenkrantz Marie*. Dillingen: Sebaldus Mayer, 1572.

Weida, Marcus von. *Der Spiegel hochloblicher Bruderschafft des Rosenkrantz Marie*. Edited by Anthonÿ van der Lee. Quellen und Forschungen zur Erbauungsliteratur des späten Mittelalters und der frühen Neuzeit 3. Amsterdam: Rodopi, 1978.

Secondary Sources

Achten, Gerard. *Das christliche Gebetbuch im Mittelalter: Andachts- und Stundenbücher in Handschrift und Frühdruck*. Staatsbibliothek Preußischer Kulturbesitz, exhibition catalogue 13. Wiesbaden: Reichert, 1980.

Amelung, Peter. *Der Frühdruck im deutschen Südwesten, 1473–1500*. 2 vols. Stuttgart: Württembergische Landesbibliothek, 1979.

Andreas, Willy. *Deutschland vor der Reformation: Eine Zeitwende*. 5th ed. Stuttgart: Deutsche Verlags-Anstalt, 1948.

Anonymous. *El Santo Rosario en la Cartuja*. Analecta cartusiana 103. Salzburg: Institut für Anglistik und Amerikanistik, Universität Salzburg, 1983.

Appelhans, Peter. *Untersuchungen zur spätmittelalterlichen Mariendichtung: Die rhythmischen mittelhochdeutschen Mariengrüße*. Germanische Bibliothek, ser. 3: Untersuchungen. Heidelberg: Winter, 1970.

Astell, Ann W. *The Song of Songs in the Middle Ages*. Ithaca: Cornell University Press, 1990.

Axters, Stephanus. *Geschiedenis van de vroomheid in de Nederlanden.* 3 vols. Antwerp: De Sikkel, 1950–56.

Baier, Walter. *Untersuchungen zu den Passionsbetrachtungen in der "Vita Christi" des Ludolf von Sachsen.* 3 vols. Analecta cartusiana 44. Salzburg: Institut für Englische Sprache und Literatur, Universität Salzburg, 1977.

Bainton, Roland. *Here I Stand: A Life of Martin Luther.* New York: Mentor, 1950.

Barth, Médard. "Die Rosenkranzbruderschaften des Elsass geschichtlich gewürdigt." *Archives de l'église d'Alsace* 16 (1967–68): 53–108.

Barthelmé, Annette. *La Réforme dominicaine au XVe siècle en Alsace et dans l'ensemble de la province de Teutonie.* Collection d'études sur l'histoire du droit et des institutions de l'Alsace 7. Strasbourg: Heitz, 1931.

Becker, Petrus. "Benediktinische Reformbewegungen im Spätmittelalter. Ansätze, Entwicklungen, Auswirkungen." In *Untersuchungen zu Kloster und Stift.* Veröffentlichungen des Max-Planck-Instituts für Geschichte 68, Germania Sacra 14, pp. 167–87. Göttingen: Vandenhoeck and Ruprecht, 1980.

—————. *Das monastische Reformprogramm des Johannes Rode Abtes von St. Matthias in Trier—Ein darstellender Kommentar zu seinen Consuetudines.* Beiträge zur Geschichte des alten Mönchtums und des Benediktinerordens, 30. Münster: Aschendorff, 1970.

Beer, Johannes. *Die Illustration des Lebens Jesu in den deutschen Frühdrucken (c. 1460–1500).* Archiv für Schreib- und Buchwesen, Sonderheft 3. Wolfenbüttel, Heckner, 1929.

Beissel, Stephan. *Geschichte der Verehrung Marias im 16. und 17. Jahrhundert.* Freiburg: Herder, 1910.

—————. *Geschichte der Verehrung Marias in Deutschland während des Mittelalters.* Freiburg: Herder, 1909.

Bertaud, Emile. "Hortus, Hortulus, Jardin spirituel." In *Dictionnaire de spiritualité,* edited by Joseph de Guibert, Marcel Viller, and Ferdinand Cavallera, 7:cols. 766–84. Paris: Beauchesne, 1969.

Bildarchiv Foto Marburg. *Marburger Index: Bilddokumentation zur Kunst in Deutschland.* Munich: Verlag Dokumentation, 1976–.

Black, Christopher F. *Italian Confraternities in the Sixteenth Century.* Cambridge: Cambridge University Press, 1989.

Blasel, Carl. "Studien zur Geschichte der Rosenkranzbruderschaft bei St. Adalbert in Breslau." *Schlesisches Pastoralblatt* 33 (1912): 1–6, 20–27, 35–44, 59–62.

Blockbücher des Mittelalters: Bilderfolgen als Lektüre, Gutenberg-Gesellschaft and Gutenberg Museum, exhibition catalogue, 22 June–1 September 1991. Mainz: von Zabern, 1991.

Bossy, John. *Christianity in the West, 1400–1700.* New York: Oxford University Press, 1985.

Boyd, Beverly. "Chaucer's Prioress: Her Green Gauds." *Modern Language Quarterly* 11 (1950): 404–16.

Brandt, Rüdiger. *Konrad von Würzburg.* Erträge der Forschung 249. Darmstadt: Wissenschaftliche Buchgesellschaft, 1987.

Bridgett, Thomas E. *Our Lady's Dowry: How England Gained that Title.* London: Burns and Oates, 1875.

Calkins, Robert G. *Illumininated Books of the Middle Ages.* Ithaca: Cornell University Press, 1983.

———. *Programs of Medieval Illumination.* Franklin D. Murphy Lectures 5. Lawrence: Helen Forsman Spencer Museum of Art, University of Kansas, 1984.

Chrisman, Miriam Usher. *Lay Culture, Learned Culture: Books and Social Change in Strasbourg, 1480–1599.* New Haven: Yale University Press, 1982.

Constable, Giles. "Twelfth-Century Spirituality and the Late Middle Ages." In *Proceedings of the Southeastern Institute of Medieval and Renaissance Studies,* edited by O. B. Hardison Jr., 27–60. Medieval and Renaissance Studies 5. Chapel Hill: University of North Carolina Press, 1971.

Conway, Charles Abbott, Jr. *The Vita Christi of Ludolf of Saxony and Late Medieval Devotion Centered on the Incarnation: A Descriptive Analysis.* Analecta cartusiana 34. Salzburg: Institut für Englische Sprache und Literatur, Universität Salzburg, 1976.

Crane, Thomas Frederick. *The Exempla or Illustrative Stories from the "Sermones vulgares" of Jacques de Vitry.* Folk-lore Society London 26. London: Nutt, 1890.

Crisp, Frank. *Mediaeval Gardens: "Flowery Medes" and Other Arrangements of Herbs, Flowers and Shrubs Grown in the Middle Ages, with Some Account of Tudor, Elizabethan and Stuart Gardens.* 2 vols. Edited by Catherine Childs Paterson. 1924. Reprint, New York: Hacker, 1966.

Daley, Brian E. "The 'Closed Garden' and 'Sealed Fountain': Song of Songs 4:12 in the Late Medieval Iconography of Mary." In *Medieval Gardens,* edited by Elisabeth MacDougall, 253–78. Dumbarton Oaks Colloquium on the History of Landscape Architecture 9. Washington, D.C.: Dumbarton Oaks, 1986.

Davis, Natalie Z. *Society and Culture in Early Modern France: Eight Essays.* Stanford: Stanford University Press, 1975.

———. "Some Tasks and Themes in the Study of Popular Religion." In *The Pursuit of Holiness in Late Medieval and Renaissance Religion,* edited by Charles Trinkaus and Heiko A. Oberman, 307–36. Studies in Medieval and Reformation Thought 10. Leiden: Brill, 1974.

Deansley, Margaret. *A History of the Medieval Church, 590–1500.* Rev. ed. London: Methuen, 1972.

de Boer, Bertilo. "De Souter van Alanus de Rupe." *Ons Geestelijk Erf* 29 (1955): 358–88; 30 (1956): 156–90; 31 (1957): 187–204; 33 (1959): 145–93.

Diehl, Patrick S. *The Medieval European Religious Lyric: An Ars Poetica.* Berkeley and Los Angeles: University of California Press, 1985.

Dobner, Joseph. *Die mittelhochdeutsche Versnovelle Marien Rosenkranz.* Borna-Leipzig: Noske, 1928.

Dorfler–Dierken, Angelika. *Vorreformatorische Bruderschaften der heiligen Anna.* Abhandlungen der Heidelberger Akademie der Wissenschaften, Phil.-hist. Klasse, Jahrgang 1992, Abh. 3. Heidelberg: Winter, 1992.

Dronke, Peter. "The Song of Songs and the Medieval Love-Lyric." In *The Bible and Medieval Culture,* edited by W. Lourdaux and D. Verhelst, 236–62. Mediaevalia Lovanensia Ser. 1, no. 7. Louvain: Louvain University Press, 1979.

Duffy, Eamon. *The Stripping of the Altars: Traditional Religion in England, c. 1400– c.1580.* New Haven: Yale University Press, 1992.

Duggan, Lawrence G. "The Unresponsiveness of the Late Medieval Church: A Reconsideration." *Sixteenth-Century Journal* 9, no. 1 (1978): 3–26.

Duval, André. "Rosaire." In *Dictionnaire de spiritualité,* edited by Joseph de Guibert, Marcel Viller, and Ferdinand Cavallera, 13:cols. 937–80. Paris: Beauchesne, 1988.

Eire, Carlos. *War Against the Idols.* Cambridge: Cambridge University Press, 1986.

Eisenstein, Elizabeth L. *The Printing Press as an Agent of Change: Communications and Cultural Transformations in Early-Modern Europe,* 2 vols. Cambridge: Cambridge University Press, 1979.

Elm, Kaspar, ed. *Reformbemühungen und Observanzbestrebungen im spätmittelalterlichen Ordenswesen.* Berliner historische Studien 14, Ordensstudien 6. Berlin: Duncker and Humblot, 1989.

———. "Verfall und Erneuerung des Ordenswesens im Spätmittelalter." In *Untersuchungen zu Kloster und Stift.* Veröffentlichungen des Max-Planck-Instituts für Geschichte 68. Germania sacra 14, pp. 188–238. Göttingen: Vandenhoeck and Ruprecht, 1980.

Engelbert, Pius. "Die Bursfelder Benediktinerkongregation und die spätmittelalterlichen Reformbewegungen." *Historisches Jahrbuch* 103 (1983): 35–55.

Engelsing, Rolf. *Analphabetentum und Lektüre: Zur Sozialgeschichte des Lebens in Deutschland zwischen feudaler und industrieller Gesellschaft.* Stuttgart: Metzler, 1973.

Esser, Thomas. "Beitrag zur Geschichte des Rosenkranzes: Die ersten Spuren von Betrachtungen beim Rosenkranz." *Der Katholik* 77 (1897): 346–60, 409–22, 515–28.

———. "Geschichte des englischen Grußes." *Historisches Jahrbuch der Görres-Gesellschaft* 5 (1884): 88–116.

———. "Über die allmähliche Einführung der jetzt beim Rosenkranz üblichen Betrachtungspunkte." *Der Katholik* 30 (1904): 98–114, 192–217, 280–301, 351–73; 32 (1905): 201–16, 252–66, 323–50; 33 (1906): 49–66.

———. *Unserer lieben Frauen Rosenkranz.* Paderborn: Schöningh, 1889.

———. *Zur Archäologie der Paternoster-Schnur.* Fribourg: Paulus, 1898.

Favis, Roberta Smith. "The Garden of Love in Fifteenth-Century Netherlandish and German Engravings: Some Studies in Secular Iconography in the Late Middle Ages and Early Renaissance." Ph.D. diss., University of Pennsylvania, 1974.

Fehrle, Ernst. *Garten, Rose und Rosengarten im deutschen Mittelalter.* Ph.D. diss., University of Heidelberg, 1924.

500 Jahre Rosenkranz, 1475–1975: Kunst und Frömmigkeit im Spätmittelalter und ihr Weiterleben. Exhibition catalogue, Erzbischöfliches Diözesan–Museum Köln, 25 October 1975–15 January 1976. Cologne: Bachem, 1975.

Fleischman, Suzanne. "Philology, Linguistics, and the Discourse of the Medieval Text." *Speculum* 65 (1990): 19–37.

Galpern, A. N. "Late Medieval Piety in Sixteenth-Century Champagne." In *The*

Pursuit of Holiness in Late Medieval and Renaissance Religion, edited by Charles Trinkaus and Heiko A. Oberman, 141–76. Studies in Medieval and Reformation Thought 10. Leiden: Brill, 1974.

Gaul, Hilde. *Der Wandel des Marienbildes in der deutschen Dichtung und bildenden Kunst vom frühen zum hohen Mittelalter.* Ph.D. diss. Philipps-Universität Marburg, 1949.

Geldner, Ferdinand. *Die deutschen Inkunabeldrucker des XV. Jahrhunderts.* 2 vols. Stuttgart: Hiersemann, 1968.

Gorce, Maxime. *Le Rosaire et ses antécédents historiques d'après le manuscrit 12483 fond français de la Bibliothèque Nationale.* Paris: Picard, 1931.

Görres, Joseph, ed. *Altdeutsche Volks- und Meisterlieder aus den Handschriften der Heidelberger Bibliothek.* 1817. Reprint, Hildesheim: Olms, 1967.

Gössmann, Maria Elisabeth. *Die Verkündigung an Maria im dogmatischen Verständnis des Mittelalters.* Munich: Hueber, 1957.

Graef, Hilda. *The Devotion to Our Lady.* New York: Hawthorn Books, 1963.

Gray, Douglas. "The Five Wounds of Our Lord." *Notes and Queries* 208 (1963): 50–51, 82–89, 127–34, 163–68.

Greenblatt, Stephen. *Renaissance Self-Fashioning: From More to Shakespeare.* Chicago: University of Chicago Press, 1980.

———. *Shakespearean Negotiations: The Circulation of Social Energy in Renaissance England.* Berkeley and Los Angeles: University of California Press, 1988.

Grimm, Jakob, and Wilhelm Grimm, et al. *Deutsches Wörterbuch.* 16 vols. Leipzig: Hirzel, 1854–1954.

Gurevich, Aron. *Medieval Popular Culture: Problems of Belief and Perception.* Translated by János Bak and Paula Hollingsworth. Cambridge: Cambridge University Press, 1988.

Haimerl, Franz Xaver. *Mittelalterliche Frömmigkeit im Spiegel der Gebetbuchliteratur Süddeutschlands.* Münchener Theologische Studien, Hist. Abt., vol. 4. Munich: Zink, 1952.

Hamm, Bernt. *Frömmigkeitstheologie am Anfang des 16. Jahrhunderts: Studien zu Johannes von Paltz und seinem Umkreis.* Beiträge zur historischen Theologie 65. Tübingen: Mohr, 1982.

Hay, Denys. *The Church in Italy in the Fifteenth Century.* Cambridge: Cambridge University Press, 1977.

Heinz, Andreas. "Eine spätmittelalterliche Exempelsammlung zur Propagierung des Trierer Karthäuser-Rosenkranzes." *Trierer Theologische Zeitschrift* 92 (1983): 306–18.

———. "Lob der Mysterien Christi. Ein Beitrag zur Entwicklungsgeschichte des Leben-Jesu-Rosenkranzes unter besonderer Berücksichtigung seiner zisterziensischen Wurzeln." In *Liturgie und Dichtung: Ein interdisziplinäres Kompendium,* edited by H. Becker and R. Kaczynski, 1:609–39. Pietas liturgica 1–2. St. Ottilien: EOS Verlag, 1983.

———. "Die Zisterzienser und die Anfänge des Rosenkranzes." *Analecta cisterciensia* 33 (1977): 262–309.

Hennebo, Dieter. *Gärten des Mittelalters.* Munich: Artemis, 1987.

Herde, Rosemarie. "Das Hohelied in der lateinischen Literatur des Mittelalters bis zum 12. Jahrhundert." *Studi medievali*, 3d ser., 8 (1967): 957–1073.

Heße, Christian, and Martina Schlagenhaufer. *Wallraf-Richartz-Museum Köln: Vollständiges Verzeichnis der Gemäldesammlung*. Cologne and Milan: Du-Mont/Electa, 1986.

Hilg, Hardo. "Marienmirakelsammlungen." In *Die deutsche Literatur des Mittelalters: Verfasserlexikon*, edited by Wolfgang Stammler and Karl Langosch, 6:cols. 19–42. Berlin: de Gruyter, 1987.

Hind, Arthur M. *Early Italian Engraving: A Critical Catalogue with Complete Reproduction of all the Prints Described*. 7 vols. in 4. 1938–48. Reprint, Nendeln, Liechtenstein: Kraus, 1970.

Hoffmann von Fallersleben, Heinrich. *Geschichte des deutschen Kirchenlieds bis auf Luthers Zeit*. Wroclaw: Grass and Barth, 1832.

Honée, Eugène, "Image and Imagination in the Medieval Culture of Prayer: A Historical Perspective." In *The Art of Devotion in the Late Middle Ages in Europe, 1300–1500*, edited by Henk van Os, 157–74. Princeton: Princeton University Press, 1995.

Hsia, R. Po-Chia, ed. *The German People and the Reformation*. Ithaca: Cornell University Press, 1988.

Huizinga, Johan. *The Autumn of the Middle Ages*. Translated by Rodney J. Payton and Ulrich Mammitzsch. Chicago: University of Chicago Press, 1996.

———. *Herbst des Mittelalters: Studien über Lebens- und Geistesformen des 14. und 15. Jahrhunderts in Frankreich und in den Niederlanden*. Edited by Kurt Köstner. Translated by Kurt Köster. Stuttgart: Kröner, 1987.

Hunt, Lynn, ed. *The New Cultural History*. Berkeley and Los Angeles: University of California Press, 1989.

Joret, Charles. *La Rose dans l'antiquité et au moyen âge: Histoire, légendes et symbolisme*. Paris, 1892. Reprint, Geneva: Slatkine, 1970.

Kaeppeli, Thomas. *Scriptores ordinis Praedicatorum medii aevi*. 3 vols. Rome: Vatican, 1970–80.

Kaes, Anton. "New Historicism and the Study of German Literature." *German Quarterly* 62, no. 2 (1989): 210–19.

Kawerau, D. G. "Gedanken und Bemerkungen. Luthers Randglossen zum Marienpsalter 1515." *Theologische Studien und Kritiken* 80 (1917): 81–87.

Keating, John J. *Outlines of Catholic Teaching*. New York: Paulist, 1955.

Kieckhefer, Richard. "Major Currents in Late Medieval Devotion." In *Christian Spirituality: High Middle Ages and Reformation*, edited by Jill Raitt, 75–108. World Spirituality 17. New York: Crossroad, 1989.

———. *Unquiet Souls: Fourteenth-Century Saints and Their Religious Milieu*. Chicago: University of Chicago Press, 1984.

Kirfel, Willibald. *Der Rosenkranz, Ursprung und Ausbreitung*. Beiträge zur Sprach- und Kulturgeschichte des Orients 1. Walldorf, Hessen: Verlag für Orientkunde H. Vorndran, 1949.

Kliem, Wolfgang. *Die spätmittelalterliche Frankfurter Rosenkranzbruderschaft als volkstümliche Form der Gebetsverbrüderung*. Ph.D. diss., University of Frankfurt, 1962.

Klinkhammer, Karl-Josef. *Adolf von Essen und seine Werke: Der Rosenkranz in der geschichtlichen Situation seiner Entstehung und in seinem bleibenden Anliegen.* Frankfurter Theologische Studien 13. Frankfurt: Knecht, 1972.

──────. "Marienpsalter und Rosenkranz." In *Die deutsche Literatur des Mittelalters: Verfasserlexikon,* edited by Wolfgang Stammler and Karl Langosch, 6:cols. 42–50. Berlin: de Gruyter, 1987.

Koch, Heinrich Hubert. *Das Dominikanerkloster zu Frankfurt am Main.* Freiburg: Herder, 1892.

Köhler, Hans Joachim, ed. *Flugschriften als Massenmedium der Reformationszeit.* Spätmittelalter und frühe Neuzeit 13. Stuttgart: Klett-Cotta, 1981.

Künstle, Karl. *Ikonographie der christlichen Kunst,* 2 vols. Freiburg: Herder, 1926–28.

Lavin, Marilyn Aronberg. *The Place of Narrative: Mural Decoration in Italian Churches, 431–1600.* Chicago: University of Chicago Press, 1990.

Le Goff, Jacques. *The Birth of Purgatory.* Translated by Arthur Goldhammer. Chicago: University of Chicago Press, 1984.

Lienhard, Marc. "Luther and the Beginnings of the Reformation." In *Christian Spirituality: High Middle Ages and Reformation,* edited by Jill Raitt, 268–99. World Spirituality 17. New York: Crossroad, 1989.

Löe, Paulus von. *Statistisches über die Ordensprovinz Saxonia.* Quellen und Forschungen zur Geschichte des Dominikanerordens in Deutschland 4. Leipzig: Harrassowitz, 1910.

Löhr, Gabriel M., ed. *Registrum litterarum pro provincia Saxoniae.* Quellen und Forschungen zur Geschichte des Dominikanerordens in Deutschland 37. Leipzig: Harrassowitz, 1939.

──────. *Die Teutonia im 15. Jahrhundert: Studien und Texte vornehmlich zur Geschichte ihrer Reform.* Quellen und Forschungen zur Geschichte des Dominikanerordens in Deutschland 19. Leipzig: Harrassowitz, 1924.

Lortz, Joseph. *The Reformation in Germany.* 2 vols. Translated by Ronald Walls. New York: Herder, 1968.

Lunzer, Justus. "Rosengartenmotive." *Beiträge zur Geschichte der deutschen Sprache und Literatur* 50 (1927): 161–213.

Lynch, Joseph H. *The Medieval Church: A Brief History.* London: Longman, 1992.

Mâle, Emile. *Religious Art in France: The Late Middle Ages.* Edited and translated by Marthiel Mathews. Bollingen Series 90, no. 3. Princeton: Princeton University Press, 1986.

──────. *Religious Art in France: The Thirteenth Century: A Study of Medieval Iconography and Its Sources.* Translated by Marthiel Mathews. Bollingen Series 90, no. 2. Princeton: Princeton University Press, 1984.

Marrow, James H. *Passion Iconography in Northern European Art of the Late Middle Ages and Early Renaissance.* Ars Neerlandica 1. Kortrijk, Belgium: Van Ghemmert, 1979.

Martin, Francis Xavier. "The Augustinian Observant Movement." In *Reformbemühungen und Observanzbestrebungen im spätmittelalterlichen Ordenswesen,* edited by Kaspar Elm, Berliner Historische Studien 14, Ordensstudien 6, 325–45. Berlin: Duncker and Humblot, 1989.

Matter, E. Ann. *"The Voice of My Beloved": The Song of Songs in Western Medieval Christianity*. Philadelphia: University of Pennsylvania Press, 1990.

Meyer, Albert de. *La Congrégation de Hollande ou la réforme dominicaine en territoire bourguignon (1465–1515)*. Liège: Soledi, 1946.

Meersseman, Gilles Gérard. "Etudes sur les anciennes confréries dominicaines, III. Les congrégations de la Vierge," *Archivum Fratrum Praedicatorum* 22 (1952): 5–176.

———. *Der Hymnos Akathistos im Abendland*. 2 vols. Spicilegium Friburgense 2–3. Fribourg: Universitätsverlag, 1958–60.

———. *Ordo Fraternitatis: Confraternite e pietà dei laici nel Medioevo*. 3 vols. Italia Sacra 24–26. Rome: Herder, 1977.

Meiss, Millard. "The Madonna of Humility." *Art Bulletin* 18 (1936): 435–64.

Meyer, Johannes. "Johannes Busch und die Klosterreform des fünfzehnten Jahrhunderts." *Jahrbuch der Gesellschaft für niederländische Kirchengeschichte* 47 (1949): 43–53.

Mézard, Denys. *Etude sur les origines du rosaire: Réponse aux articles du P. Thurston, . . . parus dans le "Month" 1900 et 1901*. Caluire: Couvent de la Visitation, 1912.

Middleton, Anne. "Medieval Studies." In *Redrawing the Boundaries: The Transformation of English and American Literary Studies*, edited by Stephen Greenblatt and Giles Gunn, 12–40. New York: Modern Language Association, 1992.

Moeller, Bernd. *Deutschland im Zeitalter der Reformation*. Deutsche Geschichte 4. Göttingen: Vandenhoeck, 1977.

———. "Piety in Germany around 1500." In *The Reformation in Medieval Perspective*, edited by Steven E. Ozment, 50–75. Chicago: Quadrangle, 1971.

Mortier, R. P. *Histoire des maîtres généraux de l'Ordre des Frères Prêcheurs*. 7 vols. Paris: Picard, 1903–14. Vol. 4: *1400–1486* (1909), vol. 5: *1487–1589* (1911).

Moschall, Joachim. *"Marien Voerspan of Sapeel": Eine mittelniederländische Bearbeitung der "Goldenen Schmiede" des Konrad von Würzburg*. Erlanger Studien 40. Erlangen: Palm und Enke, 1983.

Mussafia, Adolfo. *Studien zu den mittelalterlichen Marienlegenden*. Sitzungsberichte der kaiserlichen Akademie der Wissenschaften in Wien, Phil.-hist. Klasse, 113 (1886): 917–94; 115 (1887): 5–92, 119 (1889): fasc. ix; 123 (1890): fasc. viii; 139 (1898): fasc. viii.

Neidiger, Bernhard. "Erzbischöfe, Landesherren und Reformkongregationen. Initiatoren und treibende Kräfte der Klosterreformen des 15. Jahrhunderts im Gebiet der Diözese Köln." *Rheinische Vierteljahresblätter* 54 (1990): 19–77.

———. "Die Observanzbewegungen der Bettelorden in Südwestdeutschland." *Rottenburger Jahrbuch für Kirchengeschichte* 11 (1992): 175–96.

Nichols, Stephen G. "Introduction: Philology in a Manuscript Culture." *Speculum* 65 (1990): 1–10.

Oakley, Francis. *The Western Church in the Later Middle Ages*. Ithaca: Cornell University Press, 1979.

Obermann, Heiko A. *The Dawn of the Reformation: Essays in Late Medieval and Early Reformation Thought*. Grand Rapids, Mich.: Eerdmans, 1992.

Ochsenbein, Peter. *Das Große Gebet der Eidgenossen.* Bern: Francke, 1989.

Oertzen, Augusta von. *Maria, die Königin des Rosenkranzes: Eine Ikonographie des Rosenkranzgebetes durch zwei Jahrhunderte deutscher Kunst.* Augsburg: Filser, 1925.

Ohly, Friedrich. *Hohelied–Studien: Grundzüge einer Geschichte der Hohelied Auslegung des Abendlandes bis um 1200.* Wiesbaden: Franz Steiner, 1958.

Olsen, David R. "From Utterance to Text: The Bias of Language in Speech and Writing." *Harvard Educational Review* 47 (1977): 57–81.

Ong, Walter. *Orality and Literacy: The Technologizing of the Word.* London: Methuen, 1982.

Oppel, Arnold. *Das Hohelied Salomonis und die deutsche religiöse Liebeslyrik.* Abhandlungen zur Mittleren und Neueren Geschichte 32. Berlin and Leipzig: Rothschild, 1911.

Orlandi, Stefano. *See* Primary Sources.

Os, Henk van. *The Art of Devotion in the Late Middle Ages in Europe, 1300–1500.* Princeton: Princeton University Press, 1994.

Oudendijk–Pieterse, Frances H. A. van den. *Dürers Rosenkranzfest en de ikonografie der Duitse rozenkransgroepen van de XV en het begin der XVI eew.* Amsterdam and Antwerp: Spiegel, 1939.

Ozment, Steven. *The Age of Reform, 1250–1550.* New Haven: Yale University Press, 1980.

———. *The Reformation in Medieval Perspective.* Chicago: Quadrangle, 1971.

———. *The Reformation in the Cities.* New Haven: Yale University Press, 1975.

Pallucchini, Rodolfo. *La pittura veneziana del Seicento.* 2 vols. Milan: Alfieri, 1981.

Panofsky, Erwin. *The Life and Art of Albrecht Dürer.* Princeton: Princeton University Press, 1955.

Paulus, Nikolaus. *Indulgences as a Social Factor in the Middle Ages.* Translated by John Elliot Ross. New York: Devin-Adair, 1922.

Pearsall, Derek, and Elizabeth Salter. *Landscapes and Seasons of the Medieval World.* Toronto: University of Toronto Press, 1973.

Post, Regnerus Richardus. *The Modern Devotion: Confrontation with Reformation and Humanism.* Studies in Medieval and Reformation Thought 3. Leiden: Brill, 1968.

Quétif, Jacques, and Jacques Echard. *Scriptores ordinis praedicatorum.* 2 vols. Paris: Ballard and Simart, 1719–21.

Ranke, Kurt. *Rosengarten: Recht und Totenkult.* Hamburg: Heitmann, 1951.

Reichert, Benedictus Maria, ed. *Registrum litterarum: Raymundi de Capua, 1386–1399, Leonardi de Mansuetis, 1474–1480.* Quellen und Forschungen zur Geschichte des Dominikanerordens in Deutschland 6. Leipzig: Harrassowitz, 1911.

Reinitzer, Heimo. *Der verschlossene Garten: Der Garten Marias im Mittelalter.* Wolfenbütteler Hefte 12. Wolfenbüttel: Herzog August Bibliothek, 1982.

Rensing, Theodor. "Die Reformbewegung in den westfälischen Dominikanerklöstern." *Westfalen* 17 (1932): 91–97.

Rhodes, Jan. "The Rosary in Sixteenth-Century England." *Mount Carmel* 31, no. 4 (1983): 180–91; 32, no. 1 (1984): 4–17.

Richert, Hans-Georg. "Rosenkranz." *Zeitschrift für deutsche Sprache* 21 (1965): 153–59.

Ridderbos, Bernhard. "The Rotterdam-Edinburgh Diptych: 'Maria in Sole' and the Devotion of the Rosary." In *The Art of Devotion in the Late Middle Ages in Europe, 1300–1500*, edited by Henk van Os, 151–56. Princeton: Princeton University Press, 1994.

Ring, Grete. "Attempt to reconstruct a lost Geertgen Composition." *Burlington Magazine* 94 (1952): 147.

Ringbom, Sixten. "Devotional Images and Imaginative Devotions. Notes on the Place of Art in late Medieval Private Piety." *Gazette des Beaux-Arts* 73 (1969): 159–70.

———. *Icon to Narrative: The Rise of the Dramatic Close-up in Fifteenth-Century Devotional Painting*. Acta Academiae Aboensis, ser. A., Humaniora 31, no. 2. Åbo: Åbo Akademi, 1965.

Ritz, Gislind. *Der Rosenkranz*. Munich: Don Bosco, 1962.

Roberts, Karen Barbara. "The Influence of the Rosary Devotion on Grünewald's Isenheim Altarpiece." Ph.D. diss., State University of New York at Binghamton, 1985.

Robertson, D. W. "The Doctrine of Charity in Medieval Literary Gardens: A Topical Approach through Symbolism and Allegory." *Speculum* 26 (1951): 24–49.

Ross, Werner. "Rose und Nachtigall." *Romanische Forschungen* 67 (1956): 55–82.

Ruf, Paul. "Der Augsburger Pfarrer Molitoris und sein Holzschnittsiegel." *Zeitschrift für bayerische Landesgeschichte* 3 (1930): 387–406.

Salzer, Anselm. *Die Sinnbilder und Beiworte Mariens in der deutschen Literatur und lateinischen Hymnenpoesie des Mittelalters, mit Berücksichtigung der patristischen Literatur*. 1893. Reprint, Darmstadt: Wissenschaftliche Buchgesellschaft, 1967.

Schanze, Frieder. "Sixt Buchsbaum." In *Die deutsche Literatur des Mittelalters: Verfasserlexikon*, edited by Wolfgang Stammler and Karl Langosch, 1:cols. 1109–10. Berlin: de Gruyter, 1978.

Scheeben, Heribert Christian. "Michael Francisci ab Insulis, O. P., 'Quodlibet de veritate fraternitatis Rosarii.' " *Archiv der deutschen Dominikaner* 4 (1951): 97–162.

Scherschel, Rainer. *Der Rosenkranz: Das Jesusgebet des Westens*. Freiburger Theologische Studien 116. Freiburg: Herder, 1979.

Schiller, Gertrud. *Ikonographie der christlichen Kunst*. 5 vols. Gütersloh: Mohn, 1966–90.

Schmidt, Heinrich, and Margarethe Schmidt. *Die vergessene Bildersprache christlicher Kunst*. Munich: Beck, 1984.

Schmidt, Kurt. *"Der lüstliche Würtzgarte"*: *Ein Beitrag zur Geschichte der deutschen Mystik im Spätmittelalter*. Ph.D. diss., University of Greifswald, 1932.

Schmidtke, Dietrich. *Studien zur dingallegorischen Erbauungsliteratur des Spätmittelalters: Am Beispiel der Gartenallegorie*. Hermaea 43. Tübingen: Niemeyer, 1982.

Schmitt, Jean-Claude. "Apostolat mendiant et société; Une confrérie dominicaine à la veille de la réforme." *Annales: E. S. C.* (1971): 83–104.

Schmitz, Wilhelm. *Das Rosenkranzgebet im 15. und im Anfange des 16. Jahrhunderts.* Freiburg: Herder, 1903.

Schneider, Cornelia. "Der Alltag der Blockbücher." In *Blockbücher des Mittelalters: Bilderfolgen als Lektüre,* exhibition catalogue, 22 June–1 September 1991, Gutenberg-Gesellschaft and Gutenberg-Museum, 35–57. Mainz: von Zabern, 1991.

Schramm, Albert. *Der Bilderschmuck der Frühdrucke.* 21 vols. Leipzig: Deutsches Museum für Buch und Stift, 1920–23; Hiersemann, 1924–43.

Schreiber, Wilhelm L. *Handbuch der Holz- und Metallschnitte des XV. Jahrhunderts.* 2d ed.. 8 vols. Leipzig: Hiersemann, 1926–30.

Schroeder, Mary Juliana. *Mary-Verse in "Meistergesang."* Catholic University of America Studies in German 16. 1942. Reprint, New York: AMS Press, 1970.

Schubert, Ernst. *Einführung in die Grundprobleme der deutschen Geschichte im Mittelalter.* Darmstadt: Wissenschaftliche Buchgesellschaft, 1992.

Schuler, Carol M. "The Seven Sorrows of the Virgin: Popular Culture and Cultic Imagery in Pre-Reformation Europe." *Simiolus: Netherlands Quarterly for the History of Art* 21, nos. 1 and 2 (1992): 5–28.

Schütz, Jakob Hubert, ed. *See* Primary Sources.

Scribner, Robert. *For the Sake of Simple Folk: Popular Propaganda for the German Reformation.* Cambridge Studies in Oral Literature and Culture 2. Cambridge: Cambridge University Press, 1981.

———. *Popular Culture and Popular Movements in Reformation Germany.* London: Hambledon, 1987.

Seidelmayer, Michael. *Currents of Mediaeval Thought.* Oxford: Basil Blackwell, 1960.

Seward, Barbara. *The Symbolic Rose.* New York: Columbia University Press, 1954.

Shaw, James G. *The Story of the Rosary.* Milwaukee, Wis.: Bruce, 1954.

Simon, Eckehard. "Rosengartenspiele: Zu Schauspiel und Turnier im Spätmittelalter." In *Entzauberung der Welt: Deutsche Literatur, 1200–1500,* edited by James F. Poag and Thomas C. Fox, 197–209. Tübingen: Francke, 1989.

Smith, Wilfred Cantwell. *Towards a World Theology: Faith and the Comparative History of Religion.* Philadelphia: Westminster, 1981.

Snyder, James. *Northern Renaissance Art: Painting, Sculpture, the Graphic Arts from 1350–1575.* New York: Prentice-Hall, 1985.

Söll, Georg. "Maria in der Geschichte von Theologie und Frömmigkeit." In *Handbuch der Marienkunde,* edited by Wolfgang Beinert and Heinrich Petri, 92–231. Regensburg: Pustet, 1984.

Southern, Richard W. "The English Origins of the 'Miracles of the Virgin.'" *Mediaeval and Renaissance Studies* 4 (1958): 176–216.

———. *Western Society and the Church in the Middle Ages.* Pelican History of the Church 2. London: Penguin, 1970.

Spiegel, Gabrielle. "History, Historicism, and the Social Logic of the Text in the Middle Ages." *Speculum* 65 (1990): 59–86.

Stadlhuber, Josef. "Das Laienstundengebet vom Leiden Christi in seinem mittel-alterlichen Fortleben." *Zeitschrift für Katholische Theologie* 67 (1950): 282–325.

Stammler, Wolfgang. "Der allegorische Garten." In *"Hart, warr nich mööd"*: *Festschrift für Christian Boeck*, edited by Gustav Hoffmann and Gustav Jürgensen, 260–69. Hamburg: Fehrs-Gilde, 1960.

Stange, Alfred. *Kritisches Verzeichnis der deutschen Tafelbilder vor Dürer*. 3 vols. Munich: Bruckmann, 1967–78.

Stewart, Stanley. *The Enclosed Garden: The Tradition and the Image in Seventeenth-Century Poetry*. Madison: University of Wisconsin Press, 1966.

Strauss, Gerald. *Nuremberg in the Sixteenth Century: City Politics and Life between Middle Ages and Modern Times*. Bloomington: Indiana University Press, 1976.

Strauss, Walter L. *The Illustrated Bartsch*. Vol. 84 of *German Book Illustration before 1500*, Part V: *Anonymous Artists 1482–1483*, edited by Walter L. Strauss and Carol Schuler. New York: Abaris Books, 1983.

Swanson, R. N. *Religion and Devotion in Europe, c. 1215–c. 1515*. Cambridge: Cambridge University Press, 1995.

Szabó, Flóris, and Elisabeth Soltész. *Horae Beatae Mariae Virginis: Zwei Aufsätze über den Kodex der Erzabtei Pannonhalma*. Translated by Géza Egnl. Budapest: Kossuth, 1985.

Szövérffy, Josef. *Die Annalen der lateinischen Hymnendichtung: Ein Handbuch*. 2 vols. Berlin: Erich Schmidt, 1964–65.

Tandecki, Daniela. "Der Garten als Symbol und Refugium göttlicher und menschlicher Liebe: Versuche der Vollendung einer Tradition in den Gärten und der Lyrik Europas im XVI. und XVII. Jahrhundert." *Arcadia* 22 (1987): 113–41.

Taylor, Larissa. *Soldiers of Christ: Preaching in Late Medieval and Reformation France*. Oxford: Oxford University Press, 1992.

Tentler, Thomas N. *Sin and Confession on the Eve of the Reformation*. Princeton: Princeton University Press, 1977.

Thomas, Keith. *Religion and the Decline of Magic: Studies in Popular Beliefs in XVIth and XVIIth Century England*. New York: Scribner's, 1971.

Thurston, Herbert. "Alanus de Rupe and his Indulgence of 60,000 Years." *The Month* 100 (1902): 281–99.

———. *Familiar Prayers: Their Origin and History*. Westminster, Md.: Newman, 1953.

———. "The Name of the Rosary." *The Month* 111 (1908): 519–29, 610–23.

———. "Notes on Familiar Prayers: I. The Origins of the Hail Mary." *The Month* 121 (1913): 162–76.

———. "Our Popular Devotions: II. The Rosary." *The Month* 96 (1900): 403–18, 513–27, 620–37; 97 (1901): 67–79, 172–88, 286–304.

Toews, John E. "Stories of Difference and Identity: New Historicism in Literature and History." *Monatshefte* 84 (1992): 193–211.

Tubach, Frederic C. *Index exemplorum: A Handbook of Medieval Religious Tales*. F F Communications 86, no. 204. Helsinki: Suomalainen Tiedeakatemia, 1969.

Vauchez, André. *The Laity in the Middle Ages: Religious Beliefs and Devotional Practices.* Edited by Daniel E. Borstein. Translated by Margery J. Schneider. Notre Dame: University of Notre Dame Press, 1993.

Vetter, Ewald. *Maria im Rosenhag.* Düsseldorf: Schwann, 1956.

Vischer, Erwin. *Formschnitte des fünfzehnten Jahrhunderts in der großherzoglichen Hof- und Landesbibliothek zu Karlsruhe.* Strasbourg: Heitz, 1912.

Ward, Harry L. D., and John A. Herbert, eds. *Catalogue of Romances in the Department of Manuscripts of the British Museum.* 3 vols. 1883–1910. Reprint, London: British Museum, 1962.

Watson, Paul F. *The Garden of Love in Tuscan Art of the Early Renaissance.* Philadelphia: Art Alliance Press, 1979.

Watt, Tessa. *Cheap Print and Popular Piety, 1550–1640.* Cambridge: Cambridge University Press, 1991.

Weigel, Theodor O., and August C. Zestermann. *Die Anfänge der Druckerkunst im Bild und Schrift.* 2 vols. Leipzig: Weigel, 1866.

Whiting, Robert. *The Blind Devotion of the People: Popular Religion and the English Reformation.* Cambridge: Cambridge University Press, 1991.

Wilkins, Eithne. *The Rose-Garden Game: The Symbolic Background to the European Prayer-Beads.* London: Victor Gollancz, 1969.

Willam, Franz M. *Die Geschichte und Gebetsschule des Rosenkranzes.* Vienna: Herder, 1948.

Williams, George H. *Wilderness and Paradise in Christian Thought.* New York: Harper, 1962.

Wilmart, André. "Comment Alain de la Roche prêchait le rosaire ou psautier de la Vierge." *La Vie et les arts liturgiques* 11 (1924–25): 108–15.

———. "Les Méditations d'Etienne de Salley sur les joies de la Vierge Marie." In *Auteurs spirituels et textes dévots du moyen âge latin,* edited by André Wilmart, 317–60. Paris: Bloud and Gay, 1932.

Winter, Olaf. "Deutsche Rosenkranzklauseln und Marienlegenden als Ausdruck spätmittelalterlicher Frömmigkeit." Master's thesis, University of Freiburg, n.d.

Winston, Anne. " 'Minne' in Spiritual Gardens of the Fifteenth Century." In *Canon and Canon Transgression in Medieval German Literature,* ed. Albrecht Classen, 153–62. Göppingen: Kümmerle, 1993.

———. "Tracing the Origins of the Rosary: German Vernacular Texts." *Speculum* 68 (1993): 619–36.

Wolfgarten, Renate. *Die Ikonographie der Madonna im Rosenhag.* Ph.D. diss., University of Bonn, 1953.

Wolfs, Servatius Petrus. "Congregatio Hollandica." *Ons Geestelijk Erf* 22 (1948): 165–83.

Wood-Legh, Kathleen L. *Perpetual Chantries in Britain.* Cambridge: Cambridge University Press, 1965.

Woolf, Rosemary. *The English Religious Lyric in the Middle Ages.* Oxford: Clarendon Press, 1968.

———. "The Theme of Christ the Lover-Knight in Medieval English Literature." *Review of English Studies,* n.s., 13, no. 49 (1962): 1–16.

Wyss, Robert. "Vier Hortus Conclusus–Darstellungen im schweizerischen Landesmuseum." *Zeitschrift für schweizerische Archäologie und Kunstgeschichte* 20 (1960): 113–24.

Zschoch, Hellmut. *Klosterreform und monastische Spiritualität im fünfzehnten Jahrhundert: Conrad von Zenn OESA (+ 1460) und sein "Liber de vita monastica."* Beiträge zur historischen Theologie 75. Tübingen: Mohr, 1988.

Zumkeller, Adolar. "Johannes von Staupitz und die klösterliche Reformbewegung." *Analecta Augustiniana* 52 (1989): 29–49.

Zumthor, Paul. "The Text and the Voice." *New Literary History* 16, no. 1 (1984): 67–92.

Index

Adolf of Essen, 1, 7, 26
Ailly, Pierre d', 88
Alanus de Rupe, 24, 33, 73, 119, 136–37
  and Dominic of Prussia, 71–73
  Douai brotherhood of, 66, 77, 79, 116
  founder of the Confraternity of the Psalter of
    the Glorious Virgin Mary, 66, 136
  and methods of reciting the prayer, 65, 67
  and the Observant reform, 77, 78–79
  opposition to the name rosary, 81–82, 105,
    108
  on prayer beads, 116
  promotion of the brotherhood, 119, 122, 123
Albrecht of Mainz, Archbishop, 122
Albrecht of Scharfenberg, 103, 147
Alexander of Forli, 116, 122
Alfonso X, King, 101
Ambrose, Saint, 88
Analecta hymnica, 13, 22
Anthony, Saint, 14
Aphrodite, 82
Astell, Ann, 9, 145
Augustine, Saint, 108

Baechthold, Jakob, 148
Barthes, Roland, 151
beads, prayer, 14, 111–16
Beissel, Stephan, 7, 39, 41
Benedicta. See exempla (sermon illustrations),
  Benedicta
Bern, 142
Bernard of Clairvaux, Saint, 33, 67, 99
Der beschlossen Gart des Rosenkrantz Marie,
  103

Biblia pauperum, 34, 38
Black, Christopher, 117, 121, 144
Boileau, Etienne, 112
Bonaventure, Saint, 98
Bossy, John, 130
Brun von Schönebeck, 92
Buch der Natur, 95
Buch der Reformacio Predigerordens. See
  Meyer, Johannes
Buchsbaum, Sixt, 47–52, 128, 141
Busch, Johannes, 135

Caesarius of Heisterbach, 10–11, 15
Canisius, Peter, 60
Cantigas de Santa Maria, 101
Carthusians, 2, 66, 76–77, 131
Castello, Alberto da, 60, 61, 69, 123
chaplet, 15, 82, 100–103, 148
Chaucer, Geoffrey, 112
Christ
  as bridegroom, 9, 104, 145
  as rose, 89
  sufferings of. See joys and sorrows, of Mary
    and Christ
  as unicorn. See unicorn, Christ as
Cistercian nuns, 17
Colmar, 28, 76. See also rosary confraternity,
  Colmar
Cologne, 38. See also rosary confraternity, Co-
  logne
Compendium psalterii beatissimae Trinitatis, 7,
  33
confession, 144
Confraternity of the Psalter of the Glorious

Virgin Mary, 66. *See also* Alanus de Rupe,
    Douai brotherhood of
Conrad of Prussia, 76
Conrad von Haimburg, 99
Council of Trent, 151
Crisp, Frank, 82
Cross, the Holy. *See*, rose, tree of the

Dante Alighieri, 89
David, Gérard, 96
Davis, Natalie, 52
Devotio Moderna, 11, 27, 142
Diehl, Patrick, 24, 29
Dinckmut, Conrad, 33, 34,
*[Dis ist] Unser lyeben frowen Rosenkrantz und
    wie er von ersten offkummen*, 25, 33
Dolabella, Tommaso, 118
Domenech, Franciscus, 57, 58
Dominic, Saint, 6, 119, 124, 126
    Albigensians and, 28
    as progenitor of the rosary, 16, 72
Dominic of Prussia (Carthusian), 1, 16–17, 24,
    72, 109, 131, 132
    fifty rosary meditations (clausulae) of, 24, 25,
        68, 72–73, 100, 103, 174 n. 29
    "Liber experientiarium," 17, 72
    life-of-Christ meditations of, 22–24, 26, 72,
        103
    and the name rosary, 81. *See also* Alanus de
        Rupe, opposition to the name rosary; ro-
        sary, the name
    and variations on the rosary, 25
    "Zwanzig Exempel," 49, 100, 131
Dominicans, 66, 76, 77–78, 79, 120, 121, 144
Douai. *See* rosary confraternity (brotherhood)
Dronke, Peter, 105
Duffy, Eamon, 6, 29, 130
Dürer, Albrecht, 70, 71, 118
Duval, André, 8, 65

Eck, Johann, 140
*Ein GAR nützlich Büchlein von dem Psalter oder
    Rosenkranz Marie*, 69, 75, 118, 121, 123
Engelbert, abbot of Admont, 22, 103
Esser, Thomas, 6, 15, 16, 52, 65, 67, 69, 112
Eve, 92
Excuria, Johannes, 79
Exempelboek II, 34
exempla (sermon illustrations), 10–11, 15, 112,
    123–32
    Alexandra, 126–27, 128, 153–54
    Aves seen as Roses (The Monk and the
        Thieves), 100–102, 108, 140, 149

Benedicta, 28, 124–25
Blanche of Castile, 149
Eleodorus, 126, 158–60
Eulalia, 26, 136
Mary, the Charcoaler's Daughter, 125, 155–58
The Monk and Our Lady's Sleeves, 129, 136
The Priest Who Only Knew One Mass, 148
"Zwanzig Exempel," 49, 100, 132

Francisci, Michael, 25, 67, 70, 71, 105, 122
Frauenlob (Heinrich von Meißen), 89
Folz, Hans, 112
Frederick III, Emperor, 24
Frederick the Wise, elector of Saxony, 140

Gabriel, the angel, 94
Galpern, A. N., 130
Ganz, Peter, 148
garden
    of the annunciation, 94, 97
    of courtly love, 82–88
    of earthly paradise (Eden), 92
    enclosed, 89–96, 97, 106–7
    the heart as, 9–10, 99
    of heavenly love, 92
    "hortus conclusus." *See* garden, enclosed
    of the incarnation, 92
    Kriemhild's, 84
    Mary as, 89–92, 99
    rose, 83–84
    of the Song of Songs, 89–92
    the soul as, 99, 104, 105
    of virtues, 99
    the womb as, 92
garden allegories, devotional, 9, 99, 145
Garel von dem blühenden Tal, 84
"gaudes." *See* joys of the Virgin
Geertgen tot Sint Jans, 149, 150
Geiler of Kaysersberg, Johann, 79
Der geistliche Blumengarten, 103
German rosaries and Marian psalters, 18–21
Gertrude, abbess (daughter of Pippin I), 14
Gianetti da Salò, Andrea, 60, 62
Giovanni d'Erfordia. *See* Johannes of Erfurt
Godiva, Lady (of Coventry), 14
Goldene Schmiede, 103, 147–48
Greenblatt, Stephen, 12, 151
Gregory of Nazianzus, 101
Greifswald, 77, 78
Der große Rosengarten zu Worms, 84, 86
Guillaume de Lorris, 88
Guldin Schilling, 92
Gurevich, Aron, 10

Der Harder, 92
Heinz, Andreas, 7, 17
Hensberg, Vincentius, 109
Herolt, Johannes, 132, 144
Heynlin, Johannes, 142–43
Das Hohelied, 92
Hours, the
    of Jeanne d'Evreux, 41, 42
    of the Passion, the, 38, 41
    of the Virgin, the, 38, 41
Huizinga, Johan, 144
Hunt, Lynn, 149

illustrations and text, 52, 53–54, 64, 80
indulgences, 5, 116, 122, 127–28, 130, 137–44
Istrutione e avvertimenti per meditar i misterii
    del Rosario della Santissima Vergine
    Madre, 60

Jacquin, Franciscus, 77
Jardin amoreux de l'âme dévote, 88
Jean de Meun, 88
Jerome, Saint, 99
Jesuits, 147
Jesus Christ, name in rosary, 24
Jesus prayer, the, 27
Johannes of Chemnitz, 78
Johannes of Erfurt, 70, 78
Johannes of Paltz, 143
Johannes von Freiberg, 84
joys and sorrows, of Mary and Christ, 41,
    68–69, 70
joys of the Virgin, 38–39, 40, 41–43, 57, 68, 70,
    169–70 n. 14, 170 n. 18
Der jüngere Titurel, 147

Kaes, Anton, 133, 149, 151
Kempis, Thomas à, 142
Kieckhefer, Richard, 80
Kirfel, Willibald, 7
Der kleine Rosengarten. See Laurin
Klinkhammer, Karl-Josef, 7
Konrad von Megenberg, 95
Konrad von Würzburg, 96, 103, 147–48

Lambsheym, Johannes, 52–53, 64, 123
language and spirituality, 146–47, 151
laity, the needs of, 5, 79–80, 131–32
Landsberg, Justus, 72
Last Judgment, the, 43, 57–63, 71
Latin versus the vernacular, 29, 146–47
"laude," 70
Laurin, 84

Le Goff, Jacques, 10
Libellus perutilis de Fraternitate Rosarii, 52–53,
    123
Liber Apologeticus ad Ferricum episcopum Tor-
    nacensem, 67, 68, 71, 74
life-of-Christ meditations, 20–24, 26, 30, 38, 39,
    46–47, 140–41
    narrative form and, 26–27
Lille, 77
literacy, 31, 34, 52, 80
Livre des métiers, 112
Livre et ordonnance. See rosary confraternity,
    Douai
Loarte, Gaspar, 60
Loreto, litany of, 88
Lortz, Joseph, 134, 143
Louis IX, King, 149
Louis Marie de Montfort, Saint, 26
love garden. See garden, of courtly love
Luther, Martin, 130, 140, 144, 145, 146, 151

Mabillon, Jean, 6
Mâle, Emile, 82, 122
Mansuetis, Leonardus, 79
Marian psalters, 15, 18–22, 68
    German 18–21
    Latin, 22
"Marienlieder," 89
Marien Voerspan of Sapeel, 148
Mary, the Virgin
    as bride, 9, 92, 104, 145
    coronation of, 39, 41, 57–63, 145
    the new Eve, 92
    as rose, 1, 9, 88–89, 98, 104, 105
    as rose garden, 89
    sorrows of. See joys and sorrows, of Mary
        and Christ
Mayer, Anton, 6
Mechthild of Hackeborn, 17
media, 31
meditations (fifteen). See rosary, mysteries
Meersseman, Gilles, 41, 69
Meyer, Johannes, 77
Middleton, Anne, 6
Moeller, Bernd, 5
Molitoris, Johannes, 78
Mombaer, Johannes, 142
Münchner Minnegarten, 105

narrative rosary, 25, 26, 30, 46–47, 52, 129,
    140–41. See also life-of-Christ meditations
Neidhardt of Reuental, 84
Nichols, Stephen, 52, 53, 64

Nielsen, Michael, 116, 119
Nürnberger Garten, 98

Oakley, Francis, 5, 11
Observant reform movement, 11, 73–80
  Holland Congregation, 77, 78, 79
  Leipzig Congregation, 78
Ochsenbein, Peter, 3
Oertzen, Augusta von, 149
Om Jomfru Marie Rosenkrands, 116, 119
orality, 29–30, 31–32
Origen, 98
Orlandi, Stefano, 7, 69
Oudendijk-Pieterse, Frances, 70
Our Lady Mary's Rose Garden, 1, 98, 100, 104,
  145, 149
Ozment, Steven, 4, 5, 80, 130

Passional, 149
Passion of Christ (meditation on the), 16, 68, 147
Paternoster beads, 14, 112, 113. *See also* beads,
  prayer
Paternoster prayer, 14, 15, 67, 68, 108
Paul of Thebes, 14
Paulus, Nikolaus, 142–43
picture rosaries, 32–34, 54–64, 69
  earliest (Ulm), 33, 34, 35–37, 39, 43, 49, 69, 75
Pieters, Albertus, 78
Piety, late medieval, 5
  quantification and, 133–34, 145
  spirituality vs. calculation, 6, 134
Pinder, Ulrich, 103, 109
Polo, Marco, 14
Power, Eileen, 10, 57, 128
prayer of Saint Gregory, the, 122
Preacher of Sankt Georgen, the, 99
*Promptuarium Discipuli de Miraculis Beate
  Marie Virginis*, 132, 144
Psalms, Old Testament, 15
Psalter of Our Lady, Alanus de Rupe's, 66, 72,
  136. *See also* Alanus de Rupe, opposition
  to the name rosary
purgatory, 28, 120, 121, 127–28, 130, 137–38

Quitzkow, Hennig, 78
Quodlibet de veritate fraternitis Rosarii, 7, 67,
  74, 105, 122

Ranke, Friedrich, 148
Raymund of Capua, 73–74
"Das Redelîn," 84
Reinmar von Zweter, 147
Ringbom, Sixten, 33
Ritz, Gerlind, 112

Rode, Johannes, 2, 76–77
Romance of the Rose, 1, 88
rosalia, 82
Rosario della gloriosa vergine Maria, 60, 69, 123
Rosario della sacratissima Vergine Maria, 60
rosary, 2
  Carthusian, 66
  Christological emphasis, 49
  of Cistercian nuns, 17, 23
  earliest form of, 13–14
  mysteries, 3, 54–64, 65–71
  the name, 81–82, 101–3, 164 n. 12
  the official text, 25
  orthodoxy and, 28
  private devotions and, 27, 29
  teaching of virtue, 27, 118–19, 132
  text and context, 30, 80, 149–51
  variations, 25, 33, 54, 69, 129
rosary confraternity (brotherhood), 24–25,
  28–29, 116–22, 127–28
  Augsburg, 78, 80, 116
  Barcelona, 116
  Breslau. *See* Wroclaw
  Colmar, 28, 68, 74, 122, 125
  Cologne, 24, 67, 80, 121
  community and, 30, 120, 151
  Douai, 24, 66, 67, 68, 74, 79, 116, 119
  Florence, 78, 116
  founding of, 24
  Frankfurt, 77
  Gebweiler, 78
  Ghent, 116
  Grottkau, 78
  Haarlem, 149
  Legano, 117
  Lille, 116
  Lisbon, 116
  membership regulations, 28, 79, 117–18
  number of members, 2, 4, 80, 111
  Parabiago, 117
  promotion of, 27–28
  Rome, 78
  Rostock, 116
  as a social phenomenon, 28–29, 30
  statutes of (German), 68, 70, 120–21, 122
  Strasbourg, 78
  Ulm, 116
  Venice, 70, 75, 78, 116; statutes (Italian), 70
  Wroclaw, 78, 144
  women in, 28, 117, 118
rose, 68, 82–89, 90, 91, 146
  arbor, 89, 91, 95
  Ave Maria as, 100

chaplet, 100–103
Christ as, 89, 100
in Christian iconography, 88–89
garden. *See* garden, rose
garland, 82
golden, 34, 104, 146
Mary as, 1, 9, 88–89, 98, 104, 105
red, 34, 68, 82, 97, 98, 99, 104, 108, 145
tree of the, 89, 98
white, 68, 82, 99, 145
wounds as, 98, 104, 145
Roselli, Francesco, 57
Rosengarten des Leidens Christi, 98
"Rosenkranz," 1, 19, 84, 101
Rosetum exercitiorum, 142
Rostocker Gartengebet, 104
Ruland, Ott, 112

Saint Thomas on the Kyll. *See* Cistercian nuns
of
Das Sankt Trudperter Hohe Lied, 92
Schaur, Hans, 41, 44, 68, 74
Scherschel, Rainer, 7
Schilling, Diebold, 142–43
Schmidt, Kurt, 105
Schmitt, Jean-Claude, 7, 28
Schmitz, Wilhelm, 7
Schongauer, Martin, 91
Schubert, Ernst, 6, 47
Schütz, Jakob Hubert, 7
Schwab, Ute, 148
Scribner, Robert, 31–32, 52
sermon illustrations. *See* exempla
*Die sieben Freuden Mariae und die Leidensge-
schichte Jesu*, 43, 46
Sixtus IV, Pope, 122, 137
Song of Songs, the, 9, 98, 109, 145–46
Mary as bride of, 9, 92, 94, 104, 145
songs, rosary, 127–29, 141
Southern, R. W., 121
Speculum humanae salvationis, 34, 38, 49,
50–51, 92
Spiegel, Gabrielle, 151
*Der Spiegel hochloblicher Bruderschafft des Ro-
senkrantz Marie*. *See* Weida, Marcus von,
rosary manual of
spirituality, late medieval. *See* piety, late
medieval
Sprenger, Jakob, 24, 67, 79, 108, 117, 137
and the Observant reform, 73, 78–79
and the statutes of the rosary confraternity,
28, 68, 70, 74, 120–21, 122, 137

Stadlhuber, Josef, 47
Stöcklin, Ulrich, of Rottach, 22
Strasbourg, 148
Suso, Henry, 99
Swanson, R. N., 134

Tentler, Thomas, 134
Thomas, Keith, 129
Thomas on the Kyll, Saint. *See* Cistercian nuns
of
Thurston, Herbert, 6, 65, 72
Toews, John, 135
Traut, Wolf, 54, 56, 137–38
Trier, 17, 76

Ulm, 33, 34, 116
Ulm handbook, 33, 48, 77, 118, 123, 128. See
Vnser lieben frauen psalter (Ulm)
Ulm picture rosary. *See* picture rosaries, earliest
unicorn, 94–98
Christ as, 95–96
mystical hunt of, the, 94–96
*Unser lieben frawen psalter unnd von den dreien
rosenkräntzen*, 53
Unterlinden, cloister of (Colmar), 15
Urban IV, Pope, 143

Vauchez, André, 79, 144
Venus, 82
vernacular, 29. *See also* Latin versus the ver-
nacular
Viridarium Marianum, 109
vita Christi. *See* life-of-Christ meditations
Vitis mystica, 98
Vnser lieben frauen Psalter (Ulm), 33, 48, 77,
118, 123, 128
*Von dem psalter vnnd Rosenkrantz vnser lieben
frauen*, 25, 153
*Von der gnadenreichen, hochberümpten . . .
Bruderschaft des Psalters oder Rosenkrantz
Marie*, 60, 63, 108, 123

Wackernagel, Phillipp, 70, 127, 141
Walasser, Adam, 60, 63, 108, 116, 123
Walther von der Vogelweide, 147
Weida, Marcus von, rosary manual of, 48,
117–18, 120, 137–38, 140–41
indulgences and, 122, 130
Luther and, 130–31, 140–41
Wetzel, Conrad, 78
Willam, Franz Michel, 7, 15
women, 28, 117–18

Zumthor, Paul, 29